Spelling Trouble?

Other Books of Interest:

Linguistic Minorities in Central and Eastern Europe
Christina Bratt Paulston and Donald Peckham (eds)
Identity, Insecurity and Image: France and Language
Dennis Ager
Language Planning in Malawi, Mozambique and the Philippines
Robert B. Kaplan and Richard B. Baldauf, Jr. (eds)
Community and Communication: The Role of Language in Nation State Building and
European Integration
Sue Wright
Language Planning in Nepal, Taiwan and Sweden
Richard B. Baldauf, Jr. and Robert B. Kaplan (eds)
Language and Society in a Changing Italy
Arturo Tosi
The Other Languages of Europe
Guus Extra and Durk Gorter (eds)
Motivation in Language Planning and Language Policy
Dennis Ager
Multilingualism in Spain
M. Teresa Turell (ed.)
A Dynamic Model of Multilingualism
Philip Herdina and Ulrike Jessner
Beyond Boundaries: Language and Identity in Contemporary Europe
Paul Gubbins and Mike Holt (eds)
Bilingualism: Beyond Basic Principles
Jean-Marc Dewaele, Alex Housen and Li Wei (eds)
Ideology and Image: Britain and Language
Dennis Ager
Where East Looks West: Success in English in Goa and on the Konkan Coast
Dennis Kurzon
English in Africa: After the Cold War
Alamin M. Mazrui
Politeness in Europe
Leo Hickey and Miranda Stewart (eds)
Language in Jewish Society: Towards a New Understanding
John Myhill
Urban Multilingualism in Europe
Guus Extra and Kutlay Yagmur (eds)
Effects of Second Language on the First
Vivian Cook (ed.)

For more details of these or any other of our publications, please contact:
Multilingual Matters, Frankfurt Lodge, Clevedon Hall,
Victoria Road, Clevedon, BS21 7HH, England
http://www.multilingual-matters.com

Spelling Trouble?

Language, Ideology and the Reform of German Orthography

Sally Johnson

MULTILINGUAL MATTERS LTD
Clevedon • Buffalo • Toronto

Library of Congress Cataloging in Publication Data
Johnson, Sally A.
Spelling Trouble? Language, Ideology and the Reform of German Orthography.
Sally Johnson. 1st ed.
Includes bibliographical references and index.
1. German language–Orthography and spelling. 2. Spelling reform–Germany.
3. Language policy–Germany. I. Title.
PF3151.J64 2005
431'.52--dc22   2004016744

British Library Cataloguing in Publication Data
A catalogue entry for this book is available from the British Library.

ISBN 1-85359-785-6 (hbk)
ISBN 1-85359-784-8 (pbk)

Multilingual Matters Ltd
UK: Frankfurt Lodge, Clevedon Hall, Victoria Road, Clevedon BS21 7HH.
USA: UTP, 2250 Military Road, Tonawanda, NY 14150, USA.
Canada: UTP, 5201 Dufferin Street, North York, Ontario M3H 5T8, Canada.

Typeset by Techset Ltd.
Printed and bound in Great Britain by the Cromwell Press Ltd.

Contents

Acknowledgements

There are a number of people and organisations without whom this book would not have been possible. First and foremost, I would like to thank the Alexander von Humboldt-Foundation in Germany, who generously funded a one-year Research Fellowship during 2000–2001 (ref. IV GRO 1066520 STP), which was spent at the *Institut für deutsche Sprache* (IDS) in Mannheim and during which time the primary research was undertaken. I would also like to thank Ulrike Meinhof (Southampton), Martin Durrell (Manchester) and Philip Payne (Lancaster) for their support in obtaining this fellowship, as well as the many colleagues at the IDS for their help, not least Professor Dr Gerhard Stickel, Dr Klaus Heller, Dr Wolfgang Mentrup, Dr Annette Trabold, Karin Laton, together with Eva Teubert and her colleagues in the excellent library there. Thanks also to Dr Ricarda Wolf and Professor Dr Jannis Androutsopoulos for not only listening to my many excursions on the German spelling reform, but for providing a roof over my head as well as good wine and company on numerous occasions during that year.

As this book was largely completed while I was still working in the Department of Linguistics and Modern English Language at Lancaster University, there are many colleagues and friends there to whom I am indebted. I would especially like to thank Bob McKinlay, Tony McEnery and Francis Katamba for making it possible for me to take up the Humboldt fellowship, as well as the Faculty of Social Sciences for supporting a further trip to Mannheim in June 2003. My gratitude also extends to Marjorie Wood, the postgraduate administrator in the Department of Linguistics, whose generosity of support freed up many hours for me to continue working on this book between 2001 and 2003. Also within the Department of Linguistics, I would like to thank various colleagues who read draft chapters and/or commented on talks I gave on this topic, not least Mark Sebba, Jane Sunderland, John Heywood, Susan Dray, Roz Ivanič, David Barton, Uta Papen, Juliane Schwarz and Stephanie Suhr.

Other individuals outside Lancaster who offered their help at various stages include Chris Young (Cambridge), Stephen Barbour (East Anglia) and Lucy Macnab (Leeds). Special thanks go to Oliver Stenschke (Göttingen) and Frank Finlay (Leeds) for (almost) voluntarily ploughing their way through drafts of the whole manuscript and making many insightful suggestions for improvement, and to Jo Jackson for help with printing. Thanks also to Alison Phipps, the reviewer for Multilingual Matters, for her equally constructive comments. Although it would be all too easy to blame any shortcomings of this book on others, the usual caveats apply . . .

Finally, I would like to say a big thank you to Mike and Marjukka Grover at Multilingual Matters for being supportive publishers with realistic deadlines, and to Frank and Ben for just being there – even when I was not.

Author's Note

Following the completion of the manuscript for this book, a number of developments took place in the summer of 2004 in relation to the reform of German orthography, the contents of which could no longer be incorporated into the body of the text.

In accordance with the Fourth Interim Report of the *Zwischenstaatliche Kommission für deutsche Rechtschreibung*, a number of recommendations for minor modifications to the new orthographic guidelines were approved at the 306th plenary meeting of the German *Ministerpräsidenten* in June 2004. The main features of the revisions are as follows:

- no further new spellings to be introduced such as **Topp* (by analogy with *Tipp* or *Stopp*);
- the concept of main and subordinate variants to be abandoned in the case of foreign loans (both forms will be considered equally valid until such time as preferences are clarified by popular usage, e.g. *Ketschup/Ketchup* or *Spagetti/Spaghetti*);
- a relaxing of the rules regarding separate and compound spellings allowing both variants in a number of controversial cases such as *leidtun/Leid tun* (to feel sorry for) or *gewinnbringend/Gewinn bringend* (profitable).

These and other changes are outlined in detail in a special issue of *Sprachreport* edited by Klaus Heller and published by the *Institut für deutsche Sprache* in July 2004. (Both the Fourth Interim report and the special issue of *Sprachreport* are available at www.ids-mannheim.de/service.)

Finally, in August 2004, all newspapers published by the Axel-Springer Verlag together with *Der Spiegel* and the *Süddeutsche Zeitung* opted to revert to their own in-house versions of the old orthography (for details see, *inter alia*, Bastian Sick "Aus Neu macht alt" in *Spiegel Online* at www.spiegel.de, 6 August 2004). At the time of writing, there is ongoing debate regarding the possible need to extend the interim period for the reform's introduction that is currently scheduled to end on 31 July 2005.

Sally Johnson,
Leeds,
September 2004

Chapter 1

Introduction to the 1996 Reform of German Orthography

On 30 November 1995, a press release by the German Standing Conference of Ministers for Education and Cultural Affairs – the *Kultusministerkonferenz* or *KMK* – announced that a reform of German orthography had been approved. The proposed changes were an attempt to harmonise what was perceived to be a complex and inconsistent set of orthographic rules that were causing unnecessary problems for language users of all ages, but for young schoolchildren in particular. The reform was to be introduced from 1 August 1998 to coincide with the start of the new school year, and this would be followed by a seven-year transitionary period until 31 July 2005, during which time the old orthography would be considered 'outdated' (*überholt*) but not 'wrong' (*falsch*). However, many Federal states or *Bundesländer* chose not to delay the implementation of the reform until 1998 and instructed schools in their area to begin teaching the new rules from the start of the school year 1996/1997.

The decision to reform German orthography had not been taken lightly. Given that the first and hitherto only set of official guidelines for all the German-speaking countries had been agreed in 1901, the final proposal for their revision in 1996 was the result of almost a century of often heated debate among linguists, politicians, educationalists, lexicographers, writers, journalists, and other interested parties. Nor was the 1996 reform an exclusively German affair. From the mid-1970s in particular there had been close liaison between what were then the four main German-speaking states – the Federal Republic of Germany, the German Democratic Republic, Austria and Switzerland – a process that was then facilitated by the unification of Germany in 1990. At various points there had also been input from representatives from Liechtenstein, Belgium, Luxembourg, Denmark, Italy, Romania and Hungary.[1] On 1 July 1996, delegates from these countries (with the exception of Belgium and Denmark), together with German, Austrian and Swiss officials, met in Vienna to sign the so-called 'Vienna Declaration of Intent' (*Wiener Absichtserklärung*), thereby agreeing to implement the new guidelines.

Although the disputes surrounding state involvement in the standardisation of German orthography had never entirely abated since they first began in the mid-19th century, by the time the Vienna Declaration was signed in 1996, a new round of protest had already gathered momentum. In May of that year, Rolf Gröschner, professor of law at the University of Jena, and his 14-year-old daughter, Alena, took their case to the Federal Constitutional Court (*Bundesverfassungsgericht* – *BVerfG*) in Karlsruhe and, even though the Court rejected on a legal technicality their claim that the reform was at odds with the German Basic Law (*Grundgesetz*), their highly publicised campaign helped to fan the flames of what might reasonably be characterised as a traditional public antipathy to the idea of orthographic reform. In October of the same year, a group of eminent writers and intellectuals, including Günter Grass, put their signatures to a petition circulated at the annual Frankfurt Book Fair by the Bavarian school-teacher Friedrich Denk. This protest attracted considerable media coverage, culminating in a front-cover story by the German news magazine, *Der Spiegel.* In November 1996, Denk then went on to form a national 'citizens' action group' or *Bürgerinitiative*, entitled 'WE [the people] against the spelling reform' (*WIR gegen die Rechtschreibreform*), the aim of which was to topple the reform via a series of regional referenda (*Volksbegehren*). Later that same month, the then Federal President, Roman Herzog, famously dismissed the reform and the surrounding debates as about 'as much use as a hole in the head'.[2]

In the meantime many parents had begun to challenge the reform in the regional courts. The first victory came in July 1997 when an administrative court (*Verwaltungsgericht*) in Wiesbaden accepted one parent's application for a temporary injunction against the reform, as a result of which the state of Hesse abandoned its plans to introduce the new spellings during the coming school year. It was a watershed ruling in the context of what was to become a major public and legal battle over German orthography that would continue for at least another three years. By spring 1998 some 30 cases had been heard in the regional courts, with just under half going against the reform, and in May of that year the issue was referred back to the Federal Constitutional Court for a final hearing. However, even when this court ruled definitively in favour of the reform in July 1998, and all schools and official authorities were instructed to proceed with its implementation, the popular protest continued. On 27 September 1998 – the same day as the national elections that saw the Christian Democrat Helmut Kohl replaced by the Social Democrat Gerhard Schröder – the electorate of one Federal state, Schleswig-Holstein, voted in a referendum to opt out of the reform. Having already introduced the new guidelines in 1997, schools in Schleswig-Holstein, the most northerly German state, then reverted to the old orthography, placing themselves in a somewhat isolated position with regard to the rest of the German-speaking area. However, it was a situation that would not – and probably could not – be tolerated for long in official quarters, and following the intervention of the regional parliament, the referendum result was overturned in September 1999, and schools in Schleswig-Holstein were once again instructed to teach the new spellings.

By the end of 1999, it began to look as though the disputes over the reform had more or less abated, the process of transition having been bolstered by the conversion to the new guidelines by the press on 1 August of that year (albeit, as we shall see in Chapter 3, to somewhat modified versions of the new orthography).[3] However, in July 2000 – and just as I was about to begin writing this book – the issue hit the headlines again. One month prior to the publication of a new edition of the Duden dictionary, the Erlangen-based linguist and long-time opponent of the 1996 reform, Theodor Ickler, declared in an article in the conservative national daily, *Die Welt*, that some dictionaries were in fact being used as a vehicle for 'secretly withdrawing' various aspects of the reform (Ickler, 2000). Ickler was referring here to a number of revisions that had been made to the new Duden dictionary following discussions with the Mannheim-based 'International Commission for German Orthography' (*Zwischenstaatliche Kommission für die deutsche Rechtschreibung*), which had been set up in accordance with the Vienna Declaration. This commission, whose short-term remit was the monitoring of the reform's introduction, but which in the longer term would oversee any further necessary amendments to German orthography, had been compelled to deal with the differing representations of the new orthographic rules in a number of commercially successful dictionaries, notably the Duden and its main rival Bertelsmann. Either way, so incensed by Ickler's claims was another long-time opponent of the reform, the conservative newspaper, *Frankfurter Allgemeine Zeitung* (*FAZ*), that this paper unilaterally declared its reversion to the old orthography, a decision that, up to the time of this book's publication, has not been revoked.[4]

By 2001 it began to look as though the dispute over German orthography had finally run its course, not least following what was to be the final legal ruling on the matter. This came in June of that year when the upper administrative court in Lüneburg, Lower Saxony, ruled that the 12-year-old daughter of Gabriele Ahrens – the latter, one of the key figures in the national citizens' initiative against the reform – should no longer be taught the old orthography in accordance with a previous ruling of the administrative court in Hanover but should, like all other pupils, learn the new rules for spelling and punctuation.[5] However, popular dispute has certainly continued, and many anti-reform groups, such as the 'Organisation for German Spelling and Language Cultivation' (*Verein für deutsche Rechtschreibung und Sprachpflege*), founded in 1997, have continued to call for a reversion to the old orthography.[6] Moreover, as we shall see in the course of this book, the status of the new orthographic rules following the end of the interim period in 2005 is by no means entirely certain.

In an historical survey of written German, Wolfgang Werner Sauer and Helmut Glück (1995: 69) declared: 'Orthography is boring. It is a subject for elderly folk who love order, vote Conservative, and always keep their dog on a lead.' Their heavily ironic comment, as they then proceeded to demonstrate, could not be further from the truth. Indeed the dispute over the 1996 reform of German orthography provides ample evidence that the group of those who do not find such issues boring extends way beyond order-loving Conservatives who take their dogs for walks on leads. The question, however, is *why*? One purpose of this book is to try to answer that question by exploring a range of issues pertinent to it. At the same time I would particularly like to render this debate accessible to an English-speaking audience with little or no knowledge of German. However, before I can do any of this, I will say something about the theoretical positions that inform my particular approach to the topic.

Language Ideological Debates

In this book I propose that the 1996 reform of German orthography, together with the public protests it inspired, constitute a prime example of what Jan Blommaert (1999) has referred to as a *language ideological debate*. In the introduction to his edited volume of the same name, Blommaert (1999: 1–12) describes such debates as occurring in specific times and places where real social actors – or *ideological brokers* – have collectively disputed the nature and function of language. These ideological brokers – who 'for reasons we set out to investigate, [...] claim authority in the field of debate' (Blommaert, 1999: 9) – can then be said to have engaged in the production and reproduction of competing *language ideologies*, that is, 'sets of beliefs about language articulated by users as a rationalisation or justification of perceived language structure and use' (Silverstein, 1979: 193). At the same time, such ideological brokerage can be theorised in terms of 'bids' for *authoritative entextualisation* (Silverstein & Urban, 1996: 11), in other words, as concrete attempts to secure closure in a given debate, according to which a particular view of language would eventually achieve a naturalised, common sense status. Here we see how language ideologies represent not only *perceptions* of language and discourse, but perceptions that are themselves 'constructed in the interest of a specific social or cultural group' (Kroskrity, 2000a,b: 8). It is in this way that the concerns of language ideology theorists meld with those of critical discourse analysts, who are similarly concerned with hegemonic 'struggles to legitimise claims for the universality of perspectives, interests, projects, etc. which are particular in their origins' (Fairclough, 2003: 79). Moreover, as James Tollefson (1991) has argued, language policy and language planning – of which orthographic standardisation is one of many potential examples – can be seen as crucial areas of social life where struggles for hegemony are acted out in, and over, language as part of broader social struggles to maintain and contest dominance in social relations (see also Blommaert, 1996).[7]

Writing at the beginning of the 1990s, Kathryn Woolard noted how: 'The topic of language ideology may be one much-needed bridge between work on language structure and language politics, as well as between linguistic and social theory' (1992: 236), a view which has since been widely acknowledged in some, though not all, quarters of sociolinguistics and linguistic anthropology (more below). However, Blommaert's point of departure for the analysis of language ideological *debates* is his contention that, while there is now a substantial literature on language ideology generally (see *inter alia* Joseph & Taylor, 1990; Kroskrity, 2000a; Lippi-Green, 1997; Milroy & Milroy, 1999; Schieffelin *et al.*, 1998), and historians of language have similarly touched upon related issues: '[...] the *historiography of language ideologies* is something that remains to be constructed' (Blommaert, 1999: 1 – emphasis in original). For, in any attempt to understand how and why some views of language gradually emerge as dominant, while others are suppressed and marginalised, we need to attend to the historical processes that inform the dynamics of social power as these obtain in particular times and places (see also Blommaert *et al.*, 2003; Kroskrity, 2000). This is because, as Blommaert emphasises:

> [...] ideologies do not win the day just like that, they are not simply picked up by popular wisdom and public opinion. They are being reproduced by means of a variety of institutional, semi-institutional and everyday practices: campaigns, regimentation in social reproduction systems such as schools, administration, army, advertisement, publications (the media, literature, art, music) and so on [...]. These reproduction practices may result – willingly or not – in *normalization*, i.e. a hegemonic pattern in which the ideological claims are perceived as 'normal' ways of thinking and acting [...]. (Blommaert, 1999: 10–11 – emphasis in original)

Central to the historiographical approach advocated by Blommaert, then, is the rejection of an *idealist* view of language that treats ideational phenomena such as attitudes and ideologies as something that language users merely 'have', since this results not only in the *de*-historicisation of such phenomena, but also the mystification of the power processes underpinning them. Instead, Blommaert argues for a particular type of *materialist* view of language, that is, one that entails:

> [...] an ethnographic eye for the real historical actors, their interests, their alliances, their practices, and where they come from, in relation to the discourses they produce – where discourse is in itself seen as a crucial symbolic resource onto which people project their interests, around which they can construct alliances, on and through which they exercise power. (Blommaert, 1999: 7)

This Bourdieu-inspired approach – where the social functions and meanings of language are actively constructed, negotiated and contested (Bourdieu, 1991; Heller, 1994) – allows the theorist, in turn, to transcend mainstream perceptions of attitudes and beliefs as the possession of *individuals*, and to expose the social and political contingency of ideational phenomena, thereby contributing to their demystification (see also Gal & Woolard, 2001a). It was against this theoretical backdrop that the contributors to Blommaert's collection went on to explore a range of debates on such seemingly disparate topics as the status of Ebonics in the USA (Collins, 1999), literary production in Tanzania (Madumulla *et al.*, 1999), the 'Speak Mandarin Campaign' in Singapore (Bokhorst-Heng, 1999), translation in Corsica (Jaffe, 1999b), and the use of Castilian Spanish and Catalan at the 1992 Barcelona Olympics (DiGiacomo, 1999) (for review, see Johnson, 2001b).

Orthography as Ideology

A focus on *orthography* – literally the assumption that there is only one correct way of writing – lends itself particularly well to the kind of historical–materialist approach to language ideologies advocated by Blommaert. It is, moreover, in tune with an emerging literature within sociolinguistics and linguistic anthropology that emphasises the contingent nature of orthographic practices generally.[8] For example, Mark Sebba (1998: 35–40) describes how the dominant view of orthography has traditionally been that of a neutral, technical accomplishment whose primary function is little more than the 'reduction of speech to writing' (see e.g. Lepsius, 1981 [1863, 1855]; Pike, 1947). Yet, drawing on Brian Street's (1984, 1993) now classic distinction between 'autonomous' and 'ideological' views of *literacy*,[9] Sebba argues how an autonomous approach to orthography similarly masks the ideological nature of the choices made by real social actors in the creation and revision of writing systems. In his study of British Creole, Sebba (1998) then explores the ways in which a number of writers of Caribbean origin have tried to capture in written form a variety of speech for which there is no standard orthography. Especially interesting are the choices made by such writers in those cases where there is no *phonemic* motivation for adopting a spelling that diverges from that of the lexifier language, English, e.g. ⟨tuff⟩ (tough) or ⟨dhu/duh⟩ (do) (1998: 27). This suggests that Caribbean writers are opting for spellings that intrinsically *construct* a difference between British Creole and standard English as a way of highlighting their own distinctiveness from mainstream cultural practices.

Similar uses of orthography as a means of styling both Self and Other in the representation and construction of ethnic, regional and/or national identities have been explored in the context of, *inter alia*, Indonesian and Malaysian (Vikør, 1988, 1993), English Creole in Trinidad and Tobago (Winer, 1990), Louisiana French (Brown, 1993), Haitian Creole (Schieffelin & Doucet, 1994), Manx (Sebba, 2000a), Corsican (Jaffe, 1996, 1999a), the Hmong language in Coolaroo, Australia (Eira, 1998), the written languages of Cameroon (Bird, 2001), Sranan, an English-lexicon creole spoken in Surinam (Sebba, 2000b), and Sm'algyax, the endangered language of the Tsimshian Nation in British Columbia, Canada (Stebbins, 2001). Meanwhile, Kuniyoshi Kataoka (1997) has analysed non-conventional uses of orthography in the casual letter-writing of young Japanese women, while Jannis Androutsopoulos (2000) has demonstrated the use of non-standard orthographies as powerful indices of *youth* identities for the producers of German music fanzines wishing to locate themselves in opposition to mainstream social norms as well as rival publications. Also, whereas Romy Clark and Roz Ivanič (1997: 195–211) have critically explored the use of English spelling and punctuation as a means of disciplining language users both at school and beyond, Gunther Kress (2000) has focussed on the emergent writing practices of young children as they attempt to marry the pressure to conform to the conventional school-based practices of mainstream society, on the one hand, with the desire to deploy orthography as a conduit for personal creativity, on the other (see also Stubbs, 1992). Finally, in a special edition of the *Journal of Sociolinguistics*, Alexandra Jaffe (2000) and her contributors[10] have explored many of the assumptions underpinning the use of non-standard orthographies as a means of representing non-standard speech, thereby highlighting the ideological role played by transcription processes more generally in the construction, conscious or otherwise, of social identities (see also Bucholtz, 2000).

It is interesting to note, however, the way in which this somewhat disparate – and certainly dispersed – body of recent work in what Sebba (2000b: 926) refers to as 'the sociolinguistics of orthography' has focused on orthographic practices and values primarily in the context of *emergent*, *non-standard*, or *endangered* varieties of written language. This is perhaps inevitable when one considers that such varieties present particularly rich opportunities for observing the production of ideologies, and the construction of social identities, against the backdrop of a typically tense relationship with mainstream standards. Yet such opportunities are arguably less in evidence in the context of those varieties of written language that are already both highly standardised and widely used, for it is here that what James and Lesley Milroy (1999 [1985, 1991]) have referred to as 'standard language ideology' – the promotion of an idealised standard perpetuating the interests of dominant social groups – is probably at its most *naturalised.* Also, even though, as Deborah Cameron (1995: 39) has noted, standardisation processes can never been entirely 'finished', once a standard variety has been widely accepted, diffused, prescribed and codified – to use Einar Haugen's (1972) now classic terms – notions of orthographic (in)correctness can appear so utterly self-evident that the status of that variety as common sense is often considered, literally, *beyond debate.* It is therefore perhaps only when such conventions are subject to a form of revision or re-standardisation, as in the 1996 reform of German, that popular awareness of the contingency of orthographic norms resurfaces, and that language ideological debates in both the private and public domains are triggered once again (Coulmas, 1989: 241; Fishman, 1977: XVI).

Why Ideology?

At this juncture it is important to acknowledge how not all linguists welcome an approach to the study of language standardisation, orthographic or otherwise, that emphasises the ideological dimensions of the language planning process and/or formulation of language policy. In a discussion of his own involvement in the re-standardisation of spoken Tamil, Harold Schiffman, for example, proposes how:

> These days it is fashionable, in many circles in the west, to deny both the existence and legitimacy of standard English or other standard languages – because standards have often been used capriciously and maliciously, to deny non-standard speakers access to power. Therefore, we now hear and see a great deal about hegemony, power imbalance, linguistic prejudice, maintenance/denial of privilege, empowerment, and many other allusions to ideological control of language. (Schiffman, 1998: 368)

While Schiffman goes on to stress how standards may serve an important purpose in terms of securing the functional efficiency of a given language (not least, for example, in the case of minority languages struggling to gain or maintain recognition, or in foreign language pedagogy), he somewhat undermines his own 'anti-ideological' line of argumentation when he notes: 'The fact is that, when all is said and done, speakers of natural languages make judgments about different kinds of speech and writing of which they hear and see samples, *and some of those judgments are, like it or not, hierarchical social judgments*' (Schiffman, 1998: 369, my emphasis).

As I see it, the underlying premise of work on language ideologies and language ideological debates lies not in some kind of politically motivated contempt for sociolinguistic processes such as standardisation (as implied by Schiffman), but as a means with which to actually deepen our understanding of the 'hierarchical social judgements' to which he refers via a more holistic account of the social, cultural, political and economic contexts in which such judgements are embedded.[11] However, this invariably presupposes a degree of critical reflexivity on the role played by linguists themselves in the standardisation process.[12] This is not least because, as we will see throughout this book, language ideological debates – including, and especially, those over orthography – are frequently characterised by a situation where it is precisely linguists' own 'expert' view of language that finds itself at the centre of public controversy and, in many cases, under explicit popular attack (see also Antos, 1996; Bird, 2001; Cameron, 1995).

It is in this regard that the critical project underlying the study of language ideologies has much in common with the field of Science Studies that emerged in the 1970s (see, *inter alia*, Hargreaves, 2000; Irwin & Wynne, 1996). Here, there has been a similar concern for the apparent cleft between 'expert' and 'lay' conceptualisations of scientific knowledge within debates over the public understanding of science. And as Simon Pardoe (2000: 149) explains in his study of student writing practices, it is generally accepted within this framework that any attempt to account for potential *mis*-understandings on the part of *non*-experts is most fruitfully conducted in accordance with the 'pursuit of symmetry' (see, for example, Latour, 1993). This demands that researchers attend not only to those beliefs and practices that have traditionally been considered *rational* (e.g. expert, scientific discourses), but that they expand their 'repertoires of explanation' by showing respect for those discourses that have thereby been dismissed as *irrational* (e.g. lay understandings of science). It is in this way that researchers can work towards a better understanding of not only those beliefs and practices that have been marginalised by dominant discourses, but also of the ways in which dominant discourses have achieved their own seemingly naturalised status as common sense.

As I have argued elsewhere (Johnson, 2001a), the concept of symmetry is one that can be usefully applied to the study of public understandings of *language*. This is partly because, as is widely acknowledged within the discipline of linguistics itself, the views of linguists as *language experts* are not generally accorded a high degree of respect outside of the academy (see, for example, Aitchison, 1997; Bauer & Trudgill, 1998). On one level it is important therefore to try to understand how, and why, this might be so, not least if the academic study of language is to be of wider relevance to public practice (see, for example, Antos, 1996; Cameron, 1995; Heller, 1999; Lippi-Green, 1997; Niedzielski & Preston, 2000). However, a more focussed attempt to explore so-called 'folk' conceptualisations of language is also useful insofar as there is much that linguists can learn about the nature of language itself by exploring the views of those social actors in the 'real world' whose views have been traditionally sidelined within the discipline (see, for example, Bloomfield, 1933; 1944), as well as by acknowledging that our own work as *linguists* is itself always historically and socially situated (see Blommaert, 1999; Kroskrity, 2000a,b). That said, as Susan Gal and Kathryn Woolard have emphasised (2001b: 3), the aim of this critical project is neither to privilege folk understandings of language, on the one hand, nor to discredit traditional forms of scholarly linguistic endeavour, on the other. Moreover, such reflexivity need not entail a denial that there are indeed *facts* of language that can themselves be subject to processes of distortion and/or *mis*-representation in line with classical Marxist definitions of ideology and false consciousness (see also Lippi-Green, 1997). Rather, the aim is to explore the nature of the *claims* about language (factual or otherwise) that are proffered by disparate ideological brokers (lay or expert) in the context of the discursive struggles that invariably ensue as these compete for hegemony. This, in turn, presupposes an analytical focus on the ways in which language as an object of concern is *itself* rationalised, (re-)presented and constructed in, and through, discourse (see also Lanthaler *et al.*, 2003).

As Gal and Woolard (2001b: 2) point out, this critical project marks a significant departure from the theoretical approaches that came to dominate linguistic analysis throughout the 20th century where the emphasis was traditionally on language as a pre-given object of study, that is, as a set of structures, to be 'discovered' and analysed by *experts.* However, it is against this theoretical backdrop that we see how, in the context of a language ideological debate, the views on language put forward by both experts and non-experts alike represent equally valid epistemological sites. Moreover, acknowledging that *linguists* constitute only one of several groups of language ideological brokers, each competing for the ultimate recognition of their particular linguistic viewpoint, may well be the key to unravelling the complexities of many a language ideological debate, not least, as we shall see in this book, the dispute surrounding the 1996 reform of German orthography.

Language Ideological Debates Revisited: Theory and Method

The idea of constructing an *historiography* of language ideologies is, as we saw above, a relatively recent proposal. It is, moreover, one that has opened up a range of theoretical and methodological questions, the implications of which have yet to be fully explored. In their simplest form, these questions can be summarised as: (1) what exactly *is* a debate (language ideological or otherwise)?; and (2) how do we go about analysing one? On the first, Blommaert has the following to say:

> In the field of politics, discursive struggle and contestation are generically captured under the label of debate. The political process develops through a series of exchanges involving a variety of social actors: politicians and policy-makers themselves, academic and non-academic experts, interested members of the public, the media. Debates are, politically–ideologically, the points of entrance for civil society into

policy making: they are (seen as) the historical moments during which the polity gets involved in shaping policies. (Blommaert, 1999: 8)

He adds, however:

Though there may be a prototypical perception of political debates, it is hard to provide conclusive criteria for identifying them, both in terms of discourse event-type (identities of participants, genres, time span, setting, etc.) and in terms of their relation to the outcome of decision-making procedures. They are patterns of interrelated discourse activities [...] often with a fuzzy beginning and end, of which we usually only remember the highlights, the most intense and polarized episodes. (Blommaert, 1999: 9)

At this juncture it is important to emphasise how the 'fuzziness' to which Blommaert refers is by no means the product of an inability to define the point at which a given debate might have begun or ended. It is in fact central to the complex task of constructing an historiography of such debates that itself necessitates at least a cursory theorisation of historical *time*. According to Blommaert (1999: 3), what is needed in this regard is: '[...] a concept of time that recognises both different "objective", chronological speeds and different ways of perceiving time by subjects'. Drawing on the classic formulation by Fernand Braudel (1958), Blommaert therefore distinguishes between two main time frames, namely, *courte dureé* (or *événement*), on the one hand, and *durée*, on the other. While *courte dureé* refers to the kind of 'real' time that people can experience and control in the short term, *durée* can be described as the less visible, much more slowly evolving 'historical' time characteristic of, say, social, economic and political systems. In practice, both temporalities are relevant to language ideological debates, which typically involve intense phases of observable activity located in 'real' time but are none the less situated within much broader and protracted debates across 'historical' time. Capturing the dialectical relationship between these differing temporalities then becomes one of the central propositions when attempting to construct an historiography of such debates.[13]

This, in turn, has direct implications for a second theoretical and methodological concern, namely the most appropriate means of 'accessing' a debate for analytical purposes. As Blommaert notes:

Debates are excellent linguistic–ethnographic targets. They are textual/discursive, they produce discourses and metadiscourses, and they result in a battery of texts that can be borrowed, quoted, echoed, vulgarized etc. In sum, they are moments of textual formation and transformation, in which minority views can be transformed into majority views and vice versa, in which group-specific discourses can be incorporated into a master text, in which a variety of discursive means are mobilized and deployed (styles, genres, arguments, claims to authority), and in which sociopolitical alliances are shaped or altered in discourse. (Blommaert, 1999: 10)

Central to the study of any debate, then, are the concepts of 'text', 'discourse' and 'meta-discourse'. At the risk of oversimplifying the complex and much-contested nature of the relationship between these three terms (for further discussion, see, *inter alia*, Fairclough, 1992; Gee, 1999), I see *texts* here as stretches of spoken or written language/discourse, *discourses* as the socio-cultural frameworks that are both drawn upon and whose traces are (re-)produced within such texts, and *meta-discourses* as broader reflections/commentaries on those texts/discourses. While the overall theoretical purpose of studying a language ideological debate is to critically analyse the processes by which disparate discourses/meta-discourses struggle to become 'authoritatively entextualised', the more immediate methodological issue is one of identifying the most appropriate form of 'discourse data' that will allow us to do so (see also Woolard, 1998).

Given that all debates, historical or otherwise, are only accessible via *texts* of some description, the inevitability of some form of textual analysis is immediately apparent. The various contributors to Blommaert's (1999) collection on language ideological debates, for example, take a range of text types into account including private correspondence, in-group publications such as reports, court rulings, and articles in academic journals, as well as different forms of coverage of language-related issues in the media and on the Internet. However, not only does the notion of 'textual analysis' barely narrow down the type of approach that might be adopted (the possibilities nowadays seem endless), if textual study is to make any meaningful contribution to an historiography of language ideologies, it must also be linked to a theoretical conceptualisation of the relationship between the micro- and macro-levels of analysis. This is especially important in view of the fact that a central purpose of studying language ideological debates is to be able to describe the broader socio-political contexts in which ideational phenomena are embedded, together with the longer-term implications of such phenomena for language variation and change. In this way, we also see how the role played by texts in the production, reproduction and dissemination of language ideologies more generally is closely tied in with the relationship between real and historical *time*.

What this means in practice is that, while the analysis of specific texts generated within a language ideological debate is an important way of empirically grounding any claims that might be made with regard to the language ideologies thereby mediated, any form of textual analysis that ties itself too closely to a structural–linguistic analysis risks losing sight of the broader socio-political contexts within which their meanings are none the less generated. On one level, this may be due to practical limitations of close linguistic analysis, which may simply leave too little space for an explication of such contexts. (This is especially so where the texts concerned are long.) On the other hand, close textual analysis can sometimes, as in certain forms of discourse/conversational analysis: 'fall into the trap of situating power *inside* textual structures or discourse patterns, assuming a too self-evident stance with regard to the producers, the audience, the setting – in short, the context of the discourse' (Blommaert, 1999: 34). The issue is ultimately one of analytical strategy – albeit one that lies at the nexus between sociolinguistics/linguistic anthropology, on the one hand, and (critical) discourse analysis, on the other – namely whether to go primarily for a description of the broader socio-political processes characteristic of a language ideological debate or its moments of textual articulation (for further discussion, see Blommaert, 2001; Blommaert & Bulcaen, 2000; Blommaert *et al.*, 2003; Fairclough, 2003; Johnson, 2001b).[14]

Outline of the Book

Against the backdrop of these concerns, I take the following approach to my analysis of the language ideological debate surrounding the 1996 reform of German orthography. On the one hand, I will be focussing primarily on one particular aspect of the debate, namely the *legal* disputes surrounding the reform that took place in a specifically German context.[15] These I see as being located in an identifiable period of 'real' time, that is to say, between 1996 and 1999. As the basis for this part of the analysis I will be looking primarily at two texts, that is, the rulings produced by the Federal Constitutional Court in response to each of the two main challenges brought against the reform: the first by Rolf Gröschner and his daughter in 1996, the second by Thomas Elsner and Gunda Diercks-Elsner in 1998. The analysis will, however, be limited to a discussion of textual *content* and expanded upon with reference to the broader socio-political contexts/discourses in which these texts are none the less embedded. These include, first, the longer-term history of official attempts to standardise – and *re*-standardise – the rules of German orthography from the mid-19th century onwards and, second, the linguistic–theoretical foundations of the changes that were made to German orthography in accordance with the 1996 reform. The structure of the book is, then, as follows:

Chapter 2 – *Historical Background* – begins by looking at the earliest, and no less controversial, attempts to reach agreement on the official standardisation of German orthography in the wake of the unification of Germany by Bismarck in 1871. These disputes gave rise to the first unsuccessful proposals of 1876, eventually leading to agreement on a revised set of guidelines in 1901/1902. The discussion then sketches the continuing efforts to consolidate the standardisation process throughout the 20th century. Such attempts include the much-disputed reform of 1944 as proposed by the National Socialist Minister for Education, Bernhard Rust, as well as the post-war discussions that gave rise to the Stuttgart and Wiesbaden Recommendations of 1954 and 1958, respectively. The chapter examines finally the period of negotiation eventually leading to the 1996 reform, namely the so-called First, Second and Third Vienna Talks of 1986, 1990 and 1994, respectively.

Chapter 3 – *Linguistic Details* – begins with an account of the linguistic–theoretical approach to orthography underpinning the 1996 reform. This was grounded in a structuralist approach to the study of written language that attempted to combine both phonological and semantic principles of orthography, thereby attending to the representation of both sound *and* meaning in written German. The chapter goes on to outline the application of these principles, and the issues thereby raised, with regard to the six main areas of the reform: (1) sound/letter classifications (including the spelling of foreign loans), (2) separate and compound spelling, (3) hyphenation, (4) capitalisation, (5) punctuation, and (6) syllabification/word division at the end of lines. Finally, the chapter summarises three key themes in relation to the linguistic disputes over the 1996 changes: (1) the overall consistency of the reform, (2) the problem of variant spellings, and (3) the extent to which the reform constituted a genuine simplification of previous guidelines.

Chapter 4 – *The Constitutional Challenge* – moves on to an analysis of the two main legal challenges brought before the Federal Constitutional Court, the first in May 1996 by Rolf Gröschner and his daughter, the second in May 1998 by Thomas Elsner and Gunda Diercks-Elsner. The chapter examines the complainants' assertion that the 1996 reform was not compatible with the German constitution or 'Basic Law'. This centred on Gröschner's original claim that the proposed method of introduction – a ministerial decree – was inadequate given the *fundamental* nature of the changes made to German orthography, which in his view necessitated the involvement of the democratic legislature. The discussion also looks at the reasons for the rejection of Gröschner's claims by the Constitutional Court, highlighting the somewhat paradoxical assertions of the Court in relation to the role played by the speech community in the acceptance, or otherwise, of linguistic norms imposed by the state. These, in turn, paved the way for a series of further challenges in regional courts around the country during the period 1996–1998, which culminated in the return of the issue to the Federal Constitutional Court in May 1998, the aim of which was to bring to a conclusion the legal disputes surrounding the reform. The chapter then outlines the 1998 challenge together with the reasons for its rejection once again by the Constitutional Court, as well as sketching the repercussions of this ruling in relation to the referendum in Schleswig-Holstein and the ensuing disputes when this federal state voted to opt out of the new orthographic guidelines in September of that year.

Chapter 5 – *The 1996 Reform as Language Ideological Debate* – returns to an analysis of the disputes surrounding the 1996 reform of German orthography specifically in relation to the concept of a language ideological debate. The discussion focusses on the views of the three main groups of ideological brokers in this dispute: the complainants, the judges of the Constitutional Court, and the linguists, exploring both the differences and similarities between them *vis à vis* perceptions and/or rationalisations of the re-standardisation process. Against this backdrop, Chapter 6 – *The Trouble with Spelling? Discussion and Conclusions* – draws the analysis to a close by considering, in both theoretical and practical terms, possible alternative approaches to the reform and its overall implementation.

Notes

1. German has status as sole official language in Germany, Austria and Liechtenstein, is recognised as one of several official languages in Switzerland and Luxembourg, and is an official minority/regional language in Italy (South Tyrol), Belgium, Romania and Hungary (Ammon, 1991; Clyne, 1995; Johnson, 1998).
2. The precise expression used by Herzog was *'überflüssig wie ein Kropf'*, which translates into English rather less figuratively as 'as much use as goitre'. (See *Süddeutsche Zeitung*, 23 November 1996.)
3. The new guidelines were also formally adopted by the European Union on 1 August 2000. For a discussion of the conversion process, see also Dittmann (1999).
4. For an account of the reasons underlying the FAZ's decision to revert to the old orthography, together with a broader discussion of the protests surrounding

the reform, see *Frankfurter Allgemeine Zeitung* (2000). Interestingly, the on-line edition of the FAZ continues to use the revised orthography (see Heller in Lønnum, 2003: 53).

5. See 'Ministerium siegt mit Rechtschreibreform' in *Hannoversche Allgemeine*, 22 June 2001.
6. For details see www.vrs-ev.de. See also alternative guidelines proposed by the *Deutsche Akademie für Sprache und Dichtung* (2003). For details of ongoing discussions, especially from the point of view of the reform's opponents, see www.rechtschreibreform.com.
7. Tollefson (1991: 16) draws attention, moreover, to the traditional distinction between *language planning* as 'general' attempts to influence the structure or function of language and *language policy* as language planning specifically undertaken on the part of governments or states. However, as he also notes, the commonly held distinction between 'unofficial' and 'official' forms of language planning itself masks an uncritical perspective regarding the crucial interplay *between* public and private spheres – a relationship that will be central to the concerns of this book (see also Fairclough, 2003).
8. Seminal early collections in this field are Smalley (1964) and Fishman (1977).
9. See also *inter alia* Barton (1994), Barton and Hamilton (1998), Barton *et al.* (2001) and Baynham (1994).
10. See Androutsopoulos (2000), Miethaner (2000), Jaffe and Walton (2000), Berthele (2000) and Preston (2000).
11. See, for example, Errington (2001), Gal and Woolard (2001a,b), Milroy (2001), Milroy and Milroy (1999), and Woolard (1998) for a similar line of argument.
12. See, for example, Cameron (1995), Coulmas (1989), Joseph and Taylor (1990), Williams (1992), Blommaert (1996), Irvine and Gal (2000), Parakrama (1995), Pennycook (2001), Tollefson (1991).
13. See Stevenson (2002), who similarly situates his sociolinguistic analysis of language in pre- and post-unification Germany in terms of Braudel's formulation of historical time.
14. I would like to express my gratitude to Jan Blommaert for our correspondence on these matters. His comments have been incorporated into this section and have in many ways helped to shape my approach to this book.
15. For details of similar debates and forms of protest in Austria and Switzerland, see www.rayec.de. This study will, however, restrict itself to an analysis of the protests in the Federal Republic of Germany.

Chapter 2
Historical Background

In many respects, the debates and dilemmas that surround the standardisation of German orthography today are as old as the written language itself. Indeed they can be traced back to the general unsuitability of the Latin alphabet when it was first adopted by eighth-century monks in their attempts to spread the word of the Gospel in the vernaculars of the time, the various dialects of Old High German. From the outset, there were problems, for example, with the distinction between long and short vowels, the representation of the semi-vowels ⟨j⟩ and ⟨w⟩, combined with the need to draw on the Greek characters ⟨y⟩, ⟨k⟩ and ⟨z⟩, themselves rarely used in Latin (for further examples, see Kranz, 1998: 22; Nerius, 2000a: 277–83; Scheuringer, 1996: 14–15). That said, early attempts to write German were none the less characterised by a general commitment to both consistency in orthography (at least within individual monasteries) as well as the belief that the task of writing was ultimately to represent the spoken form of the language, as glossed in the dictum 'write as you speak' (*Schreib' wie du sprichst*). And herein lie the roots of the very issues that would permeate debates over the writing of German throughout the coming centuries: a Latin alphabet not entirely suited to the task of representing the speech sounds of a Germanic language, together with regional and situational variation in spoken German, all of which gave rise to a range of different orthographic practices.

By the end of the 14th century, the production and use of paper well established, a substantial body of written German was already in existence, the norms for which had evolved without any genuinely systematic, that is, overtly prescriptive, intervention (Scheuringer, 1996: 20; Nerius, 2000a: 288–89). However, it was with the invention of printing from moveable type by Johannes Gutenberg in the mid-15th century, and the possibilities thereby afforded for the large-scale reproduction of written texts, that the perceived need for the standardisation of German orthography gradually came to the fore – first at a regional, then supra-regional, and eventually national level. However, it was not until around the

17th century onwards that concrete attempts at standardisation began to be made by lexicographers and grammarians, although these in turn were characterised by a number of competing demands (Scheuringer, 1996: 21– 54). While some, such as Hieronymus Freyer (1675–1747) and Johann Christoph Adelung (1732–1806), wished to see an orthography firmly committed to phonetic principles, others such as Jacob Grimm (1785– 1863) were beginning to prioritise an orthography that overtly acknowledged historical traditions in the development of written German. Added to this were differing views over morphological consistency as well as the spelling of foreign words and homophones. By the middle of the 19th century, theoretical disputes such as these, together with traditionally diverse practices across the German-speaking areas, meant that different sets of orthographic guidelines had been drawn up for schools in Hanover (1854), Leipzig (1857), Stuttgart (1861) and Berlin (1871). Inevitably, this created some difficulties for any pupil or teacher who moved between those regions, especially in the light of the increasing importance attached to *dictation* in the teaching and evaluation of reading and writing, against the backdrop of a rapid rise in literacy throughout the 19th century (Wells, 1985: 346).[1]

However, the growing sense that something 'had to be done' about orthographical variability was not motivated by primarily linguistic or even pedagogical considerations. Despite the range of regional traditions in the writing of German, the ability of readers to decipher texts from other areas was largely unaffected, and within regions there was still a high degree of consistency (Wells, 1985: 349). As Wolfgang Werner Sauer emphasises (1988: 85), the prime impetus for the official standardisation of German orthography was *political*. Following the unification of the German state by Bismarck in 1871, and the concomitant process of nation-state building that thereby ensued, came the perceived need for the standardisation of many areas of social life – currency, weights and measures, postal services, railways, education and the legal system – of which language, including orthography, was an integral part.[2] It is at this point therefore that this chapter will begin its attempt to sketch the historical background essential to an understanding of the protests surrounding the 1996 reform, in general, and the legal protests, in particular.[3]

The Failed Reform of 1876

In 1898, reflecting on the state of German orthography some fifty years previously, Konrad Duden noted how: 'No two teachers in the same school and no two proofreaders in the same printing works agreed on all aspects of orthography, and there was no authority which one could have called upon.[4] That this situation would soon change, thereby triggering debates and disputes that have reverberated right up to the present day, was in no small measure down to Duden himself. However, as his biographer Wolfgang Werner Sauer notes, it is important not to lose sight of the relative minimality of the orthographic inconsistencies lamented by Duden (Sauer, 1988: 85). Although a passionate believer in an accessible 'orthography for the people' – grounded in a broad commitment to the 'write as you speak' principle – the underlying issue here was one of authority and unity in the emergent nation-state. And in the years to come it was the name of Duden that would be elevated to a status of *de facto* authority within that state in all matters orthographic.

In 1872, one year after unification, the 'problem' of orthography was raised at a conference on higher education in Dresden. There the Prussian Minister for Education and Culture, Adalbert von Falk, proceeded to commission one of the leading Germanists of the day, Rudolf von Raumer, with the task of drawing up a set of guidelines for both the standardisation (*Vereinheitlichung*) and simplification (*Vereinfachung*) of German orthography. The guidelines subsequently produced by Raumer provided the basis for the so-called 'Conference on the Establishment of Greater Standardisation of German Orthography' (*Verhandlungen der zur Herstellung größerer Einigung in der deutschen Rechtschreibung berufenen Konferenz*) held in Berlin in 1876 (see *Verhandlungen*, 1876). The participants ranged from the linguists Raumer and Wilhelm Wilmans to representatives from universities, schools, and the printing trade, and included Duden, himself a grammar-school headmaster from Schleiz in the state of Thuringia. There is no record, however, of either Austrian or Swiss participation (Schlaefer, 1981: 420–25).

From the outset, the balance of what was later to become known as the First Orthographic Conference (*I. Orthographische Konferenz*) was in favour of a broadly phonemic approach to the writing of German as symbolised not only by the appointment of Raumer, himself a leading, albeit moderate, exponent of the 'write as you speak' view, but by the simultaneous exclusion of representatives from the historical and radically pro-phonemic schools. However, there were still numerous disagreements between those in attendance. On the one hand the majority of participants, including Duden, saw the conference as a unique opportunity to undertake a comprehensive overhaul of the German spelling system. On the other hand, a significant minority, including Raumer and representatives from the printing trade, emphasised the importance of going only as far as would be feasible in the light of probable responses on the part of the press, writers, and other interested parties in the public domain. In other words, the aim should be to intervene as little as possible in the *usus scribendi* – the orthographic traditions that had developed over time – and to iron out only those major inconsistencies that were thought to be causing genuine problems for language users (Jansen-Tang, 1988: 55).

After considerable negotiation and some extremely erratic voting, the 1876 conference finally agreed a number of fairly moderate changes to German orthography (Kranz, 1998: 26; Nerius, 1975: 62–63). These included, *inter alia*, the recommendation that ⟨th⟩ be replaced by ⟨t⟩ in words such as ⟨*Theil* → *Teil*⟩ (part) or ⟨*Noth* → *Not*⟩ (need). It was decided that vowel length should only be marked following ⟨e⟩ and ⟨i⟩, since these occur in both stressed and unstressed syllables. Otherwise, the superfluous marker of vowel length ⟨h⟩ should be dropped as in ⟨*Sohn* → *Son*⟩ (son) or ⟨*Gefühl* → *Gefül*⟩ (feeling) though retained, where necessary, in order to distinguish potential homographs such as ⟨*Ruhm*⟩ (fame) and ⟨*Rum*⟩ (rum). Moreover, it was also suggested that ⟨c⟩ be replaced by ⟨k⟩ or ⟨z⟩ in foreign words such as ⟨*Classe* → *Klasse*⟩ and ⟨*Medicin* → *Medizin*⟩. The question of noun capitalisation was not, however, on the agenda. This had been a continual source of dispute ever since its prescription by Johann Christoph von Gottsched in the mid-18th century, and proved too controversial to be resolved in 1876. Even today German remains the only world language to insist on the capitalisation of *all* nouns, the same principle having been abandoned for Danish in 1948.

Hans-Georg Küppers (1984), who conducted an in-depth survey of press responses to the question of orthographic reform between 1876 and 1982, shows how journalists took a keen interest in the 1876 discussions. However, while responses were initially positive with respect to the broader aims of the conference, a number of points were raised, many of which would be repeatedly discussed and disputed over the next 100 or so years (Küppers, 1984: 65–72). Doubts were expressed, for example, regarding the legal authority of the newly-formed Empire to undertake such a reform given that there was no provision in the constitution that afforded the state the requisite powers with which to either implement, or enforce, a unified orthography. Added to this were complaints regarding the purported lack of public consultation and generally low level of publicity surrounding the conference, as well as the narrow voting margins within the conference itself. And on the linguistic side, there was a particular focus on, and objection to, the question of vowel length changes. As Küppers (1984) shows, the language of many newspapers became heated, and many sections of the press began to declare that the fundamental aims of standardisation and simplification had not been achieved *per se*. All of this would appear to have had a crucial influence not only on public opinion but on the ministers themselves, and soon Falk himself was formally airing his own doubts as to the tenability of the reform, many of which echoed those of the press.

However, the final word on the matter was to come from Bismarck himself. Furious with the matter on the grounds that the German population was already having to cope with the standardisation of currency, measurements, weights, railways, and postal services following unification only five years previously, Bismarck threatened to take action against any civil servant who used the revised spellings. Suitably intimidated, Falk declined to go ahead with the recommendations of the conference, and thus came to an end the first attempt to reform German orthography.

The Reform of 1901

The failure of the attempted reform in 1876 meant that, once again, a range of guidelines on orthography were produced in different parts of Germany, Austria and Switzerland. In recognition of this situation, Falk's successor as Prussian Minister for Education and Culture, Robert von Puttkamer, requested that a specific set of guidelines for schools in Prussia be drawn up, leading to the introduction, in 1880, of what variously became known as the 'Prussian School Orthography' (*Preuß-ische Schulorthographie*) or 'Puttkamer's Orthography' (*Puttkamersche Orthographie*) (see also Hering, 1990). These guidelines, in conjunction with the broadly similar rules produced for Bavaria and Austria one year previously, then provided the basis for Konrad Duden's 'Complete Orthographical Dictionary of the German Language' (*Vollständiges Orthographisches Wörterbuch der deutschen Sprache*) published in Leipzig in 1880. This edition of the Duden was the first in a series of dictionaries, which would become the most authoritative set of reference works on German orthography for over a hundred years, although it was not a 'dictionary' in the modern sense, given that it consisted only of a list of prescribed spellings for some 28,000 words and did not provide lexical definitions (Sauer, 1988: 92).

As Küppers shows (1984: 79–83), the question of the Prussian School Orthography was fiercely debated in the press. Many journalists emphasised what they saw as the attack on personal freedom implied by its introduction and feared a break with historical tradition in written German, which they saw as playing a crucial role in the transmission of the cultural heritage of the newly-formed nation. And once more, against the backdrop of a ministerial dispute, Bismarck made it clear that the developments did not meet with his personal approval. Until such time as a reform of German orthography had been undertaken with the full legal force of the state, Bismarck again declared that he would have action taken against any civil servant who used the new orthography. However, in spite of what has often been referred to in the secondary literature as a 'ban' on the Prussian School Orthography by Bismarck, all states were in fact free to choose whether to take action against offending civil servants, and some clearly did not (Schlaefer, 1981: 406). Moreover, most of the smaller states went on to adopt the Prussian orthography in their schools, while some of the larger ones produced their own, albeit very similar, guidelines (Wells, 1985: 351). And given the voluntary adoption of the various school orthographies by the printing trade, the press, and book publishers – together with the official adoption of the 1880 Duden by Switzerland in 1892 – the situation was such that, by the end of the century, a high degree of *de facto* standardisation in German orthography had already been achieved (Schlaefer, 1981: 415–16 and 425–30).

As Schlaefer (1981) none the less points out, it is important to emphasise how the standardisation process was not, as is often assumed, the product of 'top-down' intervention by the newly-formed nation-state, but had in fact been realised almost in spite of the best efforts of Bismarck and the authorities of the Empire to prevent it (Grebe, 1963; Kohrt, 1997: 303). Bismarck's own actions in the context of the 1876 conference and the introduction of the Prussian School Orthography of 1880, clearly illustrate the contempt in which he held such reforms. And some of the most senior civil servants of the Empire did much to hinder the efforts of the cultural and educational authorities of the individual *Länder* to standardise their various orthographies at national level, despite the fact that the *Länder* retained sovereignty over such matters under the terms of the new constitution. For example, the late 1890s saw an unsuccessful initiative, possibly emanating from the Ministry of Justice, to produce and prescribe a single, new dictionary for use by post offices around the Empire, which would be based on the orthography used in the newly-established Civil Code (*Bürgerliches Gesetzbuch* or *BGB*) and eventually replace the various school orthographies (Meder, 1997: 191–92; Schlaefer, 1981: 416–17). As we shall see in coming chapters, it would not be the last time that such rivalries and/or more general tensions between the authorities of the state at *national* level, and its various constituents at regional or *Länder* level, would permeate – even dominate – disputes over German orthography.

By the time of Bismarck's death in 1898 and in spite of such rivalries, regional differences in orthography were at a minimum, with only a few areas of uncertainty remaining, primarily with respect to individual lexical items (Schlaefer, 1981: 411–13). Differing regional pronunciations, for example, had led to variability in the spelling of words such as *Gehilfe/ Gehülfe* (clerk/assistant) or *gescheid/gescheit* (clever). There was also variation in the prescribed spellings of foreign loans such as *Billet/Billette* (ticket) or *Bureaux/Bureaus* (offices), and in the use of Gothic and Roman variants of ⟨s⟩, hence *Drechſler* (turner) in Bavaria but *Drechsler* elsewhere. None the less it was felt, not least by many teachers who were emphasising the need for absolute clarity in matters of orthography,[5] that the spelling and punctuation of German were still in need of formal attention, and in 1901 the discussions now generally referred to as the Second Orthographic Conference (*II. Orthographische Konferenz*) took place in Berlin. However, unlike in 1876, where linguistic–theoretical considerations had been at the forefront of discussion, this time linguists themselves were in the minority. The only academics in attendance were Oskar Brenner and Wilhelm Wilmanns, together with a number of school teachers (including Konrad Duden), two members of the German book trade, and political representatives from various *Länder*, with only Wilmanns and Duden having been present at the 1876 talks. Austria was represented by an observer, although Switzerland's absence has been variously accounted for as a snub following Germany's refusal to accept a Swiss invitation to participate in an international conference on orthography in 1885 (Schlaefer, 1981: 423), by its subsequent decision of 1892 to adopt the 1880 Duden as its norm, or even the late arrival of the invitation (Augst & Strunk, 1989: 232).

In practice, the outcome of the 1901 conference might well be seen as less of an explicit 'reform' and more an endorsement of the Prussian School Orthography and Duden's 1880 dictionary as the model for a unified system of German spelling (see *Protokoll*, 1901). However, some changes were agreed, among others, the shift from ⟨th⟩ to ⟨t⟩ in most words perceived to be of German origin – but not, on the insistence of the Kaiser, *Thron* ('throne') – together with the move from ⟨k⟩ or ⟨z⟩ to ⟨c⟩ in common foreign loans, both of which had been proposed in 1876. The division of certain grapheme clusters was also regulated such that, from now on, it was officially permissible to separate ⟨pf⟩, ⟨sp⟩, and ⟨tz⟩, although ⟨ck⟩ should shift to ⟨kk⟩ when split as in *Zucker → Zuk-ker* (sugar) and ⟨st⟩ should remain inseparable. None the less many issues remained unresolved. For example, although some changes were made to vowel length marking, for example, the reduction of ⟨aa⟩ to ⟨a⟩ in words such as *Waagen* → *Wagen* (car), not included was the abolition of post-vocalic ⟨h⟩ in items such as *Sohn* (son) or *Gefühl* (feeling) as proposed in 1876 (Nerius, 1975: 66). Moreover, the guidelines failed to address many of the more fundamental questions surrounding German orthography such as the general principle of phoneme–grapheme correspondence (including the spelling of foreign loans), noun capitalisation, hyphenation, the division of words at the end of lines, and – crucially – punctuation.

Following the conference of 1901, its recommendations were sent to the relevant authorities of the individual German *Länder*, as well as to Switzerland and Austria, with a request for formal approval. When this was forthcoming, the Deputy Chancellor of the German Empire, Graf von Posadowsky, wrote to the German upper house or *Bundesrat* in April 1902 requesting its approval for the official introduction of the unified orthography in 1903 by all schools and state authorities. In addition, it was requested that the Bundesrat recommend the adoption of the new orthography by municipal and non-state authorities (Augst & Strunk, 1989: 232). In July 1902 the German Kaiser, Wilhelm II, responded, freeing the way for the Bundesrat to pass a resolution to this effect in December. However, the Kaiser refused to accept the 1903 date of introduction for his own personal usage or in any correspondence directly addressed to him (so-called *Immediatberichte*), and the old orthography was ruled acceptable for such purposes until 1911 (Schlaefer, 1981: 419). Meanwhile, Austria agreed to introduce the new orthography one year earlier in 1902, while Switzerland formally repealed its commitment of 1892 to the 1880 Duden in favour of the new guidelines of 1901 (Schlaefer, 1981: 424; for further discussion of the implementation of the 1901 reform, see Kissel, 1997: 1102–103).

All in all, it was clear that the 1901 conference had achieved its purpose of formally unifying – or *standardising* – German orthography. However, the additional aim of 1876, namely that of *simplifying* the spelling system, had been marginalised from the outset, perhaps understandably so, for while the former was in many ways a question of agreeing which norm to adopt and how to enforce it, the latter required substantial intervention into actual usage for which the popular and political will – not least on the part of the authorities of the Empire – did not appear to obtain (Mentrup, 1993: 21).

After the press controversies that had surrounded the attempted reform of 1876 and the introduction of the Prussian School Orthography in 1880, public response to the 1901 reform was generally more restrained (Küppers, 1984: 92–95). The fact that only a small number of changes had been made was especially welcomed, particularly as this was felt to minimise confusion for foreign learners, for whom the language was seen by many as an important conduit for German national culture. Similarly, standardisation was greeted on economic grounds in that it would facilitate the distribution of books by publishers throughout the German-speaking areas. Moreover, there appeared to be little regret that the broader aim of simplification had not been achieved, in itself unsurprising given the view frequently expressed prior to the 1901 conference that such simplification was more or less tantamount to a level of 'dumbing down' imposed by pedagogues.

However, therein lies the more general paradox that was to permeate, even plague, discussions over the standardisation of German orthography throughout the 20th century. While a significant political compromise had been achieved via the 1901 recommendations, the problem now was that the apparent 'pragmatism' of 1901 had led to the formal prescription of a set of orthographic guidelines recognised by all involved to be imperfect, both in terms of *in*clusions as well as *ex*clusions. Duden himself was in no doubt about this, claiming in the introduction to the seventh edition of the *Orthographisches Wörterbuch* published in 1902 that his dictionary was only really an 'intermediary step' (*Zwischenziel*) on the path to further reforms. However, in spite of the fact that the 1901 guidelines had crucially – indeed fatefully – omitted to specify any formal mechanism for the ongoing revision of German orthography, even Duden would probably not have expected almost a hundred years to elapse before the next official step would – or could – be taken.

Between Reforms I: 1902–1933

Throughout the 20th century, virtually every year witnessed some form of failed attempt to achieve the ongoing standardisation – or *re*-standardisation – of German orthography in which Konrad Duden so fervently believed (Garbe, 1978; Jansen-Tang, 1988; Küppers, 1984; Nerius, 2000a). However, leaving aside a number of minor modifications to the 1901 guidelines on the part of the state, it was, ironically perhaps, Duden himself who from the outset complicated that very re-standardisation process. For example, in the seventh edition of his dictionary published in 1902, Duden's interpretation of the 1901 guidelines for the spelling of foreign loans meant that a far greater degree of optional variability was permitted than in either the sixth edition of the Duden published in 1900 or in the official guidelines themselves. There has been much speculation as to why this should have been so. Sauer (1988: 103), for example, suggests a number of reasons such as the speed with which the 1901 guidelines were incorporated into the 1902 edition of the Duden, allowing insufficient time for adequate proofreading. Whatever the case, it is clear that such optional variability presented a particular problem for one group of language users traditionally keen on watertight guidelines on all spelling-related matters, namely printers. As a consequence, 1903 saw the publication of the first edition of a separate printers' Duden: the so-called *Buchdruckerduden* (second edition, 1907). However, not only did these volumes once again reduce the amount of optional variability permitted in the spelling of foreign words – albeit going in many instances against the official guidelines of 1901 – they also incorporated a range of detailed regulations on punctuation, an area of German orthography left unregulated in 1901 (for further details, see Nerius, 2000a: 355–63).

This trend towards orthographic 'interventionism' on the part of Duden was further consolidated when, following Duden's death in 1911, the general dictionary was merged with the printers' version to produce the ninth edition of a single Duden in 1915 (the first to elevate the name of *Duden* from editor to actual dictionary title). By this time many of the inconsistencies between the 1901 guidelines, the general Duden, and the printers' Duden had been combined, resulting in a range of disparities between the 1901 rules and those subsequently contained in the various editions of the dictionary. It was an act that latterday reformer Hermann Zabel (1997b: 52) describes as the greatest 'sin' in the history of German orthography, given that the fusion of the two dictionaries led to the imposition upon the general public of a set of rules primarily intended for 'language specialists' such as printers, typesetters and proofreaders, and which were of such considerable complexity that no single language user could ever be expected to master them all. Yet such interventionism would, as Sauer (1988: 103–16) shows, repeatedly characterise the actions of the Duden corporation over the coming decades in its quasi-official capacity as arbiter of German orthography. To give but one of many examples, the guidelines of 1901/1902, while still permitting a degree of optional variability, recommended that ⟨c⟩ generally shift to ⟨k⟩ in foreign words such as ⟨*Classe* → *Klasse*⟩. However, subsequent Duden editors failed to apply this principle consistently, justifying such actions with the claim that they were simply 'documenting actual usage'. Hence while the variant spellings ⟨*Cockpit/Kockpit*⟩ were originally allowed in early editions of the Duden, these eventually gave way to ⟨*Cockpit*⟩. Moreover, recent foreign loans such as ⟨*Computer*⟩ and

⟨*Container*⟩ have not seen the 1902 principle applied at all (Sauer, 1988: 103–16; for further examples see Zabel, 1996: 357), thereby undermining previous attempts to achieve *general* orthographic rules via the introduction of *singular*, lexeme-specific rules (see Kohrt, 1987, 1997).[6]

Alongside these developments, a number of more general critiques of German orthography also began to emerge. In 1902, Oskar Brenner re-opened debates thought by many to have been settled at the 1901 conference, advocating once again that there should be much clearer phoneme–grapheme correspondence, with each speech sound represented by one character only. He also argued, *inter alia*, in favour of a greater standardisation of vowel length marking and a reduction in the level of noun capitalisation (Brenner, 1902; Jansen-Tang, 1988: 66). It was in this tradition that, O. Kosog, a school teacher from Breslau, published a brochure in 1912 that similarly demanded a more thoroughgoing reform, and that contained what became known as 'Kosog's dictation' (*das Kosogsche Diktat*). This was a passage demonstrating the virtual impossibility of mastering the finer points of German orthography, especially in the area of noun capitalisation, and Kosog showed how neither he nor many other experienced teachers of German could complete it correctly (for text, see Scheuringer, 1996: 96).[7] In conjunction with ongoing doubts surrounding the status of the Duden *vis à vis* the guidelines of 1901, the issues raised by Brenner and Kosog, along with the question of foreign loans, punctuation and hyphenation, brought together the main concerns over orthography that would reverberate throughout the 20th century.

Following World War I, the first official attempt to revise the 1901 guidelines came in 1920/1921 when representatives from Germany, Switzerland, Austria and a range of interested parties met in Berlin. A series of proposals were put forward for a comprehensive 'phonetic' (or, strictly speaking, *phonemic*) reform of German as well as the abolition of noun capitalisation (for details, see Nerius, 2000a: 371–72). However, the reform failed in the light of ailing official and ministerial support against a backdrop of widespread public and press opposition. Once again, fears of a break with the historical continuity of the language were expressed although, as Küppers shows (1984: 101–105), relatively new to the protest at this point in time were vehement personal attacks on the reformers themselves combined with the suspicion that a revised orthography was merely the first step en route to the 'Bolshevikisation' of other educational domains. Following the failure of these early reform attempts, the next most wide-reaching proposals were to come in 1931 from two different sources: teachers in Leipzig and printers in

Erfurt (Nerius, 2000a: 372–74, Lüthgens, 2002: 69–72). Each put forward their own set of suggestions, seeing the question of orthographic reform as very much in tune with the ostensibly 'liberal' mood of Weimar Germany. However, despite the generation of public interest and much discussion, the political will for reform was not ultimately forthcoming. Not for the first time, and justifiably so, it seemed that orthographic reform would emerge as too minor a concern in the light of more pressing political problems of the day (Jansen-Tang, 1988: 72–79).

Between Reforms II: 1933–1945

When the National Socialists seized power in 1933, they too had many other more pressing political concerns. That said, language was not only an undeniably important *conduit* for National Socialist propaganda but an equally potent *symbol* of German cultural heritage from the point of view of the new regime (see, *inter alia*, Hutton, 1999), an important facet of which was the written form of the language, not least its orthography (Jansen-Tang, 1988: 79–84; Küppers, 1984: 109–13). In the early days of the National Socialist regime, attitudes towards the question of ortho-graphic reform were generally positive, although concerns were expressed about the confusion for both native speakers and foreign lear-ners likely to be brought about by a switch to a new set of orthographic conventions. By the late 1930s, however, these concerns had been increas-ingly sidelined against the backdrop of the expansionist policies of the Hitler regime. Now it was felt that a simplified writing system could in fact be operationalised as a means of *facilitating* the acquisition and use of German, particularly among non-German speaking subjects in the newly-occupied territories.[8] The first significant step in this direction came in 1941 with the official abandonment of the traditional Gothic (*Fraktur*) and Sütterlin writing scripts in favour of Roman (*Antiqua*) type, and this was followed in the same year by a proposal, albeit unsuc-cessful, for orthographic reform by Fritz Rahn (Strunk, 1998a).[9] However, it was a set of suggestions for the revision of the 1901 guidelines put forward in 1944 by the National Socialist Minister for Education, Bernhard Rust, which would re-emerge as the subject of dispute some fifty years later in the context of debates over the legal status of the 1996 reform.

The so-called 'Rust reform' proposed a number of changes to German orthography, for example, the replacement in foreign loans (or, more accu-rately, items *perceived* to be of foreign origin) of the digraphs ⟨ph⟩, ⟨th⟩ and ⟨rh⟩ with the germanicised variants ⟨f⟩, ⟨t⟩ and ⟨r⟩, respectively; the reduction of three consecutive consonants to two in compound forms; the separation of verb forms such as *Rad fahren* (previously *radfahren* – to cycle); the division of syllables according to phonetic as opposed to etymological criteria; and the abolition of the comma before the coordinating conjunctions *und* (and) and *oder* (or) (Nerius, 2000a: 374). However, two of the main texts to have dealt with this period in depth – Kopke (1995a: 54) and Birken-Bertsch and Markner (2000: 9–21) – both draw attention to the way in which this particular chapter of German orthographic history has suffered marginalisation, or even outright exclusion, from mainstream historiographies of the reform process (but see also Ickler, n.d.; Simon, 1998; Strunk, 1998b). Both texts show, for example, how writers have traditionally referred to the documents pertaining to the 1944 reform as either having been 'lost' or 'destroyed' in the latter years of the war and/or the reform as having failed on account of general resistance on the part of the public, the press, and within the Nazi party (see, for example, Jansen-Tang, 1988: 82–84; Kranz, 1998: 28–29; Küppers, 1984: 110–13; Nerius, 2000a: 373–74). The net result is the downplaying, conscious or otherwise, of the legal and historical relevance of Rust's proposals. That said, the two sets of authors reach somewhat different conclusions as to what they see as the ongoing political significance of the 1944 proposals and their theoretical legacy for subsequent reform debates.

Wolfgang Kopke (1995a: 36–48) – the legal scholar whose doctoral dissertation on judicial aspects of orthographic reform afforded many of the arguments upon which the constitutional challenges against the 1996 reform were later based – draws attention to the fact that the Rust reform of 1944 was officially decreed by the Ministry for Education with respect to all schools within the territories of the Third Reich. This, he then shows, was in accordance with a law of 1934 whereby overall responsibility for educational matters had been transferred from the individual *Länder* to the central state with Hitler at its head. However, while Kopke acknowledges that the relevant edition of the legal gazette (*Reichsgesetzblatt*) containing the decree was never actually circulated throughout the Reich, and the reform was never therefore implemented in schools, he does not see this as in any way invalidating the status of the Rust proposals as a legally decreed reform. Consequently, he argues how, following the war, the 1944 guidelines on German orthography should have been formally acknowledged by the individual *Länder* of the newly formed Federal Republic of Germany to whom control of educational matters had been returned under the the constitution of 1949, the Basic Law or *Grundgesetz*.

Much of Kopke's argument in this regard revolves around the distinction between laws (*Gesetze*) versus administrative regulations (*Verwaltungsvorschriften*) or decrees (*Erlasse*) issued by the National Socialists, and their respective status *vis à vis* the Basic Law of the Federal Republic. While there are many examples of continuity in terms of *laws* between the two historical periods, it was generally the case that *administrative regulations* issued during the Third Reich were subsequently disregarded by the *Länder* authorities. Yet Kopke (1995a: 39–46) argues how, given that the distinction between the *legislature* (normally responsible for the production of laws) and the *executive* (which issues adminstrative regulations) had in any case been dissolved under the dictatorship of the Third Reich, the retrospective differentiation between the two forms of legislation in subsequent debates over orthography is ultimately inconsequential. The fact remains, according to Kopke, that it was within the jurisdictive power of Hitler, as head of state, together with his Minister for Education, Rust, to decree the 1944 guidelines and these should therefore have been formally acknowledged both by the cultural authorities of the *Länder* and orthographic reformers in the post-war period.

However, it is precisely the role of Hitler in this dispute that leads Hanno Birken-Bertsch and Reinhard Markner (2000: 107) to a rather different conclusion. Kopke's argument, they stress, fails to take into account one crucial fact: having learned of Rust's proposals from the press, Hitler ordered – via a so-called *Führerbefehl* of 24 August 1944 issued one month after being injured in an attempt on his life – that all decisions pertaining to orthographic reform be deferred until the end of the war, not least given their perceived insignificance in the context of the ensuing final phase of the German war effort. Moreover, as Birken-Bertsch and Markner show (2000: 109), unlike earlier attempts to reform German orthography from 1933 onwards, where there had been concern to act in conjunction with the Ministry of the Interior (Simon, 1998), the 1944 reform had been a largely 'clandestine' affair. Hitler is therefore thought to have been particularly antagonised by the fact that he learned about the reform from press sources, and also to have been especially concerned about proposals to germanicise the spelling of foreign loans, which, he believed, would considerably alter the visual appearance of written German. Either way, it is Birken-Bertsch and Markner's view (2000: 118) that the Rust reform was ultimately invalidated by Hitler in 1944 and it is this that undermines the legal basis of Kopke's claim that the proposals drawn up by Rust ought to have been recognised as the most recent set of state-sanctioned guidelines, not least when the Federal Constitutional Court was called upon to rule on the legality or otherwise of the 1996 reform in both 1996 and 1998.

However, the real significance of the Rust reform for latter-day debates surrounding orthography is, according to Birken-Bertsch and Markner (2000: 125–26), two-fold: first, the manner in which this particular episode clearly demonstrates the ideological nature of *all* debates surrounding orthographic reform, thereby highlighting the linguistic–theoretical imperative to see any intervention into orthography as an inherently political act; secondly, what they consider to be the largely unacknowledged degree of continuity between the 1944 proposals and the subsequent reform of 1996, together with what they see as the latter's ongoing, and theoretically outdated, commitment to orthography as a mere second-order representation of spoken language. Not surprisingly, perhaps, such proposed analogies between the intentions, linguistic or otherwise, of National Socialists, on the one hand, and latter-day reformers, on the other, have met with some hostility within reform circles (see, for example, *3. Bericht der Zwischenstaatlichen Kommission für deutsche Rechtschreibung*, 2001).

Between Reforms III: 1945–1973

In many ways, the end of World War II – despite, once again, more urgent political and economic concerns – was perhaps the ideal point at which to return to the question of orthographic re-standardisation, given that so many books had been destroyed and that, by 1944, the German publishing trade had come to a virtual standstill (Wittmann, 1999: 373–74). For once, therefore, traditional protests from printers and publishers regarding the *cost* of a potential reform and its implementation were unlikely to be heard. There was also a certain democratic impulse that saw this as precisely the time to rid the German education system of a number of arbitrary rules of spelling and the authoritarian methods used to teach them, thereby freeing up time and energy for other, more important pedagodic matters. However, the first comprehensive reform attempt – put forward in 1946 in the Soviet-occupied sector – failed amidst concerns, voiced not least in the press, of insufficient consultation between the four zones of occupied Germany as well as with Austria and Switzerland (Küppers, 1984: 113–20).[10] Once again, doubts were also expressed regarding a potential caesura with the historical tradition of German writing, not least at such a crucial point in history where language was felt by some to be all that held together an otherwise decimated German culture. And such was the brevity of this opportunity for re-standardisation that when the 13th edition of the Duden was published in 1947, thereby re-establishing the status of the old orthography, the opportunity for reform had already passed (see Jansen-Tang, 1988: 85–86).

From 1949 onwards any attempt to reform German orthography had of course to contend with the political reality of a divided Germany. However, after a number of interim reform proposals and meetings by interested parties in the late 1940s and early 1950s (Kranz, 1998: 30), the first serious attempt to bring together representatives from the two German states, Austria, and Switzerland, resulted in the publication in 1954 of the so-called Stuttgart Recommendations' (*Stuttgarter Empfehlungen*). These proposals covered eight points of German orthography: (1) The abolition of noun capitalisation and the introduction of so-called 'moderate minisculisation' (*gemäßigte Kleinschreibung*), that is, a system of capitalisation roughly akin to that used in English; (2) the standardisation of various grapheme clusters; (3) the abolition of variant spellings; (4) the writing of foreign loans according to German spelling conventions; (5) the writing of lexical items as one word or two; (6) hyphenation; (7) punctuation; (8) the writing of proper names (whereby no changes should be made) and, as an additional point, some minor alterations to vowel length marking (for comprehensive details, see Strunk 1992, 1998a).

However, as Jansen-Tang (1988: 93) notes, even this arguably pragmatic attempt on the part of the Stuttgart reformers to circumvent public antipathy via a fairly modest set of proposals failed in the context of what was probably the most vociferous public response to date, itself something of a turning point in the history of the standardisation process (Küppers, 1984: 121–29). Central to the disputes – and foreshadowing many of the controversies surrounding the 1996 reform – were the reactions of the writers Thomas Mann, Hermann Hesse, and Friedrich Dürrenmatt, who declared the reform a threat to the aesthetic and expressive functions of the language although, as has subsequently been shown (Küppers, 1984), some of their arguments were based on the misreporting of the reform's details by various newspapers. The writers' complaints were then accompanied by heated press coverage whereby the reformers were themselves variously dismissed as left-wing revolutionaries, enemies of communism, or US-imperialists, depending on the political standpoint of the publication in question.

It was clear that the public controversies surrounding the Stuttgart proposals would once again prohibit the re-standardisation of German orthography. Moreover, by the end of 1954, two separate versions of the Duden dictionary were now in print, one in the East (Leipzig) and one in the West (Mannheim). However, it was the appearance earlier that same year of a rival dictionary in West Germany, Lutz Mackensen's 'German Orthography' (*Deutsche Rechtschreibung*) commissioned by the 'Society for German Language' (*Gesellschaft für deutsche Sprache*) and published by Bertelsmann, that was to trigger a landmark ruling in the history of German orthography (Augst & Strunk, 1988).

In 1950, following the failure of early post-war reform attempts and given that the official guidelines of 1901/1902 had not been re-printed since 1942 the West German Standing Conference of Ministers for Education and Cultural Affairs – the *Kultusministerkonferenz* or *KMK* – had already stated that in so-called 'cases of uncertainty' (*Zweifelsfälle*), the Duden dictionary should be considered binding until such time as a formal revision of German orthography had been agreed. Now, in 1955, against the backdrop of the failure of the Stuttgart Recommendations and the publication of Mackensen's commercially successful rival dictionary, the publisher and editor-in-chief of the Duden, Franz Steiner and Paul Grebe, respectively, turned to the KMK requesting clarification of the situation *vis à vis* the 1901 rules. It was at this point that the KMK formally confirmed its unpublished ruling of 1950 that, until such time as revised norms were available, the 1901 guidelines – together with any subsequent official amendments – remained valid (see *Bulletin der Bundesregierung*, 20 December 1955). However, in so-called 'cases of uncertainty', the rules laid down in the Duden were to be considered binding – at least in West Germany.[11] It was in this way that Duden, a private corporation, achieved its *de facto* status as the official arbiter in matters orthographic for the subsequent four decades (Augst & Schaeder, 1997a: 5–11).

The literature dealing with these events offers a range of interpretations of the intentions that lie behind Steiner and Grebe's actions, both of whom had participated in the Stuttgart talks. Was this a case of canny commercial tactics, as suggested by Scheuringer (1996: 99), or a genuine attempt to clarify the situation in the light of a long-standing personal commitment to the orthographic re-standardisation process, as proposed by Gerhard Augst and Hiltraud Strunk (1988: 341)? And while, with the benefit of hindsight, the KMK decision might well be regarded as a highly questionable example of the state securing a trade monopoly for a private corporation (a point, as we shall see in Chapter 4, at the centre of early legal disputes over the 1996 reform), the actions of the KMK would appear to have been genuinely intended as no more than a temporary solution (Augst & Strunk, 1988). It was not widely expected at the time that the question of reform would take so much longer to resolve, even if the

KMK decision could only be welcomed by Duden, while simultaneously deplored by its commerical rivals such as Bertelsmann. The question of the 1955 KMK ruling is also linked to ongoing controversies surrounding the validity or otherwise of the Rust reform in 1944. Kopke (1995a: 47), for example, shows how, in his submission to the KMK of 1955, Paul Grebe explicitly claimed that the Duden dictionary was, unlike rival publications, based on the most recent official guidelines, namely those of 1944. In this context, the subsequent KMK ruling of 1955 with its reference to the guidelines of 1901 'together with any subsequent official amendments' must, according to Kopke, be taken as an acknowledgement of the legal validity of the 1944 regulations. However, Birken-Bertsch and Markner (2000: 118–20) take a somewhat more differentiated line. Whilst by no means able to deny the existence of the statements on the part of Grebe and the KMK to which Kopke draws attention, they doubt whether the editors of the Duden were ever in possession of a copy of the 1944 regulations and were therefore familiar with their contents (Kohrt, 1997: 306). Moreover, they show how the 1944 proposals had not in fact been integrated into the 1947 edition of the Duden, which referred only to the official guidelines of Prussia (1940), Bavaria (1940) and Austria (1935) as its sources.[12] These guidelines then continued to form the basis for the 1954 edition published in Mannheim, which made no mention as to which set of 'current regulations' had been drawn upon. Similarly, the KMK proceeded to make references to the 'current' guidelines without ever clarifying the precise referent. Thus rather than adducing the events of 1955 as further evidence of the unacknowledged validity of the 1944 regulations as proposed by Kopke, Birken-Bertsch and Markner (2000: 120) prefer to see this episode as merely exemplifying the ongoing confusion surrounding the status of official guidelines on German orthography *per se*. They imply, moreover, that the claims made by Grebe were simply part of a rhetorical tactic to persuade the KMK of the superiority of the Duden – in the context of the corporation's ongoing rivalry with Bertelsmann – via a publicly stated commitment to the 'official' guidelines, whatever these might have been (Scheuringer, 1996: 99).

Following the failure of the Stuttgart Recommendations and the KMK ruling of 1955, the question of orthography was taken up again in a series of meetings, leading to the publication in 1958 of a revised, and more moderate, set of proposals known as the 'Wiesbaden Recommendations' (*Wiesbadener Empfehlungen*). Six suggestions were made this time: (1) the introduction of moderate minisculisation; (2) freer regulation of comma usage; (3) syllable divisions based on pronunciation as opposed to etymology; (4) no variant spellings; (5) foreign loans to be written according to the German system wherever possible; (6) only genuine compounds to be written as one word, otherwise items to be separated (Strunk, 1992, 1998a). Again, in anticipation of potential public response, the question of phoneme–grapheme correspondence, in particular vowel length marking, had been sidelined and moderate minisculisation became the main demand – although this in turn similarly became the focus of widespread protest. However, unlike the Stuttgart Recommendations, which were the product of meetings involving all four German-speaking countries, the Wiesbaden Recommendations had been drawn up by a commission of West Germans only, who were themselves aware that no reform could proceed without the agreement of all those affected. And in the consultations that took place between 1961 and 1963 (Nerius, 2000a: 377–79), Austria emerged as undecided, while Switzerland came out against the reform, explicitly rejecting the demand for moderate minisculisation. East Germany, on the other hand, although apparently broadly in favour of the proposals, articulated no official response.

The failure of the Wiesbaden Recommendations did not, however, signal the end of an interest in the question of reform, and by the late 1960s the issue was once again at the forefront of discussion. This time, against the backdrop of much broader socio-political debates in the wake of the (West German) student protest movement, the initiative would come primarily from teachers (Lüthgens, 2002: 117–29). Thus in an education system where German-language teaching makes extensive use of dictation, and where pupils are required to repeat whole school years should they fail to reach a specified standard of achievement, spelling reform became a significant component of attempts to reform what were felt to be a range of discriminatory educational practices.[13] An article in the newspaper *Die Zeit* (23 February 1973), for example, suggested that three-quarters of all children made to repeat school years were being forced to do so because of their spelling – with 30% of all errors occurring in the area of capitalisation (cited in Clyne, 1995: 181–82). There was also particular concern surrounding the impact of such practices on working-class pupils, who were thought to have less contact with written German than their middle-class counterparts – a line of argument closely linked to Basil Bernstein's theory of 'restricted' and 'elaborated' codes, itself highly influential in sociolinguistic and educational debates in West Germany at the time (Barbour & Stevenson, 1990: 181–91; Bernstein, 1971; Stevenson, 2002: 26–28).

Concerns that orthography continued therefore to be used as an inappropriate means for processes of educational, and ultimately social, selection were widely voiced at this time, not least at a conference of primary school teachers in Frankfurt in 1969 (Lüthgens, 2002: 123–24), and it was in this context that the West German KMK subsequently agreed to re-visit the question of reform. This resulted in a meeting in Vienna of representatives from West Germany, Austria, and Switzerland in 1971 (the GDR declined to participate), which, as Doris Jansen-Tang (1988: 114) notes, rang in a new era of reform discussions, given that not only politicians, linguists, and publishers were invited to put forward their views but also pedagogues, psychologists and sociologists. A meeting of the KMK in 1973 then voted unanimously in favour of a reform based broadly on the Wiesbaden Recommendations and, following a further meeting in the same year in Vienna with representatives from all four German-speaking states (Nerius, 2000a: 379–82), it was agreed that the proposals be introduced in schools by 1975.

In the meantime, popular opinion was again divided. On the one hand, it appeared that significant sectors of the public were behind the reform, as illustrated not least by the formation of a citizens' initiative in 1972 – the so-called *aktion kleinschreibung* – that gathered some 50,000 signatures in favour of moderate minisculisation. On the other hand, as Küppers shows (1984: 141–51), the whole issue of orthographic reform – and particularly the symbolic significance of noun capitalisation – once again provoked considerable controversy. This time, however, the debates became specifically intertwined with more widespread antagonisms between political parties on the left and right. The Hesse branch of the Christian Democratic Union (CDU), for example, produced a pamphlet dismissing reform attempts as a conduit for Marxist indoctrination that would lead only to 'broader' social fragmentation, and similar views were taken up by the conservative newspaper, *Frankfurter Allgemeine Zeitung* (FAZ), amongst others. And so it was that just when it looked as though a reform of German orthography might finally succeed, the CDU Education Minister in Baden-Württemberg, Wilhelm Hahn, began to voice his own doubts about the reform, declaring it not least to to be 'ideologically motivated'. It was at this point that the Social Democratic (SPD) federal government of the day – despite having spoken out in favour of reform throughout 1973 – also began to waver in its commitment to what was clearly a controversial issue, not least in an election year. Thus when in 1974 the point was reached where the reform would require full-scale governmental support, it seemed that once again the political will was not forthcoming, and thus the proposals came to nothing.

From the Vienna Talks to the 1996 Reform

Despite the failure of the various reform attempts throughout the
1960s and early 1970s, the impetus for orthographic reform continued
to gather momentum in the mid-1970s, not least following the formation
in 1974 of a research group on orthography at the East German Academy
of Sciences (*Akademie der Wissenschaften*) with Dieter Nerius as its head,
and the appointment of Wolfgang Mentrup in 1977 as chief of the
newly-founded Commission for Orthographic Issues (*Kommission für
Rechtschreibfragen*) at the West German Institute for German Language
(IDS) based in Mannheim. In the meantime Austria had declared itself
in favour of moderate minisculisation, East Germany was fundamentally
behind the Wiesbaden Recommendations, and Switzerland confirmed its
intention to cooperate with any agreement reached by the other German-
speaking states.[14] Following a series of meetings in the late 1970s, and the
formulation of various sets of proposals in each of the German-speaking
countries, there now appeared to be sufficient common ground for an
international agreement. This led in 1980 to the formation of the so-called
International Working Party on Orthography (*Internationaler Arbeitskreis
für Orthographie*). In conjunction with a series of interim meetings, three
formal conferences of the Working Party were then held in Vienna in
1986, 1990 and 1994, known officially as the First, Second and Third
Vienna Talks (*erste, zweite und dritte Wiener Gespräche*), respectively, but
often collectively referred to as the 'Third Orthographic Conference'
(after 1876 and 1901).[15]

Following its initial formation in 1980, the International Working Party
on Orthography met again in 1982 and 1984, leading to the publication in
1985 of a preliminary set of reform proposals by the Commission for
Orthographic Issues (*Kommission für Rechtschreibfragen*, 1985). These proposals, which included recommendations, on *inter alia*, punctuation, capitalisation, and hyphenation, provided the basis for the First Vienna Talks
of 1986 attended by West German, Swiss and Austrian officials (the GDR
was represented by an 'observer'). In 1987 the (West German) KMK and
Federal Ministry for the Interior then requested that the Mannheim-based
Commission, together with the Wiesbaden-based 'Society for German
Language' (*Gesellschaft für deutsche Sprache*), make further suggestions
for reform in the areas of hyphenation, foreign words, and sound/spelling
relations but *not* capitalisation, given the popular opposition that this
would almost certainly arouse. In 1988 the Commission reported back
to the KMK with a set of proposals broadly based on the First Vienna
Talks of 1986 (*Kommission für Rechtschreibfragen*, 1989). These, however,

met with widespread public and media condemnation. Particularly resented, not for the first time in the history of reform attempts, was the suggestion that double vowel sequences be reduced, for example, ⟨*Aal* → *Al*⟩ (eel) or ⟨*Boot* → *Bot*⟩ (boat), although the highest level of opprobrium was probably reserved for the proposed harmonisation of diphthong spellings, resulting in changes such as ⟨*Kaiser* → *Keiser*⟩ (emperor). In fact, this one word came to symbolise the entire media furore surrounding reform attempts in the late 1980s that ultimately led to the KMK's rejection of the Commission's proposals in 1990 as documented in Hermann Zabel's 1989 book *Der gekippte Keiser* – 'The Toppled Emperor'.

Following the Second Vienna Talks and the unification of the two German states in 1990 – the latter considerably facilitating international cooperation – a revised set of recommendations were produced and published (*Internationaler Arbeitskreis zur Rechtschreibreform*, 1992). Six main areas were covered: (1) sound–letter relationships (including foreign words), whereby some of the more radical suggestions of 1988/ 1989 were dropped; (2) the writing of lexical items as one word or two; (3) hyphenation; (4) capitalisation, whereby there were three suggestions: maintaining the status quo, harmonising the existing rules of capitalisation, or adopting moderate minisculisation; (5) punctuation; and (6) syllabification. The 1992 proposals then provided the basis for a public hearing organised in 1993 by the KMK together with the Federal Ministry for the Interior in which some fifty interested groups participated, and which appeared to conclude that a reform was not only necessary but now actually feasible.[16] However, in spite of such official support, the 1992 recommendations still met with considerable public and media criticism (see Zabel, 1996, for documentation), not least the linguists' own recommendation in favour of moderate minisculisation. Further revisions were therefore made during the Third Vienna Talks in November 1994, the outcome of which was what the authors hoped would be the final set of regulations published in July 1995 (*Internationaler Arbeitskreis zur Rechtschreibreform*, 1995). The talks concluded with a declaration that a reform should be finalised by the end of 1995, introduced during the school-year 1996/1997, and fully implemented in all participating countries by 1 August 2001 (Schaeder, 1999b: 13–14; for text of declaration, see Augst *et al.*, 1997: 67–68). In December 1994 the Institute for German Language (IDS) in Mannheim then published a special edition of its in-house journal *Sprachreport* detailing the proposals, and, in an attempt to consolidate their position as the *de facto* authority on orthography, the publishers of the Duden dictionary similarly released their own 47-page booklet just before Christmas of that year (Duden, 1994).[17]

In 1995 the reform process appeared to be progressing smoothly. Indeed the Duden publishers were so confident that the reform would proceed that they had already prepared several thousand copies of a new dictionary to be launched one day after the final approval of the reform by the KMK planned for the end of September (Scheuringer, 1997b: 410–11). However, by the summer, a number of dissenting voices once again began to be heard. In August, the Saxon Cultural Minister complained of insufficient consultation with the so-called 'new' *Länder* (former East German states). In a long piece in the *Frankfurter Allgemeine Zeitung* newspaper, the Paris-based linguist, Jean-Marie Zemb, declared the reform to be a threat to the unity of the German language (see *FAZ*, 2 September 1995). Meanwhile, the Bavarian Cultural Minister, Hans Zehetmair, stepped into the debate with his own concerns about the intended 'germanicisation' of a number of foreign loans (Scheuringer, 1997b: 410–17). It was around this time that a new dimension to the anti-reform protest also surfaced as the legality of the implementation process itself began to be explicitly questioned. While the KMK had always envisaged, following the precedent of 1901 (Augst & Strunk, 1989), that the reform be introduced by a series of decrees (or *Erlasse*) issued by the individual *Länder*, this was now publicly called into question by legal experts, most notably the Jena-based law professor, Rolf Gröschner, and his former doctoral student Wolfgang Kopke (Kopke, 1995a). In Gröschner and Kopke's view, the reform would impinge in such fundamental ways upon the constitutional rights of individuals as laid down in the Basic Law that its proposed method of introduction was constitutionally untenable. What was required instead, they argued, was one or more statutory laws (or *Gesetze*) at federal and/or *Länder* level. Although the KMK did not accept this argument – which in practice would have required up to 17 individual laws – it was this aspect of the protest, as we shall see in Chapter 4, that would ultimately pose the most serious threat to the implementation of the new orthographic guidelines over the next three years.

Such was the momentum gathering against the reform that, in early September, the KMK decided to postpone the meeting at which they planned to approve the reform from the end of September to the end of November. It was against this backdrop that, at KMK meetings in October and November, a number of minor revisions were made to the original proposals, not least concerning the spelling of foreign loans (or items containing forms perceived to be of foreign origin), whereby it was agreed that some 30 individual items should continue to be written using loaned spellings, for example, *Alphabet* (not *Alfabet*), *Katastrophe* (not *Katastrofe*) and *Restaurant* (not *Restorant*). Meanwhile, discussions amongst the KMK and the conference of Prime Ministers of the 16 Länder (*Ministerpräsidentenkonferenz* or *MPK*) ensued, and in early November 1995 the IDS in Mannheim put out a press release aiming to dispel more general misapprehensions regarding the number of new rules, the alleged increase in the proportion of foreign words to be germanicised in their spelling, the cost of the reform, along with accusations of secrecy surrounding the discussions. Shortly afterwards, a further press release by the IDS announced a small number of additional revisions in the light of the 'political feasibility' of the earlier proposals, mainly, though not exclusively, in the area of foreign loans (see IDS press releases of 9 and 22 November 1995). Whilst a blow for the Duden publishers, who would be forced to pulp an undisclosed number of copies of their new dictionary, the proposed revisions appeared to satisfy both the Cultural Ministers and the Prime Ministers of the 16 Länder, the latter subsequently instructing the former to proceed with the reform's implementation. It was also at this point in the debate that the new interim period for the official introduction of the reform – from 1 August 1998 to 31 July 2005 – was confirmed (Schaeder, 1999b: 17–20).

In 1996 the proposed reform of German orthography was formally approved. In March the deadline for any veto on behalf of the individual Länder came and went, and the Prime Ministers also gave their official support. Although the then Federal Chancellor, Helmut Kohl, declined to comment specifically on matters of orthography, the Federal Cabinet similarly declared in April that it would not stand in the way of the KMK recommendations (Schaeder, 1999b: 21). In June, a petition by Rolf Gröschner and his daughter for a temporary injunction to halt the reform's introduction was rejected by the Federal Constitutional Court (more in Chapter 4). Then, in July, delegates from Germany, Austria and Switzerland together with representatives from Italy, Liechtenstein, Luxembourg, Romania and Hungary, went on to sign a 'mutual declaration of intent on the restructuring of German orthography' (*Gemeinsame Absichtserklärung zur Neuregelung der deutschen Rechtschreibung*) or the so-called 'Vienna Declaration of Intent' (*Wiener Absichtserklärung*). This declaration acknowledged the guidelines as agreed at the Third Vienna Talks in 1994 and published in July 1995 by the International Working Party on Orthography as the basis for the reform (Article I); stated that the new guidelines be introduced no later than 1 August 1998 and be fully implemented by 31 July 2005 (Article II); confirmed the setting up of an expert commission on orthography to be based at the Institute for German Language (IDS) in Mannheim. This commission (eventually convening in March 1997) would oversee the introduction of the reform and also be given the remit of monitoring the official guidelines in conjunction with general orthographic developments within the speech community, with the long-term aim of securing the preservation of orthographic unity in the whole of the German-speaking area (Article III); and, finally, the declaration stated that any other states interested in signing the mutual declaration in future would be welcome to do so (Article IV – for complete text, see Augst *et al.*, 1997: 69–70). The signing of the declaration was then followed by the publication of the official text of the new guidelines (*Deutsche Rechtschreibung*, 1996).

Of particular interest in the light of the Vienna Declaration was the decision to set up the Mannheim-based commission to oversee orthographic issues from 1996 onwards. This was a move clearly designed to tackle the question of ongoing language change that had been so fatefully neglected by the reformers of 1901, arguably paving the way for the *de facto* monopoly of the Duden corporation from 1955. It was in accordance with this particular paragraph of the Vienna Declaration that Duden specifically lost its monopoly. Moreover, while the 21st edition of the Duden revised according to the new guidelines did not appear until the end of August, their main commercial rival Bertelsmann had already published their new updated edition containing a foreword by IDS linguist and member of the International Working Party, Klaus Heller, only one day after the signing of the Vienna Declaration. It did not escape the notice of some commentators that this was a sweet 'revenge' of sorts for Bertelsmann who, along with so many other publishers, had waited over forty years for the opportunity to compete once again on equal terms with Duden (see, for example, Zimmer, 29 September 1996).

It had been a long path to the agreement of a new set of official guidelines on German orthography and in the summer of 1996 10 of the 16 Länder of the Federal Republic of Germany went ahead with the introduction of those guidelines in their schools rather than wait until the official deadline of 1998. Yet, while many participants and observers of this hugely controversial reform might have hoped that this was the end of the road, for others it turned out to be only the beginning. Over the next two years there would be some 30 court cases challenging the legality of the procedure by which the reform had been introduced. However, before turning to an analysis of these cases in Chapter 4, the next chapter will outline the actual revisions made to German spelling and punctuation in 1996 and consider some of the linguistic-theoretical disputes surrounding those changes.

Notes

1. See Fix (1994: 25–74) for a critical exploration of the relationship between the standardisation of orthography, the implementation of planned curricula in schools, and the increasing use of dictation as a means of evaluating literacy acquisition from the 19th century onwards.

2. See Meder (1997) for an informative comparative discussion of 19th-century attempts to standardise the various regional legal systems, on the one hand, and orthographic guidelines, on the other. For a discussion of efforts to specify a standard pronunciation for German, see von Polenz (1999: 255–63).

3. There are numerous texts that deal with the historical issues in far greater detail than will be possible or desirable here. For the sake of brevity and clarity, for example, I shall avoid repeating the linguistic details of each of the various reform proposals put forward from the 19th century onwards. The interested reader is therefore referred, *inter alia*, to the German texts by Jansen-Tang (1988), Kranz (1998), Küppers (1984), Mentrup (1993), Nerius (1975, 2000a), von Polenz (1999), Sauer (1988), Scheuringer (1996), Schlaefer (1980, 1981) and Veith (2000). For summaries in English, see Sauer and Glück (1995) or Russ (1994) and the sections on orthography contained in the more general histories of the German language by Keller (1978) and Wells (1985).

4. German original: 'Nicht zwei Lehrer derselben Schule und nicht zwei Korrektoren derselben Offizin waren in allen Stücken über die Rechtschreibung einig, und eine Autorität, die man hätte anrufen können, gab es nicht.' (Cited in Nerius, 1975: 61.)

5. For a detailed examination of the role played by teachers in debates over orthography from the mid-19th century to the end of the 20th century, see Lüthgens (2002).

6. For a detailed discussion of the relationship between the Duden corporation and official orthographic guidelines, see Böhme (2001).

7. The IDS linguist and head of the international reform commission, Klaus Heller (2000), has demonstrated how the 1996 reform actually resolved all of the issues in German orthography raised by Kosog's dictation.

8. In accordance with the terms used by Geerts *et al.* (1977: 206) this marks a shift from a so-called 'discouragement argument', where a reform of orthography might undermine the willingness of non-natives to learn the language, to an 'encouragement argument', where a reform would render the language easier to learn, thereby supporting the efforts of non-native learners.

9. In one sense, this move to roman type might be viewed as unexpected in the context of the more widespread National Socialist desire to preserve the kind of symbols of German cultural heritage of which Gothic and Süterlin writing scripts were such potent examples. Such concerns were, however, clearly overridden by the recognition that the *roman* script would more readily facilitate the consolidation of German in the occupied territories. As Birken-Bertsch and Markner (2000: 37–40) show, it was the fact that this paradox was not

entirely lost on the National Socialists that then led to attempts to discredit the Gothic script via a re-airing of an erroneous claim (probably first made during World War I) that such a writing system had originally been a Jewish invention.

10. See Kranz (1998: 29–30) for details of earlier reform attempts in the British zone in 1945, Berlin in 1946, Switzerland in 1946, and Leipzig in 1947.

11. The German Democratic Republic issued similar a ruling with respect to the Leipzig Duden in 1959 (Kranz, 1998: 33).

12. As Kohrt (1997: 306) notes, the incorporation of the 1944 guidelines into subsequent editions of the Duden would have required spellings such as ⟨fysisch⟩ (physical), ⟨Katolik⟩ (Catholic) and ⟨Klaun⟩ (clown), forms that neither appeared in the dictionary nor established themselves subsequently in popular usage.

13. The generally preferred variety of dictation exercise nowadays is that of *Nachschriften*, where pupils are given a complete passage a few days in advance of the dictation test and are then required to memorise the orthographic features of the passage, which is subsequently 're-written' in class under test conditions (the younger age groups work with word lists). For critical discussion of the role of dictation as a means of disciplining schoolchildren, see Jäger (1974), Spitta (1977) and Fix (1994). See Rigol (1977) for an empirical investigation demonstrating the negative impact of dictation on the overall achievement of working-class pupils.

14. For detailed discussions of the reform debate throughout this period, see Zabel (1997c) on West Germany; Hillinger and Nerius (1997) on East Germany; Blüml (1997a) and Schrodt (2000) on Austria; and Looser and Sitta (1997) and Looser (1998) on Switzerland.

15. See Zabel (1997b) for details of the meetings and their participants; see also Zabel (1995a) for an overview of press reactions to these talks.

16. Similar events were held in Austria and Switzerland, see Schaeder (1999c: 13).

17. For a detailed chronology of events surrounding the reform, and various interventions in the dispute, during the period 1994–1999, see Stenschke (2002: 112–28) and Schaeder (1999b).

Chapter 3
Linguistic Details

In Chapter 2 we saw how the fixing of a standard German orthography in 1901/1902 was followed by almost a century of attempts to revise, improve, and update the original guidelines. However, according to Dieter Nerius (2000a: 68), one of the key theoretical thinkers behind the 1996 reform, early proposals for re-standardisation tended to be driven by primarily 'social' or 'educational' concerns as opposed to a fully fledged *linguistic* theory of orthography. From the perspective of linguistics as an academic discipline, this is perhaps unsurprising when one considers the dominance of structuralist approaches to language since the early part of the 20th century. In the eyes of structuralists such as Ferdinand de Saussure (1915) and Leonard Bloomfield (1933), for example, 'real' language – and, by implication, the only legitimate focus of linguistic analysis – was *spoken* language. If dealt with by linguists at all, written language tended to be accorded a secondary status, its main function being that of *representing* speech (see for example Pike, 1947; Weisgerber, 1964).[1] Against this backdrop, it was not until the mid-1970s that orthography gradually emerged as a focus for scholarly activity in Germany following the formation of research groups in the German Democratic Republic (Rostock) and the Federal Republic (Mannheim). It was the work of these groups that then provided the linguistic–theoretical foundations for the Vienna Talks of 1986, 1990 and 1994, thereby paving the way for the 1996 reform.[2] However, as we shall see in this chapter, the reformers' attempts to re-standardise the spelling and punctuation of German were firmly grounded in *structuralist* approaches to both written language, generally, and orthography, specifically.

While drawing on a range of insights into the linguistic study of orthography, Nerius (2000a: 55–67) shows how the 1996 reform owes much to de Saussure's notion of language as a semiotic system consisting in a structured series of *signs*. These signs – the basic units of all human communication – are made up of a *signifier* (the thing that signifies) and a *signified* (the object or concept that is signified), the relationship between the two being arbitrary as opposed to fixed (de Saussure, 1915). As Nerius (2000a: 56–58) emphasises, the Saussurean view contains an in-built bias towards spoken language insofar as it is the function of speech (as opposed to writing) to record objective real-world meanings. The main purpose of writing is therefore that of representing as accurately and objectively as possible the spoken form of the language, ideally via a one-to-one correspondence between phonemes and graphemes, the minimal units of speech and (alphabetic) writing, respectively (see also Tauli, 1977).[3] According to this view, we might then see speech theorised as 'content' (or *signified*) to be represented by writing as 'form' (or *signifier*).

This notion of writing as a mere 'second-order' representation of speech was called into question by many other linguists, however, most notably functionalists working within the Prague School. In direct opposition to de Saussure, Josef Vachek (1945–1949), for example, argued strongly in favour of a relativisation of the speech/writing dichotomy, preferring to see the two codes as having distinctive communicative functions in view of their disparate positioning *vis à vis* time and space.[4] In Vachek's view, neither speech nor writing should be accorded primacy in linguistic–theoretical terms, although as Nerius (2000a: 60–62) shows, in his later work Vachek (1973) certainly noted how *one* of the many functions of writing is to represent speech, suggesting that orthography might then be seen as a kind of bridge between the two codes. However, in spite of his conviction that the optimal writing system in any language would be one based on phoneme–grapheme equivalence, Vachek was similarly aware that this was rarely achieved in practice. This means that even written languages based on alphabetic scripts must simultaneously draw on ideographic elements in the production of meaning. In other words, the orthographic representation of 'real-world' meanings need not be mediated first by speech, but can also be represented 'directly' via the visual shape of morphemes, words, and even whole texts (see also Harris, 1986, 1990, 2000). In the specific context of reading, moreover, this implies that meaning-making will be based on a combination of both phonological processing ('reading by ear') and visual processing ('reading by eye').

Acknowledging the inherent relationship between spoken and written language, while at the same time attempting to avoid the prioritisation of speech as the sole basis for writing, the linguists behind the 1996 guidelines worked with two main theoretical principles: the *phonological* and the *semantic*. According to this compromise view, orthography is posited not only as a system representing spoken language but simultaneously as a means of directly signifying a range of semantic concepts (Nerius, 2000a: 87–97). Both the phonological and the semantic principles then incorporate a sub-set of structural principles as outlined in Table 3.1.

Table 3.1 Linguistic principles underpinning the 1996 reform

Phonological principle	Semantic principle
Phonemic	Morphological
Syllabic	Lexical
Intonational	Syntactic
	Textual

Source: Nerius, 2000a: 87

In other words, decisions relating to the *phonological* principle are concerned primarily with the orthographic representation of speech-related features such as phonemes, syllables, and stress/intonation. Decisions relating to the *semantic* principle, by contrast, are linked to the way in which meaning is represented ideographically at the level of morphemes, lexemes, syntax, and textual organisation as a whole. The various linguistic levels of analysis are, moreover, locked into an overall structural hierarchy, according to which each higher level incorporates all lower levels as follows: text, sentence, lexeme, morpheme, intonation, syllable, and phoneme. However, as Nerius (2000a: 93) points out, one might wish to isolate the phonemic, morphological, and syntactic as the central levels of analysis with the syllabic, intonational, textual, and possibly lexical levels, as peripheral. Finally, in the context of orthographic reform, each linguistic level must be considered in terms of both (1) the phonological/semantic content to be *signified* and (2) its orthographic representation or *signifier*.

Achieving a workable balance between the phonological and semantic principles was not only central to the underlying linguistic philosophy of the 1996 reform, but to some extent its potential success in terms of public reception. This is because a strict adherence to the phonological principle is often thought to benefit the *writer* (especially the inexperienced writer), who can draw upon his or her knowledge of pronunciation (albeit *standard* pronunciation) to make informed decisions about the orthographic representation of particular sounds (→'reading by ear'). The semantic principle, on the other hand, is generally thought to favour the *reader* (especially the experienced reader) who, in an attempt to decode meaning, can extrapolate from already familiar visual patterns of orthographic structure across related word groups and/or text types (→'reading by eye'). A further complication in this regard concerns the more general historical development of German spelling and punctuation. Broadly speaking, the phonological principle traditionally underlying German orthography increasingly gave way to the semantic, especially from around the 16th century onwards (see Nerius, 2000a: 277–340). However, as Nerius (2000a: 91) argues, from a synchronic perspective – central to the structuralist approach underpinning the 1996 reform – this did not mean that phonological issues could be entirely sidelined given that most language users continue to perceive a link, however tenuous, between the pronunciation of a word and its spelling. It was clear, then, how any attempt to balance phonological and semantic principles within the reform package would inevitably be tested in the context of specific orthographic choices, and concomitant decisions could (and would) be readily interpreted as prioritising diachronic/ synchronic factors and the interests of either reader or writer in relation to written German.[5] The following sections now sketch the broader applications of the phonological and semantic principles to specific areas of German orthography.

Phonological and Semantic Principles of German Orthography

Phonological principles

The phonological principle incorporates three main levels of analysis: the phonemic, the syllabic and the intonational. The **phonemic** principle presupposes that the optimum alphabetic writing system will be characterised by a one-to-one correspondence of phonemes and graphemes. Leaving aside the issue as to whether such an aim is ever realisable (for discussion see Harris, 1986, 2000), German orthography has always had to contend with the same basic problem as that of English: the number of phonemes is simply far greater than the number of letters available to represent them. As a result, only three German phonemes are represented by a single grapheme – /j/ as in *ja* (yes), /h/ as in *Huhn* (chicken), and /z/ as in *sieben* (seven) – whereby ⟨h⟩ and ⟨s⟩ are also used for, or in conjunction with, other phonemes (see Russ, 1994: 154). This means that the majority of German graphemes are characterised by varying degrees of multifunctionality such that the principle of one-to-one phoneme–grapheme correspondence is flouted in three main ways. First, more than one grapheme may be used to represent a single phoneme, for example, the digraph ⟨ch⟩ for /ç/ as in *Kirche* (church) or trigraph ⟨sch⟩ for /ʃ/ as in *Kirsche* (cherry). Secondly (and conversely), more than one phoneme may be represented by a single grapheme, for example, ⟨x⟩ for /ks/ as in *Hexe* (witch). Thirdly, a phoneme may be rendered differently according to its morphophonemic environment and/or etymological status. Sometimes this will follow a pattern of complementary distribution as in the case of /ʃ/, which is written ⟨s⟩ before ⟨t⟩ or ⟨p⟩ as in *stehen* (to stand) or *sparen* (to save), respectively, and ⟨sch⟩ in most other positions.[6] On the other hand, graphemic distribution may be somewhat less systematic as in the case of /f/, which is written as ⟨f⟩ in *Feind* (enemy), ⟨v⟩ in *Vater* (father), ⟨ff⟩ in *Schiff* (ship), or ⟨ph⟩ as in *Physik* (physics).

Meanwhile the representation of vowels – and particularly vowel *length* – raises a number of related issues. Short German vowels are typically represented by a single grapheme followed by a consonant pair, for example, /I/ as in *Silber* (silver), /u/ as in *Bulle* (bull), /Y/ as in *Hütte* (hut), /œ/ as in *Hölle* (hell), /ɔ/as in *tropfen* (to drip), /ɛ/ as in *Fels* (cliff) or *Fässer* (barrels), and /a/ as in *glatt* (smooth). Long vowels, by contrast, are represented in a variety of ways. These include the use of (1) single graphemes followed by a single consonant as in *geben* (to give) or *raten* (to advise); (2) an additional grapheme, such as ⟨h⟩ as in *Stahl* (steel) or, in the case of /iː/, ⟨e⟩ as in *Lied* (song); or (3) the doubling of the vowel grapheme as in *Boot* (boat) or *Saal* (room). (For further examples, see Russ, 1994: 154–58; for a fuller account of vowel length representation, see Nerius, 2000a: 98–127; Ossner, 2001a,b; Neef & Primus, 2001; Primus, 2000.)

Leaving aside the question of proper names (which were in any case excluded from the reform), a particularly problematic area of phoneme–grapheme relations is the spelling of foreign loans. This is because such loans frequently contain phonological forms that are not native to German, such as /θ/ as in *Thriller* or the French nasal vowel /ẽ/ as in *Teint* (complexion). Alternatively, they may even be based on entirely different sound/letter correspondences as in the English loan *Nightclub*. In such cases, there are two main options. The first is to retain the foreign spelling, as in the French loan *Portemonnaie* (purse). This may be advantageous to learners and/or users of the foreign language in question, who must otherwise memorise two different spellings. Retention may even be considered to add a cosmopolitan touch and/or even aid communication in the broader international sense given that some forms, such as *City*, *Taxi*, may be widely used across different languages. The second possibility is to bring the spelling into line with German conventions, for example, *Portmonee*. Such germanicisation is particularly advantageous to those who are unfamiliar with the source language and could otherwise only decode the loan in line with native conventions of spelling/pronunciation, for example, *Por-te-mon-na-i-e*. However, this approach has the disadvantage of creating two spellings for those language users familiar with and/or learning the foreign language in question. A further complication is that, from a synchronic perspective, the rate of germanicisation is rarely systematic across word groups. This is due at least partly to the fact that the level of integration considered to be culturally desirable has itself varied diachronically. For example, the germanicisation of loaned forms was especially prevalent in the late 19th and early 20th centuries, whereas modern usage tends to favour the retention of foreign spellings, particularly where borrowings from English are concerned. Moreover, in some cases both loaned and germanicised variants are in use simultaneously although variant spellings will typically be characterised by differing semantic connotations as in the case of the English loan *Club*, which generally indexes an altogether more cosmopolitan venue/organisation than the German *Klub*. (See *Deutsche Rechtschreibung*, 1996: 10–11; for fuller discussion, see Nerius, 2000a: 127–45; Heller & Walz, 1992.)

Notwithstanding some of the major obstacles to absolute phoneme–grapheme correspondence described here – many of which are the inevitable legacy of disparate trends in the historical development of written German – the 1996 reform continued to see the phonemic principle as a broad theoretical goal, according to which some of the more problematical lack of sound–letter correspondences could be ironed out. The assumption was, moreover, that the phonological basis for German orthography would be that of *standard* German. This has the advantage that words will be written in the same way irrespective of regional variation in pronunciation, although it necessarily has as its prerequisite a knowledge of standard German on the part of all writers (and, to a lesser extent, all readers) (see *Deutsche Rechtschreibung*, 1996: 10–11).

Finally, the phonological dimension incorporates two further sub-principles, namely the syllabic and the intonational. The **syllabic** level is primarily concerned with the way in which syllables, as phonological units, are represented graphemically. This is closely linked to the question of syllabification and word division at the end of lines, and also overlaps with morphological considerations relating to the specification of morpheme boundaries. Meanwhile, the **intonational** principle deals with the orthographic representation of supra-segmental features such as rhythm, stress, intonation and pauses. Again, this is closely related to semantic principles such as the lexical question of separate and compound spelling as well as syntactic issues surrounding punctuation.

Semantic principles

Our brief discussion of the syllabic and intonational categories highlights how the phonological principle invariably melds with the semantic. This is because German orthography does not only index meaning via the representation of *speech* but also via the 'direct' representation of morphemes, words, sentences, and texts. It was this *ideographic* dimension of German spelling and punctuation that was duly acknowledged in the second theoretical tenet of the 1996 reform, the *semantic* principle. This incorporates four main levels of analysis: the morphological, the lexical, the syntactic and the textual, although, as Nerius notes (2000a: 89), these might be more accurately conceptualised as 'morphological–semantic', 'lexical–semantic', 'syntactic–semantic' and 'textual–semantic', respectively.

In direct contrast to the phonemic principle, the **morphological** (or morphophonemic) approach assumes the optimum spelling system to be one where, irrespective of differences in pronunciation, morphemes are spelled consistently. This concept of maintaining the unity of spelling across word stems – known in German as *Stammschreibung* or *Schemakonstanz* – allows the reader (and to a lesser extent the writer) to quickly establish visual links between related word groups, thereby facilitating the process of semantic decoding as in the use of ⟨a⟩ in both 'nation' and 'national' in English. The four main areas of German orthography affected by the morphological principle can be summarised as in the following.

The first is the principle of (standard) German phonology known as *Auslautverhärtung*, according to which, in closed syllables, only *voiceless* obstruents (fricatives and plosives) may occur in syllable- and word-final position. This means that voiced obstruents are automatically converted to their voiceless counterparts in final positions, as in *Tag* (day), pronounced /ta:k/, but are retained in non-final positions, as in the inflected genitive form *Tages*, pronounced /ta:gəs/. In Middle High German, such variation in pronunciation was still acknowledged orthographically, for example, *tac/Tages.* In New High German, however, the phonemic principle has been overridden by the morphophonemic imperative, hence the modern spellings *Tag/Tages.* Consequently, the six pairs of voiced/voiceless obstruents subsumed under the principle of *Auslautverhärtung* are now spelled fairly consistently across related word stems as illustrated in Table 3.2 (although for occasional exceptions see Russ, 1994: 159).

Table 3.2 Examples of _Auslautverhärtung_

Non-final →_voiced_	_Word-final_ →_voiceless_	_Syllable-final_ →_voiceless_	_English_
[b] (_Liebe_)	[p] (_lieb_)	[p] (_lieblich_)	love/kind/sweet
[d] (_Hände_)	[t] (_Hand_)	[t] (_handlich_)	hand/hands/handy
[g] (_Wege_)	[k] (_Weg_)	[k] (_Wegrand_)	paths/path/wayside
[v] (_brave_)	[f] (_brav_)	[f] (_Bravheit_)	good/good/good behaviour
[z] (_Gläser_)	[s] (_Glas_)	[s] (_Glashaus_)	glasses/glass/glass house
[z] (_beiges_)	[ʃ] (_beige_)	[ʃ] (_beigefarben_)	beige/beige/beige-coloured

Source: Hall, 1992: 28

A second area where the morphological principle generally overrides strictly phonemic considerations in modern German is that of vowel mutation or _umlaut_. This means that vowels and their mutated forms are ideally spelled consistently across related word stems as illustrated in Table 3.3.

Table 3.3 German vowels and their mutated forms

Vowel sound	_Spelling_	_Example_	_Mutated form_	_Spelling_	_Example_	_English_
/ʊ/	⟨u⟩	_Mutter_	/Y/	⟨ü⟩	_mütterlich_	mother/motherly
/uː/	⟨u⟩	_Gruß_	/yː/	⟨ü⟩	_Grüße_	greeting/greetings
/a/	⟨a⟩	_kalt_	/ɛ/	⟨ä⟩	_kälter_	cold/colder
/aː/	⟨a⟩	_Glas_	/eː/	⟨ä⟩	_Gläser_	glass/glasses
/ɔ/	⟨o⟩	_Frost_	/œ/	⟨ö⟩	_frösteln_	frost/to feel chilly
/oː/	⟨o⟩	_Floß_	/Øː/	⟨ö⟩	_Flöße_	raft/rafts
/au/	⟨au⟩	_grau_	/ɔɪ/	⟨äu⟩	_gräulich_	grey/greyish

While spellings containing ⟨ü⟩ and ⟨ö⟩ are generally consistent (although for occasional exceptions, see Russ, 1994: 157–60), there are particular problems with two other main areas. The first concerns the spelling of the short vowel /ɛ/, which can be represented by either ⟨ä⟩ or ⟨e⟩. A consistent application of the morphological principle would mean that /ɛ/ be spelled ⟨ä⟩ in word stems containing mutated forms of /a/, for example, *Wände* (walls) from *Wand* (wall), but ⟨e⟩ in other cases, for example, *Wende* (turn). Historically, however, this has not always been strictly adhered to, hence *Eltern* (parents) despite its semantic links with *alt* (old) and *älter* (older/elder). Similar problems surround the diphthong /ɔɪ/. Here a consistent application of the morphological principle would mean that /ɔɪ/ be represented by ⟨äu⟩ in word stems containing mutated forms of /au/, for example, *Häuser* (houses) from *Haus* (house), but ⟨eu⟩ in other cases, for example, *Freund* (friend). Again, however, this principle has not always been adhered to historically, hence the pre-1996 spelling of *schneuzen* (to blow one's nose) despite its apparent synchronic link to *Schnauze* (nose/mouth) and *großschnäuzig* (big-mouthed).[7]

The third area of German orthography governed by the morphological principle concerns the spelling of double consonants. These are generally retained in writing in spite of phonological factors that may lead to the assimilation or elision of the first consonant in question, for example, *fünffach* (five-fold) (pronounced ['fʏn(f)fax]). Moreover, double consonants may also function as markers of vowel length, indicating that the preceding vowel be pronounced short as in *Bulle* (bull) or *glatt* (smooth).[8]

Fourthly, there are a few additional cases where vowel sounds are spelled consistently across related word groups in spite of their differing pronunciation, for example, *vier* (four) with its long vowel /iː/ versus *vierzehn* (fourteen) and *vierzig* (forty) with their short counterpart /ɪ/ (see *Deutsche Rechtschreibung*, 1996: 11–12) (although the latter two items are sometimes similarly pronounced with a long vowel).

While an adherence to the morphological principle is generally thought to facilitate the recognition of individual words and their basic 'building blocks' on the part of readers (and to a lesser extent writers), a potential disadvantage is the degree of meta-linguistic awareness that is then required on the part of language users. Not only can language planners not presuppose such awareness – for example, to what extent is *Herbst* (autumn) derived from *herb* (harsh/bitter)? – unity of spelling has itself not always been maintained historically. This has led to a number of inconsistent forms in current usage such as the initial consonants of *voll* (full) and *füllen* (to fill) (see *Deutsche Rechtschreibung*, 1996: 12).

Such inconsistency in the relationship between spelling and meaning is especially evident in those cases where morphological considerations compete with **lexical** principles. This is particularly so where the principle of homonymy is concerned, that is, where disparate spellings are specifically employed in order to highlight the different meanings of homophones, that is, pairs of words with identical pronunciation. And here, in spite of the fact that the choice of distinguishing graphemes may appear fairly arbitrary to the language user, as in *Saite* (string of an instrument) versus *Seite* (side) or *wider* (against) versus *wieder* (again), the principle of homonymy has firmly established itself in German usage in three main ways. First, vowel sounds can be disparately represented as in pairs such as *Lid* (eye-lid) versus *Lied* (song) or *Meer* (sea) versus *mehr* (more). Secondly, the digraph ⟨ai⟩, which normally represents the diphthong /aɪ/, alternates with ⟨ei⟩ as in *Laib* (loaf) versus *Leib* (body) or *Waise* (orphan) versus *Weise* (way, manner). Thirdly, ⟨ä⟩ and ⟨e⟩ are commonly used to distinguish homophones as in *Wände* (walls) versus *Wende* (turn) or *Lärche* (larch) versus *Lerche* (lark) (see Russ, 1994: 161–62).

Lexical principles in German orthography are also concerned with hyphenation, separate and compound spelling, and capitalisation. Separate and compound spelling can itself be a useful means of distinguishing meaning in German as in the case of *gut schreiben* (to write well) and *gutschreiben* (to credit). Similarly, capitalisation has a range of lexical functions, not least the marking of proper names and the differentiation of potential homonyms such as the pronouns *Sie/Ihr* (you/your) and *sie/ihr* (they/their or she/her). However, as all nouns are written with upper-case letters in German, capitalisation is also used to mark word class, thereby assuming a syntactic function. This **syntactic** principle further incorporates sentence-initial capitalisation, which is linked to the more general area of punctuation. Meanwhile, capitalisation – especially in titles/section headings and in sentence-initial position – is also related to the **textual** principle insofar as it impacts upon the overall appearance of textual structure, thereby further assisting readers in the decoding of semantic meaning.

Details of the 1996 Reform

Against the backdrop of the theoretical principles outlined above, the 1996 reform involved changes to six main areas of German orthography:

(1)   Sound–letter classifications (including the spelling of foreign loans)
(2)   Separate and compound spelling

(3) Hyphenation
(4) Capitalisation
(5) Punctuation
(6) Syllabification/word division at the end of lines

The official text, known as the *Amtliche Regelung*, contains the 112 'new' rules for German orthography and also incorporates an index (*Wörter-verzeichnis*) of the 12,000 or so words most commonly affected by the reform intended as a guide for the spelling of further analogous items.[9] A condensed and somewhat more accessible version is, however, widely available in a special December 1998 edition of *Sprach-report*, the journal of the 'Institute for German Language' (IDS) in Mannheim produced by Klaus Heller, one of the leading theorists involved in the reform process (Heller, 1998). The following sections, which draw directly on Heller's summary, describe the main changes that were made.

(1) Sound–Letter Classifications (Including the Spelling of Foreign Loans) (*Laut-Buchstaben-Zuordnungen – einschließlich Fremdwortschreibung*)

Leaving aside the theoretical difficulties in achieving absolute phoneme–grapheme correspondence, the many attempts to reform German orthography prior to 1996 had highlighted the fact that significant interventions into sound–letter classifications were unlikely to meet with popular approval. It was partly for this reason that the reformers chose to focus their efforts on the harmonisation of existing inconsistencies within word groups containing morphologically related roots, in effect, sidelining the phonemic principle in favour of the *morphological* principle of maintaining the visual unity of spelling across word stems. Sensitive to the meta-linguistic knowledge often required on the part of language users in this context, however, the reformers chose to highlight the morphological associations as perceived by readers and writers of German in *current* usage. This meant that strictly etymological developments were in a number of cases overridden by what the reformers judged to be language users' *current* perceptions of such relationships, thereby prioritising the synchronic dimension of language usage over the diachronic.

The changes in this category affect six main areas of German orthography.

(a) Individual cases of modified vowels (umlaut) (Table 3.4)

Table 3.4 Modified vowels (umlaut)

Old spelling	New spelling	English
behende	_behände_ (as in _Hand_)	nimble, agile
belemmert	_belämmert_ (as in _Lamm_ in current usage)	miserable, awful (as in 'lamb' in current usage)
Bendel	_Bändel_ (as in _Band_)	shoe-lace (as in 'ribbon')
Gemse	_Gämse_ (as in _Gams_)	chamois (as in Austrian/ South German _Gams_)
Quentchen	_Quäntchen_ (as in _Quantum_ in current usage)	scrap, pinch, little bit (as in 'quantum' in current usage)
schneuzen	_schnäuzen_ (as in _Schnauze, großschnäuzig_)	to blow one's nose (as in 'nose/mouth', 'big-mouthed')
Stengel	_Stängel_ (as in _Stange_)	stem, stalk (as in 'pole')
überschwenglich	_überschwänglich_ (as in _Überschwang_)	effusive (as in 'exuberance')
verbleuen	_verbläuen_ (as in _blau_ in current usage)	to bash/beat up (as in 'blue' in current usage)
aufwendig	_aufwendig_ (as in _aufwenden_) or _aufwändig_ (as in _Aufwand_)	expensive (as in 'to spend' or as in 'expenditure')
Schenke	_Schenke_ (as in _ausschenken_) or _Schänke_ (as in _Aussschank_)	pub, bar (as in 'to pour out' or 'bar/ counter')
Wächte ('_Schneewehe_')	_Wechte_ (not as in _wachen_)	(snow) cornice (as in 'snowdrift' _not_ 'to watch')
But note the retention of _Eltern_ (parents) despite its derivation from _alt_ (old).		

(b) Individual cases of consonant grapheme doubling after short vowels

The forms in Table 3.5 were modified in order to harmonise spelling across morphologically related word groups.

Table 3.5 Consonant grapheme doubling after short vowels

Old spelling	New spelling	English
Karamel	*Karamell* (as in *Karamelle*)	caramel (toffee)
numerieren	*nummerieren* (as in *Nummer*)	to number
plazieren (*placieren*)	*platzieren* (as in *Platz*)	to place, position (as in 'place')
Stukkateur	*Stuckateur* (as in *Stuck*)	plasterer (as in 'piece' or 'stucco')
Tolpatsch	*Tollpatsch* (as in *toll* in current usage)	clumsy or awkward creature (as in 'mad, crazy' in current usage)

(c) ⟨ss⟩ instead of ⟨ß⟩ after short vowels

In order to harmonise the spelling of word stems containing the voiceless fricative /s/, the former practice of converting ⟨ss⟩ to ⟨ß⟩ after some short vowels, for example, *hassen* (to hate), but not others, for example, *Haß* (hate), was abandoned. According to the new rules, ⟨ß⟩ therefore continues to be used following long vowels, for example, *Maß* (measure), *Muße* (leisure) and *Straße* (street) and after diphthongs, for example, *draußen* (outside) and *beißen* (to bite), but is written as ⟨ss⟩ following all short vowels, for example, *hassen–Hass* (Table 3.6). This also means that the subordinating conjunction *daß* (that) is now spelled *dass*, thereby retaining the lexical distinction from the definite article *das* (the) and the relative pronoun *das* (that/which).

(d) Retention of root spelling in compounds

In accordance with the morphological principle of maintaining visual unity across word stems and groups, the new rule for compound spellings is that all constituent forms be written in full, thereby

Table 3.6 Spelling of word stems containing /s/

Old spelling	New spelling	English
hassen—Haß	*hassen—Hass*	hate (verb/noun)
küssen—Kuß, *sie küßten sich*	*küssen—Kuss, sie* *küssten sich*	kiss (verb/noun), they kissed one another
lassen – er läßt	*lassen – er lässt*	to let/allow – he lets/ allows
müssen – er muß	*müssen – er muss*	to have to – he must
Wasser—wässerig/wäßrig	*Wasser—wässerig/* *wässrig*	water – watery
daß	*dass*	that (conjunction)

eliminating previous inconsistencies with divided forms (Table 3.7). The same principle was also extended to the use of ⟨h⟩ preceding the suffix *-heit* (Table 3.8). Meanwhile, the form *selbständig* (independent) can be written as previously or as *selbstständig*.

Table 3.7 Compound spelling

Old spelling	New spelling	English
Flanellappen (but *Flanell-lappen* when divided)	*Flanelllappen* (or hyphenated form *Flanell-Lappen*)	flannel (cloth)
Flußsand	*Flusssand* (or *Fluss-Sand*)	fluvial sand
Balletttänzer (but *Ballett-tänzer* when divided, note also *Balletttruppe*)	*Balletttänzer* (or *Ballett-Tänzer* as in *Balletttruppe*)	ballet dancer (as in 'ballet troupe')
Stoffetzen (but *Stoff-* *fetzen* when divided)	*Stofffetzen* (or *Stoff-Fetzen*)	pieces of cloth
Previous compound spellings are retained, however, in the well-established forms *dennoch* (nevertheless), *Drittel* (third), *Mittag* (midday).		

Table 3.8 Use of ⟨h⟩ preceding -*heit*

Old spelling	New spelling	English
Roheit	Rohheit (as in roh)	brutishness (as in 'brutish')
Zäheit	Zähheit (as in zäh)	toughness (as in 'tough')
Zierat	Zierrat (like Vorrat)	ornamentation (like 'supply')

(e) Systematicisation in individual cases

The spelling of a number of individual words was harmonised in line with analogous forms as in Table 3.9.

Table 3.9 Systematicisation in individual cases

Old spelling	New spelling	English
rauh	rau (like grau, schlau, etc.)	rough (like 'grey', 'shrewd', etc.)
Känguruh	Känguru (like Gnu, Kakadu, etc.)	kangaroo (like 'gnu', 'cockatoo', etc.)

In the case of items derived from nouns ending in -*anz* or -*enz*, spellings containing ⟨z⟩ were elevated to the main variant, while spellings containing ⟨t⟩ were retained as optional, subsidiary variants (Table 3.10).

(f) Foreign loans

Finally, the spelling of foreign loans – a category that, strictly speaking, includes a range of items that are merely *perceived* as such – has, as we have seen throughout, been a traditional bone of contention in debates over orthographic reform. On the one hand, the retention of loaned spellings tends to favour educated language users familiar with the source language in question. Germanicisation, on the other hand, prioritises those unfamiliar with the source language, while creating two spellings for its users and/or learners. Although these issues are especially relevant to school-aged learners of modern languages such as French or English (for whom double spellings can be a genuine irritant), they are also closely tied in with the question of classical languages such as Greek and Latin, from which German has derived a substantial part of its vocabulary. In the latter case, germanicisation may well be interpreted as a

Table 3.10 Items derived from nouns ending in -anz or -enz

Old spelling	New spelling	English
essentiell	*essenziell* (as in *Essenz*), also *essentiell*	essential
Differential	*Differenzial* (as in *Differenz*), also *Differential*	differential (noun)
Differentiell	*differenziell* (as in *Differenz*), also *differentiell*	differential (adjective)
Potential	*Potenzial* (as in *Potenz*), also *Potential*	potential (noun)
potentiell	*potenziell* (as in *Potenz*), also *potentiell*	potential (adjective)
substantiell	*substanziell* (as in *Substanz*), also *substantiell*	substantial

form of 'dumbing down' linked to a perceived denial of the classical heritage of German. That said, germanicisation is just as likely to be associated, conversely, with an inappropriate and potentially distasteful concern to emphasise the 'Germanness' of the language thereby indexing the political, historical and cultural baggage of German nationalism. As such, it is closely tied to ongoing debates over language loyalty on the part of German speakers (Klein, 2001).

It was in an attempt to reconcile these considerations that the reformers opted to germanicise the spelling of foreign loans *only* in those cases where a process of integration was perceived to be well advanced in current usage (Table 3.11). However, it was decided that in all cases a system of optional variability should apply, according to which a series of main and subsidiary variants were specified.

(2) Separate and Compound Spelling (*Getrennt- und Zusammenschreibung – GZS*)

The question of separate and compound spelling has traditionally been one of the most controversial areas of German orthography and was left more or less untouched by the official guidelines of 1901/1902. However, a number of rules were not only incorporated into the

Table 3.11 Foreign loans

Old spelling	New spelling	English
⟨ai⟩	⟨ai⟩ or ⟨ä⟩	
Frigidaire	Frigidaire, also Frigidär	refrigerator
Necessaire	Necessaire, also Nessessär (like Mohär, Sekretär, Militär, etc., hitherto)	vanity case (like 'mohair', 'secretary', 'military', etc.)
⟨ph⟩	⟨ph⟩ or ⟨f⟩	
quadrophon	quadrophon, also quadrofon	quadrophonic
Photometrie	Fotometrie, also Photometrie	photometry
Geographie	Geographie, also Geografie	geography
Graphologe	Graphologe, also Grafologe	graphology
Orthographie	Orthographie, also Orthografie	orthography
Megafon	Megaphon, also Megafon (like Mikrofon, Fotografie, Grafik, etc., hitherto)	megaphone (like 'microphone', 'photograph(y)', 'graphics', etc.)
Delphin	Delphin, also Delfin (like fantastisch hitherto)	dolphin (like 'fantastic')
⟨gh⟩	⟨gh⟩ or ⟨g⟩	
Joghurt	Joghurt, also Jogurt	yoghurt
Spaghetti	Spaghetti, also Spagetti (like Getto, etc. hitherto)	spaghetti (like 'ghetto', etc.)
⟨é⟩ and ⟨ée⟩	⟨é⟩/⟨ée⟩ or ⟨ee⟩	
Bouclé	Bouclé, also Buklee	bouclé
Exposé	Exposee, also Exposé	outline, plan
Kommuniqué	Kommuniqué, also Kommunikee	communiqué
Varieté	Varietee, also Varieté	variety (entertainment)

(continued)

Table 3.11 *Continued*

Old spelling	New spelling	English
Chicorée	*Chicorée*, also *Schikoree* (like *Allee, Armee, Komitee,* etc., hitherto)	chicory (like 'avenue', 'army', 'committee', etc.)
⟨qu⟩	⟨qu⟩ or ⟨k⟩	
Kommuniqué	*Kommuniqué*, also *Kommunikee* (like *Etikett, Likör,* etc., hitherto)	communiqué (like 'label', 'liqueur', etc.)
⟨ou⟩	⟨ou⟩ or ⟨u⟩	
Bouclé	*Bouclé*, also *Buklee* (like *Nugat* hitherto)	bouclé (like 'nougat')
⟨ch⟩	⟨ch⟩ or ⟨sch⟩	
Ketchup	*Ketschup*, also *Ketchup*	ketchup
Chicorée	*Chicorée*, also *Schikoree* (like *Anschovis, Broschüre, Scheck,* etc., hitherto)	chicory (like 'chicory', 'brochure', 'cheque', etc.)
⟨rh⟩	⟨rh⟩ or ⟨r⟩	
Katarrh	*Katarrh*, also *Katarr*	catarrh
Myrrhe	*Myrrhe*, also *Myrre*	myrrh
Hämorrhoiden	*Hämorrhoiden*, also *Hämorriden*	haemorrhoids
⟨c⟩	⟨c⟩ or ⟨ss⟩	
Facette	*Facette*, also *Fassette*	facet
Necessaire	*Necessaire*, also *Nessessär* (like *Fassade, Rasse,* etc., hitherto)	vanity case (like 'facade', 'race', etc.)
⟨th⟩	⟨th⟩ or ⟨t⟩	
Panther	*Panther*, also *Panter*	panther
Thunfisch	*Thunfisch*, also *Tunfisch*	tuna fish
+ one individual case: *Portemonnaie*	*Portmonee*, also *Portemonnaie*	purse

'combined' Duden of 1915, but also subject to many additions and amendments in later editions of the dictionary, leading to an increasingly inconsistent set of guidelines by the end of the 20th century. After much deliberation, the reformers opted for the overall principle of viewing separate spellings as the norm, deeming therefore only compound forms as in need of specific regulation. The new guidelines also broke with the semantic principle of differentiating between literal and figurative meaning as the main criterion for specifying separate and compound spellings (which had traditionally underpinned the Duden guidelines – more below) in favour of syntactic considerations based on the generalisability and comparability across word groups (for further discussion see Augst & Schaeder, 1997b: 21–22).

According to the new rules, noun + verb compounds are now generally written separately as in Table 3.12.

Table 3.12 Noun and verb compounds

Old spelling	New spelling	English
radfahren, but *Auto fahren* and *ich fahre Rad*	*Rad fahren* (like *Auto fahren* and *ich fahre Rad*)	to ride a bicycle (like 'to drive a car' and 'I ride a bicycle')
teppichkopfen/*Teppich klopfen*	*Teppich klopfen*	to beat a carpet
haltmachen	*Halt machen*	to stop

The Duden criteria for separate and compound spellings had originally dictated that all phrases denoting literal meaning be written separately, for example, *auf dem Stuhl sitzen bleiben* (to remain seated on the chair), whereas figurative meanings be expressed via compound spellings, for example, *in der Schule sitzenbleiben* (to repeat a school year, lit. to remain seated). However, this principle had never operated entirely consistently (Table 3.13), hence *im Bett liegenbleiben* ('to stay in bed' – literal meaning but compound spelling) or *mit seinem Plan baden gehen* (literally, 'to go swimming with his plan'; figuratively, 'to fail', that is, figurative meaning but separate spelling). Moreover, while this semantic distinction might function in the case of the infinitive forms of verbal compounds, it immediately collapses in finite constructions such as the potentially ambiguous *er blieb sitzen* ('he remained seated' or 'he repeated a school year'). The 1996 guidelines therefore specified that verb + verb compounds be generally written separately, thereby relying on context of usage to clarify potential ambiguities. The same principle then applies in combinations such as those in Table 3.14.

Table 3.13 *sitzenbleiben/sitzen bleiben*

Old spelling	New spelling	English
sitzenbleiben (*in der Schule*) but *sitzen bleiben* (*auf dem Stuhl*)	*sitzen bleiben*	to remain seated (figuratively, 'to repeat a school year'; or literally, 'to remain seated')

Table 3.14 Other combinations following the principles of Table 3.13

Old spelling	New spelling	English
abwärtsgehen (*schlechter werden* – figurative) but *abwärts gehen* (*einen Weg* – literal)	*abwärts gehen*	to go downhill (figuratively or literally)

In the cases in Table 3.15, separate spellings were adopted in order to bring items into line with analogous forms. Likewise, the spelling of combinations containing *aneinander/beieinander/zueinander* (all meaning 'together') + verb were harmonised by expanding the principle of separate spellings (separate spellings having previously applied to most, but not all, such forms) (Table 3.16). The principle of spelling components separately was also extended to participial forms, thereby bringing them into line with analogous infinitive forms (Table 3.17).

Table 3.15 Cases adopting separate spellings

Old spelling	New spelling	English
gefangennehmen but *getrennt schreiben*	*gefangen nehmen* (like *getrennt schreiben*)	to take prisoner (like 'to write separately')
übrigbleiben but *artig grüßen*	*übrig bleiben* (like *artig grüßen*)	to be left over (like 'to greet courteously')

Table 3.16 Combinations containing *aneinander/beieinander/zueinander*

Old spelling	New spelling	English
aneinanderfügen but *aneinander denken*	*aneinander fügen* (like *aneinander denken*)	to fit together (like 'to think of one another')
zueinanderfinden but *zueinander passen*	*zueinander finden* (like *zueinander passen*)	to come together (like 'to go together')

Table 3.17 Participial forms

Old spelling	New spelling	English
nahestehend	*nahe stehend* (as in infinitive *nahe stehen*)	standing close to (as 'to stand close to')
laubtragende/Laub tragende (*Bäume*)	*Laub tragende* (*Bäume*) (as in infinitive *Laub tragen*)	bearing leaves (trees) (as in infinitive 'to bear leaves')

The forms in Table 3.18 were also harmonised in accordance with the principle of separate spelling. By contrast, all combinations containing *irgend* (some) were to be written together in order to maintain unity with established analogous forms such as *irgendwer* (somebody) and *irgendwo* (somewhere) (Table 3.19).

Table 3.18 Other forms harmonised with separate spelling

Old spelling	New spelling	English
soviel, wieviel but *so viele, wie viele*	*so viel, wie viel* (like *so viele, wie viele*)	so much, how much (like plural forms)

Table 3.19 Combinations containing *irgend*

Old spelling	New spelling	English
irgend etwas	*irgendetwas*	something
irgend jemand but *irgendwer, irgendwann*	*irgendjemand* like *irgendwer, irgendwann*	someone (like 'somebody, at some time')

(3) Hyphenation (*Schreibung mit Bindestrich*)

The use of hyphens serves many purposes, not least that of allowing the writer to express clusters of words/signs that might otherwise be unclear either graphically, for example, $\frac{3}{4}$-*Takt* ($\frac{3}{4}$ time) or syntactically, for example, *das In-den-Tag-hinein-Träumen* (day dreaming). The main aim of the 1996 reform was to harmonise existing inconsistencies, while at the same time allowing writers more freedom to clarify intended meaning through the use of hyphens (Table 3.20).

Table 3.20 Harmonisation of hyphenation

Old spelling	New spelling	English
Ichform, Ichsucht but *Ich-Laut*	*Ichform/Ich-Form, Ichsucht/Ich-Sucht, Ichlaut/Ich-Laut*	first person, egoism, palatal fricative (*ich-laut*)
17jährig, 3tonner 2pfünder, 4silbig 100prozentig	*17-jährig, 3-Tonner 2-Pfünder, 4-silbig 100-prozentig*	17-year-old, 3-tonner, 2-pounder, quadri-syllabic, 100 percent (adjective)
Kaffee-Ersatz Zoo-Orchester Balletttruppe Flußsand	*Kaffeeersatz/Kaffee-Ersatz Zooorchester/Zoo-Orchester Balletttruppe/Ballett-Truppe Flusssand/Fluss-Sand*	coffee substitute zoo orchestra ballet troupe fluvial sand

Polysyllabic compounds loaned from English are now generally written together (bringing them into line with the spelling of native compounds), although in most cases hyphenated forms are also permitted as a means of achieving greater clarity (Table 3.21).[10]

Table 3.21 Polysyllabic compounds loaned from English

Old spelling	New spelling
Hair-Stylist	*Hairstylist/Hair-Stylist*
Job-Sharing	*Jobsharing/Job-Sharing*
Midlife-crisis	*Midlifecrisis/Midlife-Crisis*
Sex-Appeal	*Sexappeal/Sex-Appeal*
Shopping-Center	*Shoppingcenter/Shopping-Center*

(4) Capitalisation (*Groß- und Kleinschreibung* – *GKS*)

The capitalisation of nouns is an aspect of German orthography that has traditionally caused problems for native and non-native users alike, not least due to the various inconsistencies that have arisen over the years (for history, see Nerius, 2000a: 187–221). However, reactions to reform proposals by the International Working Party in the late 1980s and early 1990s signalled that the abolition of this practice and the adoption of 'moderate minisculisation', that is, a system of capitalisation roughly akin to that used in English, was unlikely to meet with popular approval. It was in this context that reformers were obliged to opt for the less controversial strategy of harmonising the existing rules even though all were clearly dissatisfied with this outcome (Munkse, 1997a,b,c). This means that German continues to be the only language where all nouns are capitalised such that, unlike in other languages, capitalisation is used not only to identify the beginning of sentences, proper nouns, and honorifics, but is also used more comprehensively as a syntactic marker of word class.

One of the main difficulties surrounding capitalisation in German is that not only nouns must be capitalised, but also the many nominalised forms derived from words of other classes. This includes, for example, verbal nominalisations such as *das Laufen* (running), conjunctional nominalisations such as *das Wenn und Aber* (ifs and buts), or adjectival nominalisations such as *die Ewiggestrigen* (old reactionaries). In many cases, however, whether a form should be treated as nominal is not immediately obvious. For this reason, a number of inconsistencies had arisen historically as in the pre-1996 spellings *im voraus* (in advance), *es ist das beste, wenn* ... (it is for the best, if ...), *im nachhinein* (with hindsight), and *auf dem trockenen sitzen* (to be in a tight spot, i.e. financially). Moreover, nouns can themselves be subsumed into other word class groups and have not therefore traditionally required capitalisation, for example, *mittags* (at midday) or the adverbial phrases *heute abend* (this evening) and *trotz seiner Krankheit* (in spite of his illness).

Against this backdrop the aim of the 1996 reform was to smooth out as far as possible existing inconsistencies surrounding capitalisation practices, according to which the possibility for use of an article with the item in question (the so-called *Artikelprobe*) becomes the main grammatical test for nominal status, and hence capitalisation. The new regulations specify that nouns are to be capitalised in all preposition + noun constructions, for example, *auf Grün* (on green), *in Bezug* (with regard), *mit Bezug* (with regard) and all noun + verb constructions, for example, *Rad fahren* (to ride a bicycle) or *Tennis spielen* (to play tennis) (Table 3.22).

Table 3.22 Noun + preposition and noun + verb constructions

Old spelling	New spelling	English
in bezug auf, but *mit Bezug auf*	*in Bezug auf* (like *mit Bezug auf*)	with regard to
radfahren, but *Auto fahren*	*Rad fahren*, (like *Auto fahren*)	to ride a bicycle (like 'to drive a car')

With the exception of their usage in constructions containing the verbs *sein* (to be), *bleiben* (to remain) and *werden* (to become), the nouns *Angst* (fear), *Bange* (fear), *Gram* (ill-will), *Leid* (sorrow), *Schuld* (blame) and *Pleite* (bankruptcy) are also to be capitalised (Table 3.23).

Table 3.23 *Angst/Bange/Gram/Leid/Schuld/Pleite*

Old spelling	New spelling	English
angst (and *bange*) *machen* but *Angst haben*	*Angst* (and *Bange*) *machen* (like *Angst haben*)	to make anxious (like 'to be anxious')
schuld geben	*Schuld geben*	to blame
pleite gehen	*Pleite gehen*	to go bankrupt
	(but *bange sein, gram bleiben, pleite werden*)	(but 'to be afraid', 'to bear ill-will', 'to go bankrupt')

The following forms are also subject to capitalisation (Table 3.24):

(1) Nominalised adjectives used as ordinals, for example, *der Erste und der Letzte* (the first and last one), *der Nächste* (the next one) and *jeder Dritte* (every third one);
(2) Indefinite numeral adjectives when combined with indefinite pronouns, for example, *alles Übrige* (everything else) and *nicht das Geringste* (not the least);
(3) Nominalised adjectives in fixed word combinations, for example, *im Klaren* ('clear', i.e. 'about something'), *im Folgenden* (in the following), *im Nachhinein* (with hindsight), *des Näheren* (the precise details), and – in both the literal and figurative senses – *im Dunkeln tappen* (to grope in the dark) and *im Trüben fischen* (to fish in troubled waters).

Table 3.24 Forms of adjectives subject to capitalisation

Old spelling	New spelling	English
der, die das letzte	der, die das Letzte	the last (one)
der nächste, bitte	der Nächste, bitte	next, please
alles übrige	alles Übrige	everything else
nicht das geringste	nicht das Geringste	not the least
im großen und ganzen	im Großen und Ganzen	on the whole
des näheren	des Näheren	the precise details
im allgemeinen	im Allgemeinen	in general
es ist das beste (= am besten), wenn...	es ist das Beste	it is best (= the best, if...)
auf dem trockenen sitzen (in finanzieller Verlegenheit sein)	auf dem Trockenen sitzen	to be in a tight spot (financially)
den kürzeren ziehen (Nachteile haben)	den Kürzeren ziehen	to pick the short straw (to be disadvantaged)

Forms denoting times of the day are now also capitalised (Table 3.25) when used in conjunction with *heute* (today), *gestern* (yesterday), *vorgestern* (the day before yesterday), *morgen* (tomorrow), and *übermorgen* (the day after tomorrow). Nominalised compounds combining 'weekday' plus 'time of day' are also written with upper-case letters, for example, *am Sonntagabend* (on Sunday evening) but not adverbial forms such as *sonntagabends* (on Sunday evenings).

Table 3.25 Forms denoting times of the day

Old spelling	New spelling	English
heute mittag	heute Mittag	midday today
gestern abend	gestern Abend	yesterday evening
am Sonntag abend	am Sonntagabend	on Sunday evening
Sonntag abends	sonntagabends	on Sunday evenings

Forms consisting in preposition + language/colour are also now capitalised (Table 3.26). The same goes for pairs of undeclined adjectives denoting people (Table 3.27). On the other hand, superlatives used in conjunction with the preposition *aufs* can be written with either upper- or lower-case letters (Table 3.28).

Table 3.26 Preposition + language/colour

Old spelling	New spelling	English
auf deutsch, but *bei Grün*	*auf Deutsch* (like *bei Grün*)	in German (like 'on green')

Table 3.27 Pairs of undeclined adjectives denoting people

Old spelling	New spelling	English
groß und klein	*Groß und Klein*	big and small
jung und alt, but *Arm und Reich*	*Jung und Alt* (like *Arm und Reich*)	young and old (like 'rich and poor')

Table 3.28 Superlatives used in conjunction with *aufs*

Old spelling	New spelling	English
aufs beste	*aufs beste/aufs Beste*	in the best way possible
aufs herzlichste	*aufs herzlichste/aufs Herzlichste*	most sincerely

In fixed adjective + noun constructions, the adjective is now generally written with a lower-case letter (Table 3.29). However, adjectives continue to be capitalised in the following:

(1) Proper names such as *der Stille Ozean* (the Pacific Ocean; literally, 'the calm ocean');
(2) Titles such as *Regierender Bürgermeister* (governing mayor);
(3) Biological classifications such as *Roter Milan* (red kite);
(4) Feast days such as *Heiliger Abend* (Christmas Eve);
(5) Historical events such as *der Westfälische Friede* (the Treaty of Westphalia).

Table 3.29" Fixed adjective + noun constructions

Old spelling	New spelling	English
das Schwarze Brett	das schwarze Brett	notice board
der Weiße Tod	der weiße Tod	death in the snow (literally 'the white death')
die Erste Hilfe	die erste Hilfe	first aid

Meanwhile, adjectival forms derived from people's names, for example, *ohmsch* (ohmic), are now generally written with lower-case letters even when referring to a phenomenon named after the person in question, for example, *das ohmsche Gesetz* (Ohm's Law). If, however, the name is itself stressed (as opposed to the accompanying noun), then it may also be capitalised, but should be set apart from any declinational suffix by an apostrophe, for example, *die Grimm'schen Märchen* (Grimms' fairy tales) (Table 3.30).

Table 3.30 Adjectival forms derived from people's names

Old spelling	New spelling	English
das Ohmsche Gesetz, but der ohmsche Widerstand	das ohmsche Gesetz (like der ohmsche Widerstand)	Ohm's Law (like 'ohmic resistance')

Finally, the use of capital letters in familiar forms of address was abolished although the polite forms *Sie* and *Ihr* (and declined forms in the latter case) continue to be capitalised (Table 3.31).

Table 3.31 Forms of address

Old spelling	New spelling	English
Du, Dein, Dich, Dir, etc.	du, dein, dich, dir, etc.	you, your, you (accusative), you (dative) – second person singular, familiar form of address
Ihr, Euer, Euch, etc.	ihr, euer, euch, etc.	you, your, you (accusative/dative) – second person plural, familiar form of address

(5) Punctuation (*Zeichensetzung*)

Punctuation was a further area not incorporated into the guidelines of 1901/1902, although a number of rules were introduced by the 1915 Duden and expanded upon in subsequent editions of the dictionary (see Chapter 2). The gist of the 1996 proposals was to simplify those regulations and allow greater freedom of choice for language users. One of the main changes was in the area of commas, which are no longer required before coordinating conjunctions such as *und* (and) and *oder* (or) in order to separate two main clauses (Table 3.32).

Table 3.32 Comma use before *und* and *oder*

Old spelling	New spelling	English
Der Schnee schmolz dahin, und bald ließen sich die ersten Blumen sehen, und die Vögel stimmten ihr Lied an.	*Der Schnee schmolz dahin und bald ließen sich die ersten Blumen sehen und die Vögel stimmten ihr Lied an.*	The snow was melting away and soon the first flowers could be seen and the birds began to sing.

In the case of infinitive and participial clauses, commas are only required in the following specific contexts:

(1) Where the clause is preceded by a referential demonstrative word group as follows: *Darüber, bald zu einem Erfolg zu kommen, dachte sie lange nach* (she thought for a long time about becoming successful soon).

(2) Where the clause is followed by a referential demonstrative word group as in: *Bald zu einem Erfolg zu kommen, das war ihr sehnlichster Wunsch* (to be successful soon, that was her greatest wish).

(3) Where the clause does not fit into the standard sentence structure as in: *Sie, um bald zu einem Erfolg zu kommen, schritt alsbald zur Tat* (she, in order to become successful soon, quickly stepped into action).

Finally, the 1996 regulations recommended that commas be used as and when necessary for purposes of clarity and/or disambiguation as in the following examples:

(1) *Sie begnetete ihrem Trainer(,) und dessen Mannschaft musste lange auf ihn warten* (she met her trainer(,) and his team had to wait a long time for him).

(2) *Ich rate ihm, zu helfen* (I recommend that he helps) versus *Ich rate, ihm zu helfen* (I recommend that he be helped).

(6) Syllabification and Word Division at the End of Lines (*Worttrennung am Zeilenende*)

Finally, four main changes were made to the way in which words can be separated at the ends of lines. First, the rule according to which ⟨st⟩ should not be separated was abandoned, bringing it into line with analogous grapheme clusters that were previously separable such as ⟨sp⟩ as in *Wes-pe* (wasp) and ⟨sk⟩ as in *Mas-ke* (mask) (Table 3.33).

Table 3.33 Separation of ⟨st⟩

Old spelling	New spelling	English
We-ste	Wes-te	waistcoat
Ka-sten	Kas-ten	box, case
Mu-ster	Mus-ter	model, sample

Secondly, the rule whereby ⟨ck⟩ must be converted to ⟨kk⟩ when divided was similarly abandoned (Table 3.34).

Table 3.34 Division of ⟨ck⟩

Old spelling	New spelling	English
(Zucker→)Zuk-ker	Zu-cker	sugar
(lecken→)lek-ken	le-cken	to lick
(Backe→)Bak-ke	Ba-cke	cheek

Thirdly, whereas foreign loans – or items perceived to be of foreign origin – had previously only been divided in accordance with etymological criteria, it was agreed that pronunciation conventions should also be acknowledged, thus allowing foreign loans to be divided according to the same phonological principle as words of German origin (Table 3.35).

Finally, the former principle of disallowing forms of word division resulting in syllables of only one vowel was abandoned (Table 3.36).

The Reform and its Critics

The changes to German orthography introduced by the 1996 reform attracted a substantial body of criticism. This came not only from those

Table 3.35 Division of foreign loans

Old spelling	New spelling	English
Chir-urg (but *Si-rup*)	*Chir-urg/Chi-rurg*	surgeon (as previously, or like 'syrup')
Si-gnal (but *leug-nen*)	*Si-gnal/Sig-nal*	signal (as previously, or like 'to deny')
Päd-agogik (but *ba-den*)	*Päd-agogik/Pä-dagogik*	pedagogy (as previously, or like 'to bathe')
par-allel (but *Pa-rade*)	*par-allel/pa-rallel*	parallel (as previously, or like 'parade')
Heliko-pter (but *op-tisch*)	*Heliko-pter/Helikop-ter*	helicopter (as previously, or like 'optic(al)')

Table 3.36 Division into syllables of only one vowel

Old spelling	New spelling	English
Ufer (inseparable)	*U-fer*	(river)bank
Ofen (inseparable)	*O-fen*	oven, heater

opposed to the idea of orthographic reform *per se*, but similarly from many linguists broadly in favour of reform, who none the less questioned the underlying theoretical principles and/or specific recommendations of the new guidelines. The *linguistic* disputes over individual aspects of the reform are too numerous to be detailed here in their entirety,[11] but what unites most criticism is scepticism regarding the ability of the changes to contribute to the reform's basic aim. As stated in the official guidelines (*Deutsche Rechtschreibung*, 1996: 10), that aim was to harmonise the basic rules of punctuation and spelling by formulating a new and unified conception of German orthography. Those basic rules would then be accorded greater validity, leading to the elimination of many previous inconsistencies and exceptions. However, Werner Veith, one of many linguists who believed that neither a genuine re-standardisation (nor concomitant simplification) of German orthography had ultimately been achieved, structured his critique of the reform around three main themes as follows (Veith, 1997).

Consistency of the reform

Veith's (1997: 25–28) first concern was the extent to which the reform was linguistically, that is, structurally, consistent. Veith questioned, for example, the reformers' particular application of the morphological principle as a means of achieving a simplification of sound–letter classifications. This was primarily because the emphasis on language users' current perceptions of semantic relations led, in his view, to a series of problems. Even though the reformers emphasised how an item such as *belämmert* (awful) is not strictly derived from *Lamm* (lamb) (Augst & Schaeder, 1997a,b: 16), in other cases, the etymological relationship supposedly acknowledged by the new spellings was both inaccurate *and* inconsistent. For example, the spelling of the verb *nummerieren* (previously *numerieren*, 'to number') was brought into line with its cognate noun *Nummer*. However, the Latin *numerus* from which both items are derived was not only written with a single ⟨m⟩, but other related forms in German such as *Numerale* (numeral) and *numerisch* (numerical) continued to be written thus (Veith, 1997: 25).[12] Such morphological inconsistencies were further compounded by the decision not to bring the spelling of *Eltern* (parents) into line with the form from which it is clearly derived, namely *älter* (older) (for further examples, see Ickler, 1997b: 101). Veith (1997: 25) therefore questioned whether even those language users with a genuine understanding of the morphological principle would be well served by its seemingly inconsistent application within the new guidelines.

A second point criticised by Veith (1997: 25) in relation to sound–letter classifications concerned the changes made to the spelling of ⟨ss⟩ and ⟨ß⟩, whereby the former is to be written after all short vowels, the latter after long vowels and diphthongs. Veith's main objection was that the emphasis on a phoneme–grapheme relationship based on *standard German* pronunciation may well lead to some difficulties for speakers of other varieties. He cited here the example of *Gas* with its standard long vowel, which is none the less pronounced short in many parts of the German-speaking areas, especially in colloquial usage (note, however, the plural form *Gase* with its long vowel). Moreover, as Helmut Berschin (1998: 45) pointed out, the new rules on ⟨ß/ss⟩ failed to eliminate the main source of user error, that is, the need to distinguish between the subordinating conjunction *dass* (that) and the relative pronoun *das* (that/which). Such potential confusion was exacerbated by the fact that in Switzerland the grapheme ⟨ß⟩ was officially abandoned in 1938, a fact duly acknowledged by the new guidelines such that Swiss usage continues to be characterised by the almost exclusive use of ⟨ss⟩ (Gallmann, 1997a).[13]

Finally, Veith (1997: 26–28) noted some of the apparent inconsistencies in the new rules on capitalisation. Here the main grammatical test for nominal status, hence capitalisation, is the so-called *Artikelprobe*, that is, the possibility for use of an article with the item in question. For Veith, a potential inconsistency in this regard was the continued requirement for lower-case letters in nouns when used in denominalised constructions containing the verbs *sein* (to be), *bleiben* (to remain) and *werden* (to become). While *grammatically* consistent, this means that language users must continue to distinguish orthographically between constructions such as *ich habe Schuld daran* ('I am guilty'; literally, 'I have guilt' – nominalised *Schuld*) versus *ich bin schuld daran* ('I am guilty' – denominalised *schuld*). As Veith pointed out, this was not in keeping with the reform's general trend of *increasing* capitalisation as a means of harmonising the rules, whereby the same can be said for the decision to abandon capital letters for the second person familiar forms of address *du* (singular) and *ihr* (plural). Meanwhile, the rules for capitalisation in the case of hyphenated forms are complex to say the least. Here Veith noted how the writer is now required to capitalise only the first component of a hyphenated compound together with any nouns occurring within it, while any other components are to be written with lower-case letters, hence the pre-1996 form *das Entweder–Oder* (either–or) shifts to *Entweder–oder*. While such advanced meta-linguistic awareness is a lot to ask of language users when dealing with German compounds – consider, for example, the pattern of capitalisation in *das In-den-Tag-Hineinträumen* (day dreaming, lit. 'dreaming one's way into the day') – the demands are even greater where foreign loans are concerned. Thus writers are required to differentiate between the structure of English loans such as *das Walkie-Talkie* and *das Make-up*, the former with a noun (*Talkie*), which requires capitalisation, the latter with a prepositional adverb (*up*), which does not. As Veith observed (1997: 28), such rules are likely to create difficulties even for the most experienced writers.

The problem of variants

A second area of concern from Veith's point of view related to the question of variants, particularly where foreign loans (or those forms perceived as such) were concerned (1997: 28–32). Here, for example, the reformers specified a series of main and subsidiary variants, according to which the integrated, germanicised form would function as the main variant only in those cases where a process of integration was considered well advanced in current usage. This has inevitably led to confusion for language users, not least because the specification of the main versus subsidiary variants differs in the case of each individual lexeme. So, while the integrated spelling *Ketschup* is specified as the main variant with the loaned spelling *Ketchup* as its subsidiary, in the case of 'spaghetti' the situation is reversed, and the loaned spelling *Spaghetti* is the main variant, the germanicised *Spagetti* its subsidiary. As Veith noted, this potentially places language users in the dubious position of trying to second guess the reformers' own perceptions of the relative integration of each of the two variants. Yet even such highly developed meta-linguistic skills were unlikely to lead to an entirely correct spelling of loaned forms given the many inconsistencies across groups of related items. Thus while *Phonologie/Fonologie* were originally specified as the main and subsidiary variants respectively, in the case of *Phonem* and *Phonetik* only the original ⟨ph⟩ spellings were permitted. The same goes for a series of variants containing ⟨rh/r⟩ and ⟨th/t⟩, hence *Katarrh/Katarr* (catarrh) but only *Rhythmus* (rhythm), and *Panther/Panter* (panther) but only *Anthologie* (anthology).[14]

In an attempt to clarify the thinking behind this situation, the reformer Hermann Zabel (1997d) describes how the reformers' original intention had in fact been to make the integrated spelling the main variant in each and every case with the loaned variant its subsidiary. This would have involved the creation of integrated spellings where these did not already exist, on the one hand, and the eventual phasing-out of outmoded foreign variants, on the other. However, although this plan was effectively vetoed on account of public and media objections to the germanicisation of many foreign loans in the late 1980s (for documentation, see Zabel, 1989), the resulting decision to specify main and subsidiary variants on an individual, as opposed to a strictly rule-governed basis, was undoubtedly rather unsatisfactory. Moreover, this question of variance affected a number of other areas such as hyphenation (*Hairstylist/Hair-Stylist*), syllabification (*Si-gnal/Sig-nal*) and aspects of capitalisation (*aufs beste/aufs Beste*, in the best way possible).[15] All in all, Veith calculated (1997: 28–29) that approximately 10% of the 12,000 items in the word list accompanying the new guidelines were characterised by some form of optional variability.[16]

As Julian Rivers and Christopher Young (2001: 181) note, one group of language users particularly affected by this problem is schoolteachers (and, by implication, their pupils) (see also Lüthgens, 2002). In the case of loaned forms, for example, teachers not only have the unenviable (if not, impossible) task of knowing which items are characterised by optional variability in the first place, but must then differentiate between the main and subsidiary variant with regard to each individual lexeme. Moreover, when encountering subsidiary variants in pupils' work, teachers are now required to note the main variant in the margins, but without deducting any points from the overall score awarded. This quickly led to a scenario whereby main variants became known as *bevorzugt* (preferred) and secondary variants as *erlaubt* (permitted), a situation that the reform opponent Friedrich Denk (1997: 42–43) feared would lead to a social stratification of written usage (see also Kopke, 1995a: 199–200). In practice, however, this was (and is) highly unlikely, given that a prerequisite for such stratification would itself be a shared understanding within the speech community as to precisely which is the main and subsidiary variant in each and every case (and which is to be afforded social prestige), a consensus that is clearly not forthcoming. That said, the situation was and is exacerbated during the transitional period 1998–2005 by the fact that the new guidelines coexist alongside the old ones.[17] Added to this, teachers must in any case employ their professional judgement regarding the most appropriate point at which to instruct their pupils in the finer points of the new rules (Sitta, 1997: 223) – something which similarly applies to teachers of German as a foreign language.[18]

In practice, it seems that, in order to apply the rules on main and secondary variants correctly, most language users would be obliged to refer to a dictionary. And, while one might pity both pupils and their teachers forced to do so several times in the course of preparing or marking a piece of written work, even here there were originally a number of problems. As Rivers and Young (2001: 181–82) demonstrate in a brief comparison of the two main rival dictionaries published by Duden and Bertelsmann in 1996, decisions as to how best to re-present the question of variants were far from uniform. While both dictionaries listed the loaned spelling first followed by the integrated variant, only Bertelsmann specified which was the main and subsidiary variant in each case, for example, '*Ketchup* (subsidiary) → *Ketschup* (main)' or '*Spaghetti* (main) → *Spagetti* (subsidiary)'. Duden, on the other hand, omitted to indicate which of the two variants was primary, noting only its status as loaned or integrated, for example, '*Ketchup* → germanicised *Ketschup*' or '*Spaghetti* → germanicised *Spagetti*'. The whole question as to whether dictionaries accurately interpreted and reported the issue of main and secondary variants was widely debated and disputed (e.g. Augst & Schaeder, 1997b: 10–11;

Bünting & Timmler, 1997; Güthert & Heller, 1997; Scholze-Stubenrecht, 2001; Sitta, 1997). Accordingly, this was one of the first issues dealt with by the newly-formed International Commission for German Orthography. Following consultation with the Commission, the Duden editors then revised the representation of main and secondary variants in the 22nd edition published in August 2000 in a way that more systematically reflected the 1996 guidelines (for review of this, and Ickler's alternative dictionary – Ickler, 2000 – see Niederhauser, 2001).

However, even allowing for the fact that the expectation of homogeneity between different dictionaries is in itself unrealistic – and that the question of variants may well have been strategically exaggerated as a means of undermining the reform – it was clear that most users had, and continue to have, some difficulty interpreting the rules on variants. Unsurprisingly, perhaps, this has led to a range of 'local' practices, not least within the press, which in most cases converted to the new orthography on 1 August 1999. For example, many newspapers and publishers, prompted by their need to use electronic search engines efficiently, tended to opt for one or other of the variants, thereby forging (not for the first time, however) their own 'house styles'. And the press agencies, following their own assessment of foreign loan etymology, in many cases opted for the use of those variants specified as *subsidiary* by the 1996 guidelines.[19] As Rivers and Young (2001: 183) note, this may well constitute a source of conflict for pupils who will be taught to favour main variants such as *Ketschup* in a school context, but who will frequently encounter the use of subsidiary variants such as *Ketchup* outside of the classroom, notably in the press. It is a level of confusion, moreover, which – ironically perhaps – can and will only be compounded by any further potential interventions on behalf of the Commission for Orthography to remedy such matters following the end of the interim period in 2005.

Finally in this context, it is important to distinguish between the type of 'restricted variation' or so-called *gezielte Variantenführung* (Zabel, 1997d) that characterises the spelling of foreign loans and other items (e.g. hyphenation, syllabification, and some areas of capitalisation) and the 'freer variation', which is now permitted in the case of punctuation. Here, Rivers and Young (2001: 179) are again sceptical of the extent to which such liberalisation will genuinely support language users in their attempts to write correctly, noting, in particular, the hidden rules and traps that appear to surround the use of infinitive and participial clauses. Thus, while many such constructions are characterised by optional commas, for example, *Ein altes Lied singend (,) kam er aus dem*

Zimmer (singing an old song, he came out of the room), in some cases the commas are in fact compulsory, for example, *Er kam aus dem Zimmer, ein altes Lied singend* (he came out of the room singing an old song). Although such 'freer variation' brought about by the use of so-called 'stylistic' as opposed to 'grammatical' commas was intended to liberate language users from excessive normification in the area of punctuation, as with foreign loans, this seems likely to lead only to further instances of what Rivers and Young (2001: 178) refer to as 'pre-programmed confusion'. Overall, it seems doubtful that the degree of variability incorporated into the 1996 guidelines genuinely resulted in a *simplified* set of guidelines for German orthography, and Augst and Schaeder (1997b: 42–44) concede that this is a further area requiring attention from the Mannheim-based Commission.

Rules and their applications

The notion of 'hidden rules and traps' brings us to the third and last of Veith's concerns, namely the extent to which the reform has brought about a simplification of German orthography in *quantitative* terms (Veith, 1997: 33–42). In other words, do the new guidelines contain fewer rules than previously? The question is by no means straightforward when one considers the difficulty in identifying an entirely comparable pre-reform set of guidelines against which to evaluate the new ones. However, if (following Berschin, 1998: 44–45) one takes as the most pragmatic point of comparison the 212 rules contained in the last version of the Duden published prior to the reform (20th edition, 1991) one might reasonably claim – as the reformers have frequently done (e.g. Heller, 1998) – that the 1996 package with its 112 rules does indeed constitute a *reduction* in number.

Leaving aside the different types of rules contained in these two publications (Berschin, 1998: 44; Veith, 1997: 33), the main dispute here centres on the number of allegedly 'hidden rules' contained within the 1996 guidelines in the form of additional 'rules for application' (see also Ickler, 1997b), which take a variety of forms such as sub-rules, specifications, authorisations, conditions, word lists, and cross-references. Thus using as his main example §34 of the official guidelines on separate and compound spelling, Veith shows how what might initially appear to be a 'single' rule is in fact characterised by no less than 71 additional rules for its application (for further discussion, see also Ickler, 1997e). Indeed, as Renate Baudusch (2001) shows, the whole area of separate and compound spelling quickly emerged as one of the most controversial aspects of the reform (e.g. Zemb, 2001). Critics variously lamented, for example, the fact that the move to separate spellings ran in many cases counter to the more general historical trend towards compounding. They were also perturbed by the impact of increased word division on the appearance of written German, as well as by the purported effect on the referential potential of the written language, as signalled, for example, by the way in which many previous compounds 'lost' their own individual dictionary entry. These complaints combined with what Veith in any case saw as the 'hidden rules' surrounding separate and compound spelling, according to which it was still necessary to write many items together, for example, *wiederkommen* (to come back) continues to be distinguished from *wieder kommen* (to come again, i.e. once more). Although this does not in fact amount to a system of optional variability as in the case of, say, foreign loans or punctuation, the disparate interpretation of the many rules on separate and compound spelling led to considerable confusion where dictionaries were concerned, which, in turn, resulted in a much-criticised degree of misreporting of the new guidelines. And, following extensive discussions with the new International Commission for German Orthography, it was the clarification of these errors (together with the representation of variant forms) in the new edition of the Duden, published in August 2000, that sparked Ickler's public accusations in *Die Welt* newspaper of a 'secret withdrawal' of certain aspects of the reform, thereby prompting the reversion to the old rules on the part of the *FAZ* newspaper (FAZ, 2000).

Although not all areas of the reform are as complex as those for separate and compound spelling, nor attracted the same level of public controversy, Veith (1997: 36–40) proceeded to calculate a total of 1106 special 'rules for application' *in addition to* the original 112. As Berschin (1998: 45) points out, no pupil would in practice be expected to learn such rules in their entirety: in all probability they would concentrate on particular sub-sections. However, more important, in his view, is the fact that pupils learn the rules of spelling primarily via their ability to visualise the correct forms of individual items (or groups of related items) – drawing, in other words, on the ideographic/semantic dimensions of spelling. However, even here Veith (1997: 40–42) offers little consolation. According to his calculations the 1106 rules for application contain 105 word lists with no less than 1180 individual lexical items that fall *outside* of any specific rule. When one adds to these the 1100 or so items characterised by optional variability (as discussed above), Veith calculates that around one-fifth of the 12,000 items in the accompanying word list cannot be explained with regard to the rules described within the guidelines, but must be memorised on an individual basis.[20]

Even allowing for the possibility of a degree of 'anti-reform' hyperbole, Veith's characterisation of the new guidelines does not present a particularly optimistic account of the reform's ability to achieve its fundamental aim of *simplifying* the rules of German orthography. Like Berschin (1998: 44), Veith sees the reform as characterised by greater, as opposed to, reduced complexity. However, for Berschin a further – and crucial – criterion against which to evaluate the proposed simplification of the new guidelines would be their improved efficiency in pedagogic terms: in other words, do young pupils make fewer mistakes when writing German than previously? In this sense, one might concede that even a greater number of rules (hence greater apparent complexity) might none the less lead to an overall simplification from the learner's point of view. However, it is precisely this issue which is so difficult to address, given that no empirical study was commissioned by the reformers and/or the KMK in order to ascertain the comparative learnability of German orthography before or after the reform's introduction.[21] This leads Berschin to distinguish between two overlapping but potentially competing interpretations of the reform's key aim of simplification. First, there is the question of *systematising* the rules via the formulation of a unified concept for German orthography, that is, by attempting to iron out as many exceptions and irregularities as possible. Secondly, there is the desire to improve the *learnability* of those rules on the part of, say, young pupils. As Berschin (1998: 45) points out, whilst the aim of systematisation might well be seen as primarily *linguistic* (in a strictly structural sense), the desire to improve learnability is more broadly *political.*

The extent to which the 1996 reform was perceived to have constituted a simplification of German orthography, thereby enhancing overall learnability, is one of many themes that would emerge in the ensuing legal debates. This is linked, moreover, to the question of the *quantitative* impact of the reform on the written language overall. Although estimates have inevitably varied, the broad consensus is that the new guidelines, excluding the changes to ⟨ss/ß⟩, affected no more than around 0.5% of an average written text (see e.g. *Bundesverfassungsgericht*, 1998: 239). And in a legal sense, the question of quantitative impact revolved at least partly around the extent to which the reform was considered sufficiently fundamental so as to have (1) genuinely improved learnability, and (2) required proper statutory legislation as opposed to a simple decree on the part of the Education Ministers.

On a more general note, many would argue that if the impact of the reform was genuinely so minimal, then why such seemingly exaggerated concern and debate? On the other hand, can such a minimalist reform have possibly been justified in view of the upheaval clearly brought about by both the planning and transition process? This relates not least to the concomitant financial costs, which, although objectively incalculable, were undeniably considerable. One need only think of the many working hours on the part of linguists and politicians, the cost for both publishers and schools of revising and replacing dictionaries and schoolbooks,[22] as well as the loss of working/learning hours for teachers and pupils. To these, however, one would then be forced to add the cost of the thousands of hours spent by lawyers and state authorities when faced with the lengthy legal challenge that would be brought against the reform. It is to that challenge that we now turn in the next chapter.

Notes

1. Such views are, of course, still present in latter-day approaches to language. As Langer (2000: 18), for example, emphasises: 'To oversimplify slightly: orthography is not part of language because it is an artificial system, consciously invented and developed by people. Language, on the other hand, is naturally acquired in processes that are even today unclear to us. Crucially, however, to say that orthography is part of the language would be to say that a language without orthography is missing something. Clearly this is not the case, as evidenced by the hundreds of (complete) languages in the world that are not written.'

2. For further details, see, *inter alia*, Augst (1985, 1986), Kohrt (1983, 1985, 1986), Looser (1998), Mentrup (1979, 1983), Nerius (1975, 1986), Nerius & Scharnhorst (1980), Schrodt (2000), Strunk (1998a) and Zabel (1987).

3. It is important to stress at this juncture how the view of writing as a means with which to represent speech is considerably older than de Saussure's work, dating back, as Harris (2000) shows, to Aristotelian views of written language. For a much broader discussion of the linguistic–theoretical relationship between speech and writing, see also Harris (1986: especially Chapter 4), who demonstrates, *inter alia*, how the main difficulty with the concept of phoneme–grapheme correspondence is that the inventory of graphemes is generally well defined, where its phonemic 'equivalent' remains a matter of ongoing debate. For a critique in the specific context of German and the reform of its spelling system, see Kopke (1995a: 251–61).

4. For further discussion of the 'speech–writing' dichotomy, see, for example, Barton (1994, 1995), Barton and Hamilton (1996), Harris (1986, 2000) and Stubbs (1980).

5. See Duden editor Scholze-Stubenrecht (2001) for a discussion of the main difficulties associated with implementing those dimensions of the new guidelines based on morphological principles in the new editions of the Duden, not least where these conflict with phonological principles. As

Scholze-Stubenrecht shows, what were ostensibly purely technical, linguistic decisions on the part of the Duden editorial board were easily mis-construed by the reform's opponents as attempts to re-write the 1996 guidelines.

6. Note also the use of ⟨ch⟩ in French loans such as *Champagne* and ⟨sh⟩ in loans from English such as *Shop*.

7. For further details, see Nerius (2000a: 155–56). For a detailed account of the problematic relationship between the diachronic and synchronic levels of analysis in cases such as these, see Scholze-Stubenrecht (2001) and Munske (1997c: 303–307).

8. For a detailed critical discussion of the representation of double consonants, see Eisenberg (1999, 2000), Ramers (1999a,b) and Sternefeld (2000).

9. See *Deutsche Rechtschreibung* (1996). For a discussion of the structure of the guidelines and index, see Augst and Schaeder (1997a), Gallmann and Sitta (1997), Heller and Scharnhorst (1997).

10. As we shall see later in this chapter, the question of optional variability, as in the case of hyphenated forms, was one aspect of the reform causing particular problems for dictionary editors and therefore subsequently revisited by the Mannheim-based Commission. In each of the cases listed here (with the exception of *Jobsharing*, which is now the only permissible variant), compound forms have been subsequently specified as the *main* variant, with hyphenated forms as *secondary*; see Duden, 2000).

11. For collections dealing with the reform in general, see Augst *et al.* (1997), Augst and Schaeder (1997b), Eroms and Munske (1997), and Schaeder (1999a). For critiques of each of the six main areas of the reform, see Berschin (1998), Veith (1997), Fuhrop *et al.* (1995), and Ickler (1997a). For alternative reform concepts, see *Studiengruppe Geschriebene Sprache* (1997), Zemb (1997) and Ickler (2000) and *Deutsche Akademie für Sprache und Dichtung* (2003), while for a response to critics on each of the main areas of the reform, see Augst and Schaeder (1997b). On the individual areas of the reform, see Augst and Stock (1997) on phoneme–grapheme classifications generally, Eisenberg (1997a) and Maas (1997) on the representation of vowel length, and Poschenrieder (1997) and Gallmann (1997a) on the use of ⟨ß⟩ and ⟨ss⟩. On the representation of double consonants, see Eisenberg (1999, 2000), Ramers (1999a,b), and Sternefeld (2000). On the spelling of foreign loans, see Zabel (1997a,b,c) and Rivers and Young (2001). On separate and compound spelling, see Baudusch (2001), Eisenberg (1997b), Günther (1997), Herberg (1997) and Schaeder (1997). On capitalisation, see Augst (1997a), Ewald and Nerius (1997), Gallmann (1997b), Kopke (1995a: 332–70) and Munske (1997a). On punctuation, see Baudusch (1997a,b), Gallmann (1997c), Primus (1997) and Rivers and Young (2001). Finally, on syllabification/word division at the end of lines, see Augst (1997b).

12. These were the kinds of issues subsequently addressed in discussions between dictionary publishers such as Duden and Bertelsmann and the newly-established Mannheim-based International Commission for German

Orthography, which in turn sparked the controversies in the summer of 2000 (see Chapter 1) when the reformers were accused by their opponents of 'secretly withdrawing' certain aspects of the reform. The problem, of which the reformers were always aware, is at least partly related to the impossibility of providing an exhaustive word list in conjunction with the new guidelines. The original list could only ever serve as a basic model upon which dictionaries could then generalise, whereby different dictionaries would inevitably generalise in differing ways and to differing extents. To this day, the orthographic representation of related word groups remains the subject of discussion and potential revision. The 22nd edition of the Duden published in July 2000, for example, listed *nummerisch* (numerical) as a permissible variant of *numerisch*, though *Numerale* continued to be written with only one ⟨m⟩. For further discussion, see Scholze-Stubenrecht (2001).

13. See Augst and Schaeder (1997: 15), however, who point out how attempts to eliminate the distinction between *dass* and *das* on the part of the International Working Party were blocked in the early 1990s. They similarly note how the question of entirely abandoning the grapheme ⟨ß⟩ was never on the agenda given the desire from the outset to avoid changes that significantly altered the appearance of the written language. For further discussion of *daß*/*dass*, see Reiffenstein (2000) and Kranich-Hofbauer (2000).

14. Augst and Schaeder (1997: 20) acknowledge the discrepancies here and describe the particular difficulties encountered by the reformers when dealing with so-called 'expert' registers, an area requiring further attention on the part of the Mannheim-based Commission. As with the earlier examples of *nummerisch*/*Numerale*, these are problems closely connected to the impossibility of providing an exhaustive word list to accompany the rules themselves. Indeed, the question of ⟨ph⟩ spellings was one of the first to be addressed by the Commission such that ⟨f⟩ spellings are now permitted as subsidiary variants of *Phonem* and *Phonetik*, although *Rhythmus* and *Anthologie* continue to function as the only possible forms (see Duden, 2000). For further discussion, see also Scholze-Stubenrecht (2001).

15. As noted above, however, many of these cases were subsequently revisited by the Mannheim Commission.

16. See Haugen (1966: 117–18) and Gundersen (1977: 255) for a discussion of the problems that similarly surrounded variant spellings or 'doublets' in reforms of Norwegian orthography.

17. In a questionnaire survey of 11 primary school teachers, Weinberger (2001) showed how no teacher scored higher than 50% in terms of familiarity with main and subsidiary variants in the case of foreign loans. Such teachers were, as was to be expected, extremely sceptical of the value of liberalising spellings in this way, arguing that such variability merely increased, rather than decreased, the likelihood of pupil error. See also Geerts *et al.* (1977: 199), who describe similar problems experienced by teachers concerning the implementation of variants in Dutch spelling reforms in the 1950s and

1960s. For an in-depth study of teachers' responses to the 1996 reform, see Lüthgens (2002).

18. For a discussion of the reform's impact on the teaching of German as a foreign language, see Drewnowska-Vargáné and Földes (1999), Földes (2000) and Stuppnik-Bazzanella (2000).

19. In a statement dated 21 June 1999, the German-speaking news agencies declared their adherence to those loaned forms derived from *living* languages such as English, French and Italian (e.g. *Ketchup*, *Portemonnaie* and *Spaghetti*). In the case of Latin and Greek loans, however, they would adhere to loaned spellings in the context of 'expert' scientific registers only (e.g. *demographisch*, *homophon* and *Photosynthese*) but would use integrated spellings where these were in common everyday usage (e.g. *Typografie*, *Megafon* and *substanziell*). Moreover, the agencies confirmed their decision to adopt hyphenated variants over compounds loan forms (e.g. *Centre-Court*, *Job-Sharing*, *Moto-Cross*) as well as their adherence to, *inter alia*, the pre-1996 rules of punctuation together with the capitalisation of pronominal forms such as *Du*, *Ihr*, and so on (for details, see Duden, 2000: 119–20; see also Nürnberger, 2000). For an overview of the new guidelines as implemented by the press, see also section five of the third interim report of the *Kommission für deutsche Rechtschreibung* (2001).

20. On the specific question of the word list accompanying the new guidelines, see Scholze-Stubenrecht (2001), who argues that many of the problems surrounding the reform would be best dealt with via a more detailed word list as opposed to revision of the guidelines themselves. See also *Deutsche Akademie für Sprache und Dichtung* (2003), which published its own revised set of guidelines and word list.

21. See, however, Geerts *et al.* (1977: 201–202) who highlight a similar weakness where Dutch spelling reforms were concerned. Indeed as Bird (2001: 153) notes, it is by no means uncommon to find such a lack of empirical evidence where the creation and revision of writing systems are concerned although this may, of course, relate to the difficulty in providing such evidence *per se* insofar as it is singularly difficult to assess the efficacy of a new system prior to its actual implementation. See also the third report of the *Zwischenstaatliche Kommission für deutsche Rechtschreibung* (2001), whose authors refute the controversial claim made by Marx (1999) that, at least as far as the new rules on ⟨ss⟩ were concerned, students were experiencing *greater* difficulties than previously. See, however, the critical response by Richter (2001), who notes how Marx's study deals only with so-called *Umlerner*, that is, pupils converting to the new rules after having learned the old ones.

22. Hans-Joachim Gelberg, owner of a small publishing company in Dortmund specialising in children's literature, estimated the costs to his firm alone of the transition to the new orthography at around DM 500,000–600,000, that is, approximately £200,000 (Gelberg, 1997).

Chapter 4
The Constitutional Challenge

In Chapter 2 of this book I began by sketching the historical background to the more recent debates over the re-standardisation of German orthography. Chapter 3 then turned to a description and analysis of the changes to German spelling and punctuation that were proposed as part of the 1996 reform. In this chapter, I now move on to a consideration of the legal challenges that were brought against those changes during the period 1996–1999. Legal disputes such as these provide a particularly fruitful site for the study of a language ideological debate as outlined in Chapter 1 (see for example Lippi-Green, 1997: 152–70; Phillips, 2000; Shannon, 1999). This is not least because the adversarial nature of the judicial process in itself creates a discursive space in which a range of potentially conflicting views on language can be aired by the various participants. It is a process, moreover, that invariably presupposes some form of *verdict*, that is, a ruling that ultimately prioritises and thereby legitimises one or more views of language over others. Against this backdrop, it is possible to track the ways in which the language ideological standpoints of particular individuals and/or groups of ideological brokers may be authoritatively entextualised. That said, it is important to note how the actual achievement of such entextualisation by no means guarantees the wholesale acceptance of those views that have gained hegemony in a formal – in this case *juridical* – sense. As will become clear, this would certainly be true of the legal disputes surrounding German orthographic reform, where the ruling of the Federal Constitutional Court in favour of the revised orthography and its subsequent implementation continued to be widely contested.

The legal challenge brought against the 1996 reform can be seen in terms of four main phases, which themselves provide the overarching structure for this chapter. The first section will examine the initial challenge that was brought before the Federal Constitutional Court in 1996. The second section summarises the period 1996–1998 during which the reform continued to be contested in the regional courts as well as finding itself at the centre of a campaign for referenda organised by citizens' initiatives around the country. The third section examines in detail what reformers and opponents alike hoped would be the final ruling on the reform in May 1998 when the case was referred back to the Federal Constitutional Court.[1] Finally, the fourth section describes the referendum that took place in September 1998 in which the reform was successfully overturned in Schleswig-Holstein, leading to a subsequent opt-out by schools in that state, a situation that was (by no means uncontroversially) reversed by the regional parliament there one year later.

The Constitutional Challenge of 1996

In May 1996 the first legal challenge against the reform was brought before the Federal Constitutional Court by Rolf Gröschner, a professor of law at Jena University, together with his then 14-year-old daughter, Alena. As a basis for this section of the analysis, I shall critically discuss the document containing the official ruling of the Court on these two cases, *1 BvR 1057/96* and *1 BvR 1067/96*, published on 21 June 1996. However, it is important to note at the outset how, in the years leading up to his petition, the central complainant, Rolf Gröschner – himself a scholar of cultural jurisprudence (see Gröschner, 1982, 1992, 1995) – acted as the supervisor of a doctoral dissertation on constitutional aspects of orthographic reform by Wolfgang Kopke (Kopke, 1995a). Many of the ideas underpinning Gröschner's challenge, along with those of subsequent cases brought against the reform therefore draw directly upon Kopke's work. The thrust of these ideas – which subsequently became known as the 'Jenenser critique of the spelling reform' – is summarised in various papers (e.g. Gröschner, 1997; Gröschner & Kopke, 1997; Kopke, 1995b, 1996, 1997) and critically evaluated in a number of others (for example Häberle, 1996; Hufeld, 1996; Hufen, 1997; Jäkel, 1996; Knobloch, 1998; Kolonovits, 1997; Meder, 1997; Menzel, 1998a,b; Munske, 1997a; Rivers & Young, 2001; Roellecke, 1997; Roth, 1999; Schneider, 1998; Zabel, 1996). However, it is worth noting that central to all the arguments put forward throughout this legal challenge was Kopke's claim that the Basic Law in itself prevents the state from adopting a pro-active role where cultural (and, by implication, linguistic) matters are concerned. According to Kopke (1995a: 372–411), this is because state action is limited to the function of 'respecting and protecting' (*achten und schützen*) the language as traditionally used within the speech community as opposed to intervening 'actively', that is, at a *structural* level, in its development.

The complaints

In the first section of his complaint, Gröschner disputed the role played by the Duden dictionary in trying to secure the implementation of the 1996 reform. The Duden, as we saw in Chapter 2, was declared in 1955 by the Standing Conference of the West German Ministers for Education and Cultural Affairs (or KMK) to be binding in so-called 'cases of uncertainty' until such time as a further reform of the 1901 guidelines had been agreed. Meanwhile, the KMK resolution of 30 November 1995 had explicitly stated that the 1955 ruling would not be revoked until 1 August 1998. Since, however, the individual federal states or *Länder* were technically permitted to introduce the new guidelines at a time of their choosing in the two-year period *between* 1 August 1996 and 1 August 1998, and an edition of the Duden dictionary revised according to the new regulations was already planned for the summer of 1996, it was Gröschner's contention that the Duden would effectively function as a lever for the reform's implementation during this two-year transitionary period.

Kopke has argued at length how the original 1955 ruling of the KMK almost certainly infringed the then West German Constitution or Basic Law of 1949 that was subsequently adopted by the newly-unified German state in 1990 (Kopke, 1995a: 48–65; 1995b: 878–80). For example, Article 12 of the Basic Law states that 'The practice of trades and professions may be regulated by law' – that is to say, *only* by law. By the early 1990s, however, anxious about the ensuing loss of their 40-year monopoly, and not having participated in the drawing up of the new guidelines, the Duden editors were especially eager to be seen publicly to have played a central role in the new reform, thereby continuing to convey the impression of the authoritative status of their dictionaries (see Munske, 1997c: 288). For example, in a pamphlet outlining the new guidelines (Duden, 1994), Duden declared their self-appointed task of helping to secure the implementation of the reform, and their editor-in-chief, Günter Drosdowski, was happy to proclaim, in an interview in the news magazine, *Der Spiegel* (19 June 1995), the role of his company as the 'long arm of the state' in matters orthographic (see also Böhme, 2001; Scholze-Stubenrecht, 1997). All in all, Kopke was of the opinion that the position of the Duden publishers *vis à vis* the state was itself in need of statutory regulation, particularly since the 1996 reform was, in his view, tantamount to a recommendation to the population *by the state* to purchase an updated version of the Duden – in itself, a potential

further breach of Article 12. Only through the full and open public discussion that would necessarily accompany the drawing up of proper statutory legislation on the whole question of orthographic reform would
other publishers, Kopke believed, be afforded their rightful opportunity
to compete openly and fairly with Duden.

Of course, Gröschner's argument tended to overlook the fact that by
1996 many other revised dictionaries would also be available for public
purchase, including that of Duden's main rival, Bertelsmann. In this
regard, Gröschner and Kopke have been widely criticised for over-
estimating the significance of the Duden spelling dictionary in the
process of reform, together with the role played by its editors (e.g.
Zabel, 1996: 359–60; Hufeld, 1996: 1076). But whether those other
dictionaries would ever really be able to compete on a level playing
field with the Duden, given the latter's long-term position of authority,
was open to debate. Central to Gröschner's and Kopke's argument was
their belief that the Duden was seen *by the wider population* as authoritative
in questions of orthography, not least in view of the authority afforded to
it by the 1955 ruling (see also Böhme, 2001).

The three additional complaints put forward by Gröschner concerned
various claims that the 1996 reform of German orthography constituted
an infringement of his own constitutional rights as laid down in the
Basic Law.

Gröschner maintained first that the reform, together with the purportedly unlawful role played by the Duden in securing its implementation,
were an infringement of Article 2, Paragraph 1, of the Basic Law, which
stipulates that 'everyone has the right to the free development of his personality insofar as he does not violate the rights of others or offend against
the constitutional order or the moral code'. In addition, Gröschner cited
Article 1, Paragraph 1, of the Basic Law, which states that 'The dignity
of man is inviolable. To respect and protect it is the duty of all state authority'. It was Gröschner's contention that the spelling reform breached
these constitutional rights because one of the basic conditions for the
free development of his personality was what he referred to as 'linguistic
integrity'. The spelling reform, he argued, impinged upon that integrity
because he would eventually be required, not only in his professional
capacity as a civil servant himself (most school teachers and university
professors have civil servant status in Germany), but even in his *private*
correspondence to adopt the new orthographic rules in order to avoid
the 'social embarrassment' that generally accompanies an inability to
spell correctly (see Drosdowski in Duden, 1994: 4). Gröschner therefore
claimed that it is the duty of the state, as enshrined in Article 1, to

respect and ultimately protect the dignity arising from such linguistic integrity.

Kopke (1995a: 277–93) had developed this notion of 'linguistic integrity' by arguing how, although Article 2, Paragraph 2, of the Basic Law explicitly guarantees only the *physical* inviolability of the individual, Article 2, Paragraph 1, taken together with Article 1, could also be interpreted as guaranteeing *psychological* inviolability. He then draws on recent research on written language and orthography, particularly within psycho- and neuro-linguistics, demonstrating that writing is not merely, as traditionally maintained, a second order representation of spoken language underpinning the dictum 'write as you speak'. This, he claims, is because readers do not make sense of the written word by simply decoding graphemes as direct representations of individual speech sounds but, *in addition*, by coming to recognise over time the meaning of lexical items as complete semiotic units, which are then stored in the brain and subject to a cognitive process of retrieval (Kopke, 1995a: 261–76). Prioritising the semantic over the phonological principle underpinning German orthography (see Chapter 3), Kopke therefore argued that, if writing can be demonstrated to constitute a system in its own right, then to demand that civil servants and pupils such as Gröschner and his daughter *replace* the system they have previously acquired, and crucially stored in their 'mental lexicon', is tantamount to a constitutional breach of their right to the free development of their personality.

Returning to the legal challenge, Gröschner argued, secondly, that the spelling reform impinged on his constitutional rights as laid down in Article 5, Paragraph 3, of the Basic Law, which guarantees that 'Art and science, research and teaching are free'. Gröschner considered that this freedom would be curtailed should he not be permitted in his professional capacity as an examiner in state law examinations to evaluate the new spellings as incorrect.

Thirdly, Gröschner maintained that the reform contravened his constitutional rights as specified in Article 6, Paragraph 2, of the Basic Law, which states that the 'Care and upbringing of children are the natural right of the parents and a duty primarily incumbent on them'. Gröschner went on to argue how, while decrees on the part of the KMK had traditionally constituted an adequate means by which to introduce revisions to school curricula, the current reform was different. Because his daughter would be learning what he considered to be an orthography *fundamentally* different to the one he had learned himself, the reform impinged upon his parental right to educate his daughter as he wished. He then argued that such a conflict of parental authority need not be tolerated without the approval of the democratic legislature, in other words, a statutory law as opposed to a ministerial decree, whereby Kopke had cited the laws passed as a means of implementing the Dutch spelling reform of 1947 as a model in this regard (Geerts *et al.*, 1977: 198; Kopke, 1995a: 206). Gröschner's arguments were broadly reiterated by his 14-year-old daughter, who claimed that she too considered the spelling reform an infringement of the right to the free development of her own personality, since she would similarly be forced to use spellings other than those she had previously learned at home and school, and had therefore stored in her 'mental lexicon'.

At this juncture, some further contextualisation becomes necessary given that this need, as perceived by Gröschner and his daughter, for a statutory regulation of orthography is in fact tied into the much broader historical and political question of the relative powers of the legislature and the executive with respect to the German constitutional monarchy of 1901, on the one hand, and the post-war parliamentary democracy of (West) Germany, on the other. Whereas Augst and Strunk (1989) had argued that the 1901 mode of implementing an orthographic reform via ministerial decree afforded an appropriate precedent for 1996, this was severely disputed by Gröschner and Kopke (Gröschner, 1997; Gröschner & Kopke, 1997; Kopke, 1995a,b). Thus, while control over educational matters in both periods remained primarily in the hands of the executive of the *Länder*, Kopke argued how this by no means guaranteed the *equivalence* of powers in the two historical periods. Indeed it was Kopke's view that, under the constitutional monarchy of 1901, the powers of the executive were significantly *greater* than in the new (Berlin) Republic for two main reasons.[2] First, Article 7 of the Basic Law states 'The entire education system is under the supervision of the state' – although, as we shall see later, the definition of both 'supervision' and 'state' remains open to interpretation. Secondly, the rights of the individual *vis à vis* the state are much more firmly embedded in the post-war constitution than in 1901. This means that German citizens are now better positioned to demand action on the part of the legislature – in other words, the statutory enforcement of executive action – wherever they consider the enjoyment of their basic rights to be impinged upon to a 'disproportionate' (*unverhältnismäßig*) extent. And it is a point of additional interest that, unlike in 1901, when the rights of civil servants and school pupils such as Gröschner and his daughter were afforded little or no protection, this has *not* been the case since 1949 when the rights of both groups have been constitutionally guaranteed (Kopke 1995a: 163, 215), albeit, as we shall see later, with a number of caveats.

The post-war model of a federal constitutional democracy embodies, however, a crucial tension – one that is familiar to students of the US constitution, which itself provided the inspiration for the (West) German Basic Law of 1949. One of the main aims of the Basic Law was to rectify the flaws in the Weimar constitution that had structurally facilitated the seizure of power by the National Socialists in 1933 (see Dürig, 1998: ix–xvi). This was to be achieved particularly via Article 20, with its proposition that 'All state authority emanates from the people' together with its constitutional guarantee of a separation of legislative, executive, and judicial organs. The problem here is that those constitutional structures originally intended as a means of strengthening the democratic influence of the *people* against the potentially totalising forces of the *state* simultaneously run the risk of an ever-increasing juridification of social life, which itself threatens to stifle the possibility for political action on the part of the state (see Ossenbühl, 1989: 325). This occurs as citizens increasingly contest the authority of the *executive* (in this case, the KMK) with recourse to the *judiciary* (in this case, the Federal Constitutional Court) in order to demand action on the part of the *legislature* (in this case, either the national or *Länder* parliaments) – a trend that has increased notably since the 1970s (see Ossenbühl, 1989: 337–38). And it is precisely in an attempt to counter the potential for such 'over'-juridification that there has been frequent recourse in recent decades to the so-called 'principle of fundamentality' (*Wesentlichkeitsprinzip* or *-doktrin*). This posits that rulings by the legislature, in the form of parliamentary statutes, are required only in those cases where the decisions to be made are too *fundamental* to be left to the executive (see Ossenbühl, 1989; Staupe, 1986).[3] Moreover, the legislature is not permitted to transfer to the executive any form of 'blanket authorisation' regarding specific areas of social life such as, say, education. Instead executive measures must be evaluated on an issue-by-issue basis with regard to the potential for fundamental infringements of citizens' rights as laid down in the Basic Law (Gröschner, 1997).[4] Of course, the crux of all such disputes then lies in the extent to which any such measure is deemed to be fundamental.

In a series of constitutional debates over educational issues since the 1970s, the principle of fundamentality has generally been interpreted thus: the KMK may stipulate changes to the content of school curricula by means of decree provided that such changes are fairly limited and gradual, affecting only minor curricular details (so-called *Feinlernziele*). Where broader, more *fundamental* pedagogic aims and objectives (so-called *Groblernziele*) are affected, action is required on the part of the legislature. In this regard a benchmark has been the extent to which curricular innovations were thought to have an impact extending *beyond* the limited realm of school pupils that then impinged to a disproportionate extent on the constitutional rights of citizens in the wider community (*Außen-* or *Breitenwirkung*). This was the case, for example, in 1977, when changes to the sex education curriculum proposed in Hamburg – involving a shift from broadly religious to secular principles – were deemed to impact upon the constitutional rights of individuals outside of the classroom (notably parents) to a sufficiently fundamental degree as to require a statutory ruling on behalf of the regional parliament there (see Kopke, 1995a: 157–62; Ossenbühl, 1989: 334–36).

Returning to the specific question of orthography, it was Gröschner's belief that the 1996 reform did indeed affect broader pedagogic aims and objectives, thereby fulfilling the condition of fundamentality, in two main ways (Gröschner, 1997). First, he argued that the reform had resulted in an orthography fundamentally different to the previous standard. In his view, the guidelines of 1901/1902 had not really constituted a reform at all, but had simply documented an 'organic' and already completed process of language change, for example, the move from *Thür→Tür* (door). This, he believed, was in stark contrast to the 1996 reform, which had introduced a number of previously entirely non-existent spellings as a result of new guidelines on, for example, sound–letter classifications (e.g. *Känguru⇐Känguruh*), separate and compound spelling (e.g. *sitzen bleiben⇐sitzenbleiben*), capitalisation (e.g. *in Bezug auf⇐in bezug auf*), punctuation (e.g. via the abolition of compulsory commas preceding *und* and *oder*), and word division at the end of lines (e.g. *O-fen⇐Ofen*) (see Chapter 3; see also Munske, 1997a). Gröschner's views on the nature of the 1901/1902 reform have been vehemently (and correctly) refuted by many commentators, keen to stress how the 1901/1902 guidelines did indeed constitute an active intervention into orthographic structure on the part of both the state and linguists as opposed to merely documenting a process of naturally occurring language change (e.g. Mentrup, 1998; Menzel, 1998a: 1179). None the less it was the complainants' conviction that pupils would from now on be required to learn a version of German orthography that was so *fundamentally* different from the previous one that a ministerial decree was an inadequate means with which to secure its implementation.

The second reason concerns the much-disputed question of the relationship between school curricula, on the one hand, and their implications for the wider community, on the other. Here Gröschner was convinced that the 1996 reform would have implications extending beyond schools, which would impinge to a disproportionate extent upon the constitutional rights of the wider population, not least parents. Not only did Article III of the Vienna Declaration clearly state that the longer-term aim of the reform would be to work toward the preservation of orthographic unity in the whole of the German-speaking area, further evidence was provided, he believed, by the role of the Duden corporation in helping to secure the implementation of the reform right across the speech community.

For both of these reasons, Gröschner was convinced of the need for a statutory law on orthographic reform at either national or *Länder* level. And although there has been some disagreement in the literature as to what *kind* of legislative action was being demanded by Gröschner and opponents of the reform more generally, Menzel (1998a: 1183) notes how this need not have involved the detailed specification of a standard orthography on the part of the state, merely a parliamentary ruling clarifying overall responsibility for such issues (so-called *parlamentarische Leitentscheidung*) (see also Kopke, 1995a: 296).[5] Indeed Kopke's own preference was for a state-sanctioned system whereby existing orthographic practices would be first tracked and *only then* recommended as authoritative to schools and the civil service. This amounted, in other words, to a system not unlike that which operates informally in the UK – hence the occasional glossing of opponents' views as 'the English way' (*der englische Weg*). As Rivers and Young suggest (2001: 173), although Kopke did not himself draw the analogy, what he was proposing ultimately amounted to a German version of the 'Oxford English Dictionary'.

The Court's response

Section II of the document outlines the response of the Constitutional Court, which is formally obliged to accept complaints by individuals in conjunction with two sections of the Law of the Federal Constitutional Court (*Bundesverfassungsgerichtsgesetz* or *BVerfGG*). The first of these, §93a (Paragraph 2), states that complaints can be accepted only where *fundamental* significance in terms of constitutional rights can be attached to the complaint – and the Court rejected that such significance was evident in Gröschner's case. Given their inadmissibility, the complaints therefore could not be considered in relation to §90 (Paragraph 1), which states that every individual has the right to bring a complaint to the Constitutional Court should he or she believe that the actions of state authorities disproportionately impinge upon constitutional rights. The Court justified its refusal to accept Gröschner's complaint as follows: for an individual to be *fundamentally* affected by a breach of

one or more constitutional rights, he or she must (as a minimum requirement) be 'personally, currently and directly' affected by the action in question. The Court then ruled that this was not the case where Gröschner was
concerned and dealt with his complaints in reverse order.

The first reason for the rejection of Gröschner's claim that he was
directly affected by the spelling reform related to the question of parental
rights together with Gröschner's contention that a ministerial decree was
an insufficient basis for its introduction. The Court ruled that the spelling
reform was, at the time when the complaint was made, limited to a
mutual obligation entered into by the Ministers for Education and Cultural Affairs of the 16 *Länder*, who would subsequently be responsible
for its implementation in schools. However, since at the time of Gröschner's complaint such implementation had not yet begun, Gröschner
could not yet claim to be either *personally* or *currently* affected – indeed,
nobody could. In other words, the complaint was dismissed because it
was prematurely lodged. It was a legal technicality, which, not surprisingly, infuriated opponents of the reform (e.g. Ickler, 1997c: 136), who
argued that by the time the reform had in fact been introduced they
would be dealing with a *fait accompli*, which (as they correctly anticipated)
would be even harder to reverse. Moreover, as Hubertus Gersdorf (2000:
10) shows, although complainants must normally demonstrate that they
are *currently* affected by the measures in dispute, there is none the less
provision within Law of the Federal Constitutional Court allowing
them to present their case in advance of the implementation of such
measures. This is permissible in two main circumstances: first, where it
would be difficult to reverse the measures in question following their
actual implementation and, second, where the measures would be
implemented in the relatively near future – both of which would
appear to have applied in the case of the spelling reform.

The second reason why the complaint was rejected concerns the
requirement stipulated in §90 (Paragraph 2, Sentence 1) of the Law of
the Federal Constitutional Court that, prior to lodging a complaint, complainants must first have taken their case to the lower courts and
exhausted the requisite legal channels. However, the same paragraph
goes on to state that complainants may proceed *directly* to the Constitutional Court should they consider themselves to be severely and una-
voidably disadvantaged by first proceeding through the lower courts.
In this case, the Court did not believe that such a disadvantage was forthcoming and again ruled Gröschner's complaint to be inadmissible.

After stating that the actions of the Standing Conference of Ministers
for Education and Cultural Affairs (KMK) could not be considered to

constitute a breach of parental rights, the Court proceeded to rule that the actions of neither the Standing Conference of the Prime Ministers of the 16 *Länder* (*Ministerpräsidentenkonferenz* or *MPK*) nor the Federal government could, for the same reasons, be considered to affect the complainant directly. Nor would Gröschner's rights be directly impinged upon by the signing of the declaration of intent planned for 1 July 1996 in Vienna. This declaration, the Court claimed, would neither function as a legally binding agreement for the Federal Republic, nor would it directly affect the implementation of the reform. However, in Kopke's opinion (1997: 112–13), this merely highlighted the general unenforceability of the reform, since in his opinion no legal action could be taken against any country or federal state that subsequently failed to secure its implementation, whereby one means of securing the requisite legislative authority would have been via parliamentary approval of the Vienna Declaration itself (see Kopke, 1995a: 207).

Finally, in this section of its judgement, the Court dealt with the disputed role played by the Duden dictionary *vis à vis* the 1996 reform. The Court thereby reiterated the KMK ruling of 1955 that the 1901 guidelines remained valid until such time as a further reform had been implemented, and that *only* in so-called 'cases of uncertainty' should reference be made to the supplementary rules contained in the Duden. The Court ruled that, in those *Länder* where the reform had not yet been introduced, any version of the Duden that did not conform to the 1901 guidelines (i.e. one already revised according to the new rules) was clearly not covered by the ruling of 1955 and therefore disqualified itself from use in the classroom. This meant that, in the two-year period between 1 August 1996 and 1 August 1998, teachers in the 'pre-reform' *Länder* would be required to refer to pre-1996 versions of the Duden in 'cases of uncertainty'. While this might initially appear to be an undesirably complex situation, in reality, this was precisely what happened. This is because such 'pre-reform' *Länder* would not have acquired new, updated dictionaries until such time as the reform had actually been introduced, therefore undermining Gröschner's argument that teachers would in practice be obliged to *distinguish* between the pre- and post-1996 editions of the Duden during the interim period (see also Menzel, 1998a: 1181).[6]

Having dismissed Gröschner's assertion that the reform required a statutory law to secure its implementation (and having rejected his daughter's case on the same grounds), the Court then addressed the substantive aspects of Gröschner's complaint. First, the Court rejected outright Gröschner's claim that his freedom of teaching would be curtailed, since it did not accept that he was either directly affected by the reform or that his duties with regard to state examinations were embraced by this aspect of the Basic Law. Secondly, the Court dismissed Gröschner's complaint that the reform constitute a breach of his constitutional right to the free development of his personality. Again, apart from the fact that Gröschner could not yet claim to be directly affected because the complaint was itself premature, the Court did not accept his suggestion that he would be forced to adopt the new orthography in his private correspondence in order to avoid 'social embarrassment' in the eyes of the speech community. This, according to the Court, was so because the speech community does not base its views regarding the correctness of particular spellings specifically on rulings made by the *state*. Instead, perceptions of orthographical correctness depend primarily on those rules considered to be binding by the *speech community* itself. The Court therefore proposed that those members of the speech community who had already learned to read and write would not in fact conclude that Gröschner was writing incorrectly should he continue to use the old spellings: they would merely assume that he was adhering to the traditional, as opposed to the revised, rules.

From Gröschner's perspective, the ruling of the Court arguably missed the point since, as becomes clear elsewhere (Gröschner & Kopke, 1997: 299), underpinning his complaint is precisely the fear that the speech community would conclude that he was adhering to the *traditional*, pre-reform spellings. He then argued how, through continuing to use the old orthography, he would in fact be 'outing' himself as conservative in view of the social stratification of orthography that would eventually obtain against the backdrop of two competing sets of norms (see also Denk, 1997: 42–43). However, of particular theoretical interest for present purposes is the distinction made by the Court between *de jure* rulings on orthographical correctness (i.e. by the state) and *de facto* perceptions of correctness (within the speech community), whereby precedence is given to the latter. In doing so, the Court would appear to have side-stepped – at least at this stage in the debate – the all-important question of the relationship between these two spheres and their relative significance for the individual language user.

With regard to Gröschner's alleged breach of his personality rights meanwhile, the Court ruled once again that, because the reform had not yet been introduced into schools, there was no actual basis for a constitutional complaint at that point in time. However, the judges went on to add that, even though the writing practices of the wider community were unlikely to remain unaffected in the longer term by the version of orthography taught in schools at any one time, the constitution would never ultimately be in a position to offer the complainant *protection* from confrontation with such spellings.

It is in this regard that the comments of the Court highlight a potential paradox. By drawing attention to the fact that the Basic Law could never really protect the complainant from new spellings taught in schools, the Court appeared to be conceding that the reform was indeed of consequence for individuals within the wider speech community, *potentially* reinforcing Gröschner's claim that the reform impinged upon constitutional rights of individuals within that community. Clearly, the longer-term effects of a reform cannot be limited to school-aged children and official authorities (over which the KMK has jurisdiction) but are always intended to percolate through to the wider speech community (over which it does not) – an intention made explicit, moreover, within the Vienna Declaration. But leaving aside for the time being the obvious question as to what the purpose of a school education is meant to be, if not to prepare pupils for later life as part of the wider community (and what are pupils, in any case, if not already a part of that community?) as will become clear later in this chapter, it is the actual *extent* to which the reform could be said to impact on the constitutional rights of individuals within the speech community that would emerge as the crux of this intriguing dispute.

Opposition to the Reform: 1996–1998

Despite the rejection of the constitutional challenge brought by Gröschner and his daughter in June 1996, and the fact that schools in 10 of the 16 *Länder* began teaching the new orthography from August of that year (Stenschke, 2002: 117), the public disputes surrounding the proposed reform of German orthography continued. The next significant protest took place in the context of the Frankfurt Book Fair in October 1996, and it was here that the name Friedrich Denk first became widely associated with the anti-reform campaign.

In September 1996, Denk, a schoolteacher from the Bavarian town of Weilheim, had just received guidelines from his regional education authority, instructing all colleagues to begin with the implementation of the new orthographic rules. No stranger to controversy,[7] Denk (1997: 41) describes how he studied the guidelines 'briefly but intensively', along with the revised editions of the Duden and Bertelsmann dictionaries, and proceeded to formulate 20 arguments against the reform, a copy of which was sent to 50 writers and academics. A shorter version containing ten objections was then produced in the form of a flyer, 2000 copies of which were distributed at the Frankfurt Book Fair during the first week of October. This so-called 'Frankfurt Declaration on the Spelling Reform' (*Frankfurter Erklärung zur Rechtschreibreform*) criticised the reform on the following grounds (Denk, 1997: 41–44):

(1) The impact of the reform on written German would be too minimal as to merit the inevitable upheaval brought about by its implementation.

(2) Many of the new rules were superfluous and did not render German orthography easier to learn.

(3) The changes would lead to a reduction of 'semantic potential' in the German language overall (notably via the new rules on separate and compound spellings).

(4) The new rules would damage the reputation of the German language abroad, leading to a reduction in the number of foreigners wishing to learn German.

(5) The reform would disadvantage less well-educated language users, particularly in view of the uncertainty brought about by the existence of variant spellings.

(6) A generation of children/pupils would suffer years of confusion and aggravation as a result of the reform.

(7) The new orthography was ugly, particularly those forms containing three identical graphemes such as *Schifffahrt* (boat trip) or *Kaffee-ersatz* (coffee substitute).[8]

(8) The consequences for German literature would be catastrophic. The necessary revision of literary works would lead not only to an increase in cost to the reader, but would in many cases actually interfere with the referential potential of such texts, threatening the potential enjoyment of German literature overall.

(9) The new guidelines – frequently glossed as *Neuschreib* (New-write) – had been imposed by the state upon an unwilling population in an Orwellian fashion.

(10) The cost of the reform would run into millions of German marks/ Euros. Only printers, publishers of dictionaries and schoolbooks, and software manufacturers would benefit, while the tax-payer stood to lose via the millions of working hours consumed by the introduction and acquisition of the new spellings.[9]

A summary of the Frankfurt Declaration, together with some 450 signatures, was later published in the *Frankfurter Allgemeine Zeitung* newspaper (19 October 1996), calling for a halt to the reform and highlighting the way in which the reform had been drawn up by a 'primarily anonymous group of experts' (Denk, 1997: 46). One week later the KMK replied with their own so-called 'Dresden Declaration', containing a detailed refutation of the Frankfurt accusations (KMK, 25 October 1996). Particularly disputed by the ministers was the claim regarding insufficient consultation. They noted how not only had drafts of the reform proposals been made available to the public in 1988 and 1992, but that these had been widely commented upon in the press. Moreover, in May 1993, the KMK in conjunction with the Ministry of the Interior had organised a public hearing, to which many interested parties had been invited to submit their views in writing. While some had indeed responded, there had been no reply from the German branches of the international writers' association, PEN.[10]

However, it was undoubtedly the pre-eminence of a number of its signatories that allowed the Frankfurt Declaration to gain such widespread media coverage. Amongst those who had signed were leading writers such as Günter Grass (subsequently awarded the Nobel Prize for Literature), Siegfried Lenz, Martin Walser, Hans-Magnus Enzensberger and Walter Kempowski, along with many other well-known intellectuals, publishers, academics, journalists and historians. Thus it was on the 14 October 1996 that the title page of the national news magazine, *Der Spiegel*, famously implored its readers to 'Save the German Language!' (*Rettet die deutsche Sprache!*), while the header dismissed the reform as 'nonsense' (*Schwachsinn*) and proclaimed 'The Writers' Revolt' (*Der Aufstand der Dichter*). The accompanying illustration, with echoes of the March revolution of 1848, depicted a group of writers armed for battle, amidst a pile of books, one of which was the Duden spelling dictionary impaled on a bayonet. Towering above the scene as a whole stood a resolute Günter Grass proudly bearing the German national flag, an image that perhaps more than any other in the course of the reform debate captured the extent to which this was by no means a dispute about orthography alone, or even the written language generally. What was clearly at stake here – for some at least – was the German language in all its force as an index of cultural and national unity.[11]

Following an unsuccessful challenge against the reform which he brought before the administrative court in Munich in early November 1996, Friedrich Denk went on to form the nationwide citizen's initiative 'WE [the people] against the spelling reform' (*Initiative WIR gegen die Rechtschreibreform*).[12] In April 1997 this organisation then published its so-called 'Munich Declaration', outlining the aim of the initiative, which was to oppose the reform of German orthography by means of a national campaign for regional referenda (*Volksbegehren*).[13] This was in accordance with *Länder* constitutions that allow petitions for such referenda to be drawn up on any issue. A designated proportion of the electorate are then required to sign, although the precise number varies (e.g. 5% in Schleswig-Holstein ≅ 106,000 signatures; 10% in Lower Saxony ≅ 580,000 signatures). Over the next year, petitions were organised in a number of *Länder*, and should the requisite number of signatures be collected, there would be a legal obligation on the part of the *Land* in question to hold a referendum within approximately nine months.[14]

Meanwhile, many politicians also continued to voice their concerns surrounding the reform. In February 1997 a group of 34 members of the Bundestag declared their support for a cross-party initiative organised by Detlef Kleinert (FDP) with the aim of halting the reform, and this gave rise to a lengthy parliamentary debate in April 1997 that led to the referral of Kleinert's application to a number of sub-committees for further discussion. In a meeting of the budgetary committee in May, a majority of politicians then spoke out against the reform, and this was followed by a public hearing on the part of parliamentary legal committee in June, in which linguists (including Theodor Ickler) and legal experts (including Rolf Gröschner) were invited to submit their views on the legality or otherwise of the reform. And it was on the basis of the recommendations of this hearing that, in March 1998, the Bundestag formally recorded its concern about the reform process and the surrounding disputes, noting, *inter alia*, that since the German language ultimately belonged to 'the people' (*das Volk*), it should be allowed to develop 'organically' on the basis of consensus within the speech community (see Bundestag plenary protocoll, 13/224).

During this period many parents of school-aged children continued to challenge the reform in the lower administrative courts (*Verwaltungsgerichte*) and upper administrative courts (*Oberverwaltungsgerichte*) of the various *Länder*. By spring 1998 some 30 cases had been heard, and in 12 of these, judges agreed with parents that fundamental constitutional rights were indeed infringed by the reform (Mentrup, 1998: 2). In the summer of 1997, for example, an administrative court in Wiesbaden (Hesse) had been the first court to grant a temporary injunction against the implementation of the new orthography on the grounds of insufficient legislative basis, thereby preventing the introduction of the reform in schools there, originally planned for 1 August 1997.[15] Three months later, the first case against the reform was successfully brought to an *upper* administrative court, this time in Lüneburg, Lower Saxony, and, having already introduced the new rules during the school-year

1996/1997, this state subsequently became the first to actually revert back to the teaching of the old orthography pending some form of agreement at national level concerning the future of the reform. However, in December 1997, two further challenges to rulings against the reform on the part of the upper regional courts in Hamburg and North-Rhine Westphalia were once again rejected by the Federal Constitutional Court (see *Bundesverfassungsgericht, 1 BvR 2264/97* and *1 BvR 2368*).

Finally, in May 1998, the case against the reform was referred back to the Constitutional Court for what it was hoped by all involved in this dispute would be a conclusive hearing – not least in view of the impending deadline of 1 August by which time all schools were expected to have begun teaching the new orthography. This time the complaints were brought by Thomas Elsner and Gunda Diercks-Elsner, the parents of two children of primary-school age in Schleswig-Holstein, Germany's most northerly federal state. However, the case was never going to be straightforward. In June, it emerged that the petition for a referendum on the reform in Schleswig-Holstein had gained the support of some 10.5% of the population (i.e. well over the requisite 5%) and that a referendum would therefore take place on 27 September, the same day as the forthcoming federal elections. Moreover, in a controversial twist, the complainants actually withdrew their case one week prior to the publication of the final ruling in July 1998, protesting that the verdict was already widely known in official circles, and had even been announced in the news magazine *Focus* (6 July 1998). In any case the ruling of the Court was now meaningless, they declared, in view of the forthcoming referendum in their own state. It was against this backdrop, therefore, that the Federal Constitutional Court was to make its ultimate bid for 'authoritative entextualisaton' in an attempt to bring to a conclusion the ongoing language ideological debate surrounding the 1996 reform.

The Constitutional Challenge of 1998

The complaints

Prior to bringing their case against the reform to the Federal Constitutional Court, Thomas Elsner and Gunda Diercks-Elsner (the former himself a lawyer) had seen their request for a temporary injunction against the introduction of the reform in schools in Schleswig-Holstein rejected by the lower regional court in March 1997, a ruling which was then upheld by the upper regional court in Schleswig in August. As we shall see below, the case brought before the Constitutional Court in 1998 was argued on broadly similar grounds to those of Gröschner's protest in 1996. However, unlike in Gröschner's case, the couple's protest now met with the formal requirement that, before bringing a case to the Constitutional Court, complainants must first have proceeded through the lower courts and exhausted the requisite legal channels. This time, therefore, the case was accepted for hearing. The ruling itself is recorded in the document, *BVerfG, 1 BvR 1640/97*, and the complaints, which are contained in Section III of the document, can be summarised as follows (for discussion see also Wagner, 1998a,b).

First, the couple claimed, like Gröschner, that the state is not permitted, without the approval of the democratic legislature, to engage in a regulation of German orthography that actually *intervenes* in orthographic practices, thereby going beyond a mere documentation of existing usage. This is because, according to the rule of law and the democratic principle, all decisions of a fundamental nature must be made by the legislature. However, in the complainants' view, the 1996 reform – allegedly the first orthographic reform of its kind[16] – was indeed a fundamental intervention insofar as pupils were now required to learn a form of spelling and punctuation that was substantially different from that acquired by their parents, and that had introduced a range of previously non-existent forms in a purported attempt to make German orthography easier learn. In this context, the couple added how the introduction of the new orthography in itself not only amounted to a decision of fundamental educational importance but also one that constituted a *lowering* of educational standards. This was exemplified, *inter alia*, by the way in which schoolbooks were now employing commas only in those contexts specifically stipulated by the new guidelines, but were allegedly omitting to use those commas specified as optional by the 1996 guidelines (see Chapter 3). All in all, the reform, itself the product of explicit intervention on the part of linguists, could not be considered a continuation of previous orthographical practices, but an entirely new departure. In this sense, the reform clearly entailed what was indeed, in the complainants' view, a shift in broader pedagogic aims (*Groblernziele*) as opposed to minor details of curricular implementation (*Feinlernziele*). Moreover, as the upper administrative court in Schleswig had conceded in its previous ruling, the reform did not only aim to change the writing practices of those in schools and official authorities but also the wider speech community across the whole of the German-speaking area. Finally, it was noted how the requisite law need not in itself lay down the correct rules for German orthography but should at least clarify the body responsible for such matters together with the appropriate procedures for the modelling of such rules on the basis of *de facto* usage within the speech community.

Secondly, the couple argued that the reform constituted a breach of constitutional rights as guaranteed by Article 2, Paragraph 1, of the Basic Law on freedom of personality and Article 1, Paragraph 1, on human dignity insofar as the reform impacted upon both their own 'linguistic integrity' as well as that of their children. Given that the human personality is characterised by the right to self-determination, the Basic Law could be expected to protect complainants from any measures that impinged upon their ability to transform 'intellectual concepts' (*geistige Lebensentwürfe*) into 'concrete actions' (*konkrete Handlungen*). That such an ability is linked to linguistic integrity is self-evident, they argued, when one considers that language is itself a prerequisite for the development and expression (*Entfaltung*) of individual freedom. Moreover, even allowing for the fact that the reform is binding in a *legal* sense for schools and state authorities only, the new rules impinge none the less on the 'expressive needs' (*Ausdrucksbedürfnisse*) of the speech community as a whole in such a way that the personality rights of each and every language user are infringed.

Thirdly, the complainants returned to the question of parental rights as guaranteed by Article 6, Paragraph 2, of the Basic Law. Whereas, traditionally, parents had themselves learned the same basic material in school as their children, this would no longer be the case following the introduction of the reform. Like Gröschner, the complainants argued how, as a consequence of the reform, they would no longer be able to offer their children the necessary educational support in ways that *complemented* pedagogic practices within schools. In addition, the complainants feared that they would no longer be able to pass on books to their children as a means of supporting the school-based acquisition of literacy, not least since their children were likely to be disconcerted by the old orthography contained in such texts, the use of which in school-work would then be criticised. The complainants were also concerned that their children would be less inclined *per se* to read books written in the old orthography, thereby endangering parental attempts to introduce them to classical German literature (see also Kopke, 1995a: 192). In addition, they had a right to expect that children attending state schools be taught according to curricula that were fully compatible with constitutional requirements on education. In this context, they noted how as far as German schools overseas and offices of the Goethe Institute were concerned, it was to be expected that statutory legislation be required in order to secure the implementation of the reform, given that such institutions were outside of the jurisdiction of the KMK.

Fourthly, and finally, the couple argued how their rights had been infringed in accordance with Article 103, Paragraph 1, of the Basic Law, which states that 'In the courts every person shall be entitled to a hearing in accordance with the law'. In its previous ruling on their petition for a temporary injunction against the reform, the upper regional court in Schleswig had noted that the complainants would indeed have a right to prevent the teaching of the new orthography, provided it could be demonstrated that the reform was of central importance for language education in general. The complainants had therefore expected the court to address this issue in the course of its deliberations, but it had not. Instead, the judges had noted that the teaching of a new orthography did not affect the content of German language teaching but merely involved a transition to a revised norm, which would none the less enjoy validity in the near future. Moreover, the complainants had been surprised by the court's claim that legislative approval of the reform was not in fact necessary insofar as orthography in the German-speaking areas is based on rules that are themselves 'outside of the domain of law'.

The Court's response

Before proceeding with its ruling, the judges of the Constitutional Court explained, in section VI, how the complainants' withdrawal of their case prior to the announcement of the verdict in July 1998 was itself invalid. Although complainants do have the right to retract complaints, the Court may refuse to permit this where a hearing has already been held and where the issue at hand is deemed to be of sufficient general relevance. Given that the case brought by Thomas Elsner and Gunda Diercks-Elsner would lead to the clarification of a number of similar disputes, as well as having implications for judicial questions surrounding school curricula in general, the Court chose to override the complainants' withdrawal and went ahead with its ruling.

Prior to the hearing in the Constitutional Court, a number of interested parties, including political, legal, linguistic and business representatives, had responded to the Court's request to give a written assessment of the following areas, which in turn provided the basis for the hearing that was held: the historical development of orthography; the justification, content and implementation of the proposed changes; practical experiences of the reform so far; anticipated orthographic developments; and finally, economic implications, including those of a possible retraction of the reform. A selection of these representatives then also provided evidence in person at the hearing, which was held on 12 May.[17]

The most significant section of the ruling was dedicated to the question of parental rights as guaranteed by Article 6 of the Basic Law (see section VI). Here the Court noted how, while parents clearly enjoy constitutional rights in relation to the education and upbringing of their children, in practice these have to be balanced against the rights of the state to oversee the education of those children as laid down in Article 7. The task of the judiciary is then to decide on the nature of that balance. And in this regard the Court did not concur with the complainants' view that the reform impinged upon parental rights to a degree that was sufficiently disproportionate as to merit the involvement of the legislature.

As a preliminary, the Court noted how constitutional means cannot in any case be used to assess the necessity, content, value and purpose of the reform, since the Basic Law itself has nothing to say on spelling and punctuation nor on the value of different orthographies. At the same time, however, there is nothing in the Basic Law that actually *prevents* the state from attempting to influence and/or regulate orthographic practices. In this sense, the idea that the German language belongs to 'the people' is, the judges argued, irrelevant to the argument at hand for the state is clearly not prevented from taking normative action upon areas of social life that are not actually in its 'possession'. Similarly, the notion that language develops organically does not in itself preclude action on the part the state. In this regard, the Court declared language to be no different from any other 'rule-governed area of social life' – the state is restricted only by the type and extent of any normative regulation it may wish to perform, not by its ability to take action *per se*. In accordance with Article 7 of the Basic Law the state may therefore regulate written language, for example, in ways that help to clarify and/or simplify problematical areas of usage since teachers and pupils need clear guidance on such matters. Moreover, historically, this has always been the case where orthography is concerned. As the judges correctly acknowledged, the state has since the mid-19th century engaged in the normification of orthography in ways that traditionally went beyond the mere documentation of language change occurring organically within the speech community. The same could be said for the role played by the Duden spelling dictionary: once a particular variant was 'described' as the most widely used within the speech community, this in itself became tantamount to an act of *pre*scription – an act, moreover, which from 1955 onwards was itself state-sanctioned. In this sense, as the Court noted, it is only with some difficulty than one can formally distinguish between acts of *de*scription and *pre*scription where language usage is concerned. Finally, the responsibility for matters orthographic had always been with the *Länder*, whereby the fact that such regulation might be part of a broader attempt to standardise German orthography as a model for *all* users is largely irrelevant. The aim of schools, the judges argued, is to prepare pupils for life in a constantly changing world outside of the classroom. In this sense it is self-evident that what pupils learn in schools will eventually impact upon the outside world. However, while the *Länder* were themselves constitutionally obliged to coordinate their activities with one another (and are permitted to sign treaties with other nations as in the case of the Vienna Declaration) the judges noted how *absolute* agreement between the *Länder* is not in itself a prerequisite of such activities. The fact that one federal state might opt out of teaching the new rules, as in the case of Lower Saxony hitherto (or, by implication, Schleswig-Holstein in the forthcoming referendum) did not of itself prevent the *Länder* from working towards the aim of achieving overall orthographical unity or indeed invalidate any decisions reached in the course of that process.

In sum, the judges ruled that the state of Schleswig-Holstein did not require action on the part of the legislature in order to instruct its schools to teach the new orthography. This was not only because the teaching of reading and writing is a basic educational activity, the responsibility for which falls within the remit of the *Länder*, but because the content, extent and consequences of the reform were simply not sufficiently fundamental as to require statutory regulation. At this juncture the Court reiterated its definition of 'fundamentality': in order to be considered fundamental the disputed measure must impinge to a *disproportionate* extent upon the ability of citizens to enjoy their constitutional rights as laid down in the Basic Law. It is not sufficient for an issue to be in itself politically controversial and/or simply 'relevant' for the wider community nor should the 'principle of fundamentality' itself be interpreted in such a way as to lead to a decision-making monopoly on the part of the legislature (see also Kopke, 1995a; Menzel, 1998a,b; Ossenbühl, 1989). Central to the principle of fundamentality is also the requirement that measures be taken by the most *appropriate* organ of the state and, in the case of the spelling reform, this was clearly the *Länder* executive, that is, the KMK.

Bearing in mind this definition of 'fundamentality', the judges went on to rule that the 1996 reform could not be seen to impact in any fundamental way upon the rights of either parents, pupils or third parties.

First, although *parents* have a natural right to try to promote and develop the linguistic competence of their children, the teaching of orthography, the Court argued, is primarily the responsibility of schools. Whether or not the reform makes changes to orthography that go beyond the mere documentation of organic change within the speech community is, in this context, beside the point. What counts is whether the effect of those changes is such that parental rights are infringed to a degree that requires the approval of the democratic legislature. As the complainants themselves conceded, from a quantitative point of view, the changes are clearly minimal. However, even if, as the complainants (together with some linguists at the hearing) had argued, certain areas of the reform such as the new rules on separate and compound spelling made the learning of orthography more difficult as opposed to easier, the overall *qualitative* impact of the reform was still minimal. It was not, for example, evident that communication between users of the old and new orthography would be seriously impeded. Consequently, the judges did not find evidence to substantiate the complainants' assertion that their children would no longer be able, or indeed wish, to read their parents' books, thereby potentially alienating the younger generation from the canon of classical German literature. Moreover, in view of the seven-year interim period between 1998 and 2005 that allowed considerable time for the transition from the old to the new rules, parents need not initially fear that the academic achievement of their children would suffer since use of the old spellings would not be penalised in school. Only after 2005 would the continued use of the old orthography impinge upon the marks awarded to pupils and even here the KMK ruling of November 1995 had made provision for the potential extension of the interim period should any further difficulties emerge. Likewise, via the setting up of the Mannheim-based International Commission for German Orthography, the Vienna Declaration had established a mechanism for the ongoing monitoring and possible adaptation of orthographical rules in the light of potential problems. At this juncture the judges conceded how it was not possible to predict the extent to which parents themselves would eventually come to accept the new rules or even apply them in their own usage. That said, parents could not generally expect to keep pace with everything their children learn at school – it is only natural that children will acquire knowledge that differs and/or goes beyond that of their elders. And while the reform clearly impacted upon the school curriculum, resulting in curricular content that was indeed modified, the changes were so minimal in both a quantitative and qualitative sense that they could not be seen to impact in any fundamental way on the broader pedagogic aim of teaching pupils to read and write. Moreover, given that these are pedagogic and linguistic questions relating to school-based practice, the monitoring and regulation of which traditionally lies with the remit of the *Länder*, it is clear that the executive as opposed to the legislature constitutes the most appropriate organ to decide upon the necessity, content, extent, and timing of a spelling reform.

Secondly, the Court similarly ruled that the rights of *pupils* could not be seen to be disproportionately infringed by the reform. Although pupils similarly enjoy constitutional rights in relation to Articles 1 and 2 of the Basic Law (which, the Court acknowledged, were certainly *affected* by the reform) as with parents, the rights of pupils themselves had to be balanced against those of the state. And in this context the Court was satisfied that the educational authorities of Schleswig-Holstein had taken the potential infringement of pupils' constitutional rights sufficiently into consideration. The authorities had, for example, implemented the new rules in the belief that they were in the best interests of pupils insofar as they would make the written language easier to learn, that the readability of texts in the new spelling would not be affected, and that communication between users of the old and new orthographies would not be fundamentally affected.

Thirdly, the Court ruled that the rights of *third parties* were similarly not infringed in any disproportionate sense by the reform in accordance with Article 12, Paragraph 1, of the Basic Law, which states that 'All Germans have the right freely to choose their trade or profession their place of work and their place of training. The practice of trades and professions may be regulated by law.' Here we are back to the issue raised by Gröschner in 1996 in relation to the activities of the Duden – does the reform impinge upon the practice of trades and professions in such a way that presupposes the need for statutory legislation? And in this respect the judges declared, once again, that this was not the case given that the impact on those businesses clearly affected by the reform (such as publishers, press agencies, manufacturers of electronic spell-checkers or any company employing such technology) was not *so* great as to impinge disproportionately upon their professional/commercial freedom. While it could not be denied that the transition to the new orthography would involve the incurrence of additional costs, no company was obliged in any formal/juridical sense to adopt the new rules. Should a company therefore choose to move to the new orthography on the basis of what was happening in schools and other state authorities, then that decision would be made on the basis of an assessment of market conditions alone as opposed to any formal legal requirement.

Finally, as far as the complaints concerning any potential infringement of constitutional rights in relation to Article 2 (personality rights) and Article 1 (human dignity) were concerned, these were rejected on the same grounds as those identified in relation to Article 6 on parental rights generally. In other words, the Court ruled how complainants' own rights were not affected to any constitutionally significant extent since the introduction of the reform by the educational authorities in Schleswig-Holstein pertained only to schools. Even though writing practices within the wider community were unlikely to remain unaffected in the longer term by the new version of orthography now taught in schools, outside of the classroom, individuals remained free to write as they chose. This was particularly true, the Court noted, for the transitional period between 1998 and 2005 during which time the use of both versions of German orthography remained acceptable within schools, such that it was not possible to see how the adherence to the old orthography by individuals outside of schools would lead to their negative evaluation in any personal sense. However, even with regard to the period after 31 July 2005, it was still not apparent how or why this should be the case. Written language, the Court argued, would continue to develop in spite of the rules officially laid down according to the reform, and many established spellings would in any case continue to function as permissible variants of new forms. At most, a few individual items would be replaced by new forms either already contained in the 1996 regulations or later recommended by the International Commission for German Orthography, and in the latter case these would in all probability be items already considered to have established themselves within speech community usage. Against this backdrop, it was not clear how the constitutional rights of those who wished none the less to continue using the old orthography would be disproportionately affected.

The Referendum in Schleswig-Holstein

The constitutional propriety of the 1998 ruling together with its broader language ideological implications are crucial issues to which I shall return in more detail in Chapters 5 and 6. However, the ruling of the Constitutional Court by no means marked the end of the dispute for, despite the pro-reform verdict, it remained within the remit of any regional parliament in Germany to pass a law obstructing the implementation of the new orthography and/or for any electorate to vote against the reform's introduction at *Länder* level (Rivers & Young, 2001: 175). And this was precisely what happened in the autumn of 1998 when 56.4% of voters in Schleswig-Holstein rejected the introduction of the new orthography in schools there (with a turnout of approximately 60% of the total electorate).

While it would be inaccurate to claim that attitudes towards orthographic reform were consistently divided along party political lines throughout the disputes described thus far, this had certainly been the case where the referendum in Schleswig-Holstein was concerned, its success having been in no small measure down to the explicit support of the conservative Christian Democratic Union (CDU).[18] And having lost the elections at federal level on the same day, one CDU politician is reported as noting somewhat wryly that at least his party had *'something to celebrate'* (*Der Spiegel*, 5 October 1998). However, it has also been speculated as to whether the ruling of the Constitutional Court earlier that year had itself precipitated the 'no' vote in Schleswig-Holstein. Given that the Court had already addressed the possibility of one or more *Länder* opting out of the reform (and insisted that the reform would still go ahead in the light of such an eventuality) this may well have been seen by some sectors of the population as a *carte blanche* to register their disgruntlement with the reform more generally (see *Der Spiegel*, 5 October 1998). Either way, the result meant that the state of Schleswig-Holstein now found itself in a somewhat unusual position of orthographic isolation *vis à vis* the rest of the German-speaking areas, although Matthias Dräger, owner of the publishing house, Leibniz, and speaker for the citizens' initiative behind the referendum, was keen to stress that such isolation had at no time been the intention of the anti-reform campaign. On the contrary, his initiative always saw the wider aim of its popular protest as paving the way for an overall rejection of the reform followed by a return to the old orthography throughout the German-speaking areas. With this in mind, Dräger immediately called for a special meeting of the KMK in order to consider the future of the reform nationally (and, presumably, internationally). However, according to the news magazine *Der Spiegel* (5 October 1998) such a meeting seemed unlikely from the outset and, if anything, the situation in Schleswig-Holstein appeared only to harden the resolve of the other *Länder* to push through the reform.

The task of dealing with the immediate consequences of the referendum was one that fell to the Education Minister in Schleswig-Holstein, Gisela Böhrk (SPD). In spite of her own personal dismay (she believed that a reversal to the old orthography could only be detrimental to young people) Böhrk found herself constitutionally obliged to issue a parliamentary decree instructing schools to revert back to the teaching of the old rules from 1 November 1998 (having already introduced the revised rules in 1997). However, this in itself did not bring the issue to a close, for this new-found isolation of Schleswig-Holstein raised a number of questions. First, would schools there now be required to provide separate textbooks exemplifying the old orthography for their pupils and, even if this were technically possible, could they afford to do so? Secondly, what would happen to pupils who moved between schools in Schleswig-Holstein and the other German-speaking areas where the reform was

going ahead? Would this, for example, lead to a downgrading of qualifi-
cations obtained in Schleswig-Holstein, particularly with regard to the
status of the *Abitur* as the prerequisite for entry into higher education?
Moreover, what would be the effect on the study of German as a whole,
particularly among pupils in Schleswig-Holstein – interestingly, the one
group not permitted to vote in the referendum? For those pupils living
in border areas (whose peers attended schools in Lower Saxony,
Hamburg or Mecklenburg-Western Pomerania and were therefore learning the new rules), the cultural relativity of orthographic norms was particularly exposed. While this might have been an apposite illustration of
a fact emphasised by reformers throughout the debate – namely that
notions of orthographic correctness have always been subject to variation
across time and space – some parents and teachers genuinely feared that
the situation might well lead to a broader sense of educational disillusion-
ment among pupils, whereby 'if nothing right is really right, and nothing
wrong is really wrong, then why bother learning at all' (*Der Spiegel*,
5 October 1998).[19]

While these were the broader cultural issues raised by the referendum
result, a number of more immediate constitutional implications remained.
In her decree instructing schools to revert to the old rules (*Umsetzungser-
lass*), Böhrk declared that, although the old orthography would now be
taught, the new rules would none the less continue to be tolerated for
she could not envisage a situation where practices considered to be
correct in the rest of the German-speaking areas would actually be evaluated as *in*correct in Schleswig-Holstein (a situation which, as Rivers and
Young, 2001: 176, point out, in itself created an intriguing hierarchy of
'preferred' and 'permitted' variants where foreign loans were concerned).
However, even here the referendum's organisers were able to raise
objections for, strictly speaking, it was possible to argue that there was
no constitutional obligation to even *tolerate* the new rules given the
wording of the referendum paper itself, which had stated that: 'Schools
should teach the version of spelling which is generally customary. The
version of spelling generally considered customary is the one which has
long since been recognised as such by the population and is used in the
majority of available books.'[20]

In many ways therefore it was the question of which books were available that became central to the dispute: for as long as the majority of titles
were still printed in the old orthography, teachers in Schleswig-Holstein
could not be constitutionally required to even tolerate the new rules.
With this in mind Böhrk then turned to the organisation representing
the German book trade, *der Börsenverein des Deutschen Buchhandels*, to

enquire as to how long it would take before the majority of books would be printed in the *new* orthography, thereby 'liberating' the authorities in Schleswig-Holstein from the wording of the referendum. However, the organisation replied that it was not within the remit of publishers to act as arbiters in such matters – besides it was simply not possible to quantify the exact proportion of books available in the old or new orthography within the Federal Republic at any one time. And this in itself raised a further interesting dilemma, for a decree that, as a result of its inherent lack of clarity, could not be policed was almost certainly unconstitutional. In other words, if there was no possibility to check whether the *majority* of books were published in the old or new spellings at any one time, then the referendum and subsequent reversion to the old orthography in Schleswig-Holstein were arguably invalid (see *Der Spiegel*, 5 October 1998).[21]

Moreover, not everyone in Schleswig-Holstein was happy with the current situation – after all, only 60% of the electorate had participated. Of these voters, 29.1% had rejected the proposal to revert to the old orthography and a further 14.6% had not considered the use of a referendum an appropriate means of resolving the dispute *per se*, such that only around 30% of the electorate overall had actually voted against the reform. It was against this backdrop that the dispute was once again returned to the Federal Constitutional Court in July 1999, when a father and his two school-aged children argued that the renewed teaching of the old orthographic rules in Schleswig-Holstein constituted a breach of *their* basic rights, not least their right to freedom of movement around the German-speaking areas as guaranteed by Articles 11 and 12 of the Basic Law (see *Bundesverfassungsgericht, 1 BvQ 10/99*). Central to the complainants' concerns was whether the fact of having learned to read and write in Schleswig-Holstein according to the old orthographic rules might diminish young people's opportunities to study and/or work elsewhere in the German-speaking areas. However, the case was rejected on the grounds that the situation in Schleswig-Holstein was not incompatible with the Basic Law: as stated in the 1998 ruling, decisions relating to orthography and its teaching ultimately remained in the hands of the *Länder*. Besides, it was not within the Court's remit to rule on the relative disadvantages to citizens where the *Länder* diverged in terms of educational provision as they so frequently did in the case of the Federal Republic.

By this time, however, it was clear that no other federal state was going to follow the example of Schleswig-Holstein and opt out of the teaching of the new orthography, as the referendum organisers had originally hoped.

In March 1999, the ruling of the Federal Constitutional Court of July 1998 had been confirmed by the Federal Administrative Court (*Bundesverwaltungsgericht*) in Berlin (see *BVerwG, C9/98, VR 2000*, 24.3.1999). Moreover, two further attempts to organise petitions for referenda against the reform in Bremen and Berlin had similarly failed (see Stenschke, 2002: 127–28). And when the press announced its conversion to the new rules from 1 August 1999 (albeit, as became clear in Chapter 3, with certain caveats), and the minister for internal affairs declared that all government submissions to the Bundesrat would similarly be presented in the new orthography, it became apparent to all the political parties in Schleswig-Holstein, including the Christian Democrats, that the imperative for orthographic unity was considerable and that the current situation was probably not in the best interests of pupils there. In September 1999 the decree instructing schools to teach the old rules was therefore repealed, and the civil service and schools were told to base their usage on the new guidelines as from 1 October and 1 November, respectively. As Rivers and Young (2001: 176) have noted, the 'constitutional propriety' of a decision to reverse the popular will in this way remains to this day uncertain. However, when challenged before the Federal Constitutional Court in November 1999 by the citizens' initiative '*WIR gegen die Rechtschreibreform*', the Court once again confirmed the question of orthography to be solely a matter for the executive (see *Bundesverfassungsgericht, 2 BvR 1958/99*). And it was in this way the legal controversies surrounding the reform finally drew to a close.[22]

Notes

1. In July 1998, the Austrian Constitutional Court (*Verfassungsgerichtshof*) rejected a case against the reform brought on broadly similar grounds to those in Germany (for details, see ruling 98/97 available at www.vfgh/entscheidungen). However, the analysis here will focus on the protests that took place in a specifically German context. For further information on protests in Austria and Switzerland, see www.raytec.de/rechtschreibreform and www.rechtschreform.com.

2. See Ossenbühl (1989: 320), who emphasises the historical contingency of *any* interpretation of the relationship between the legislature and executive, depending as it does on the nature of both the state and constitution in question. In this sense, the disputes over the spelling reform are indicative of a much broader, indeed classic, tension in federal constitutional jurisprudence.

3. It is important to note that the concept of 'fundamentality' as applied here is by no means novel. As Ossenbühl (1989: 337) shows, the idea that fundamental issues should fall under the remit of the legislature, as opposed to the executive, has a long tradition that goes back to liberal constitutional

movements in the early 19th century, notably of the *Vormärz* period between 1815 and the March revolution of 1848. But what *is* new – occurring against the backdrop of an increasing tendency since the 1970s for citizens to challenge the authority of the executive before the Federal Constitutional Court – is the elevation of the principle of fundamentality to the status of juridical theory in its own right. This has brought the whole question of what constitutes a *fundamental* measure to centre stage as in disputes such as the one described here.

4. Ossenbühl (1989: 334-35) notes how the development of constitutional juris- prudence in 19th-century Germany was in many respects fuelled by a per- ceived need to protect the rights of the individual from the actions of a democratically unelected and increasingly bureaucratic *executive*. By the late 20th century, however, and in view of the tendency towards political homogeneity of elected parliamentarians, on the one hand, and the executive, on the other, the emphasis shifted more towards the need to insist that the democratically elected legislature take action itself as opposed to *delegating* responsibility to the executive.

5. See Ossenbühl (1989: 332–37) for a detailed discussion of the relationship between the role of the democratic legislature generally and any specific role accorded to parliament, that is, the possible tensions between *Gesetzes-* and *Parlamentsvorbehalt*, respectively.

6. The need to distinguish between pre- and post-1996 official guidelines and dictionaries would, however, arise later in the dispute for those teachers working in schools in Lower Saxony and Schleswig-Holstein, *Länder* that sub- sequently reverted to the old orthography after having already introduced the new rules.

7. A profile by Harald Martenstein, in *Der Tagesspiegel*, 20 October 1996, describes Denk as the author of two books, one on the manipulation of the public by the liberal press, and one on the press in the Third Reich, in which he argued that the National Socialist regime had permitted a comparatively greater degree of freedom for writers and intellectuals than the German Democratic Republic. Denk was also the coordinator of a series of high-profile literary readings and the annual Weilheim literary prize, for which he himself received the *Kul- turpreis* of the *Bild-Zeitung*. In 1993, the winner of the Weilheim prize, Gertrud Fussenegger, was widely criticised for what Martenstein describes as her incontrovertibly anti-Semitic writings during the years of the Nazi regime.

8. This argument consistently overlooked the fact that hyphenated spellings were also permitted in the case of such forms, for example, *Schiff-Fahrt* or *Kaffee-Ersatz*.

9. Cf Geerts *et al.* (1977: 202–206) for a classification and analysis of the argu- ments cited by opponent to reforms of Dutch orthography, which follow an almost identical pattern to those of the Frankfurt Declaration.

10. At that time, there were still two branches of PEN, one in eastern and one in western Germany.

11. Moreover, the editors of *Der Spiegel* proudly declared that the new orthography would never be adopted in their own publication, a declaration upon which they were forced to renege, however, when their publishers *Gruner & Jahr* subsequently converted to the new spellings (or modified versions thereof) along with the rest of the German-language press on 1 August 1999 (see *Der Spiegel* editorials, 14 October 1996 and 2 August 1999).

12. The title of this organisation contains a direct reference to the slogan chanted by many East Germans in the weeks before the collapse of the German Democratic Republic (GDR) in the autumn of 1989. While the GDR government had always insisted that its primary concern was to act in the interests of 'the people' (*das Volk*), the crowds gathered around the Brandenburg Gate in East Berlin could be heard chanting in opposition to the regime: 'WE are the people' (*WIR sind das Volk*). A key turning point came when the definite article *das* (the) mutated to its indefinite form *ein* (one), resulting in the new mantra 'We are ONE people' (*Wir sind EIN Volk*), thereby precipitating calls for the unification of the two German states. Taking this intertextual reference one step further, the Berlin branch of the newly-formed initiative declared (though presumably not without some irony): 'WE are the spelling people!' (*WIR sind das Rechtschreibvolk!*). For further details of the various anti-reform initiatives, see www.raytec.de/rechtschreibreform.

13. See press release by '*Initiative WIR gegen die Rechtschreibreform*': '*Münchner Erklärung zur Rechtschreibreform*', 25 April 1997.

14. For details of the various referendum campaigns, see *Focus*, 32, 4 August 1997 (p. 41) and www.raytec.de/rechtschreibreform.

15. See Menzel (1998a,b) and Hantke (2001) for critical comparative discussions of the various regional rulings.

16. Again, the notion of the 1996 reform as the 'first reform of its kind' contains the controversial presupposition that the 1901/1902 guidelines did not in fact constitute a *bona fide* reform. What is particularly interesting in this context is the question of the Rust reform of 1944. While, as became clear in Chapter 2, much has been made in recent literature of the changes proposed by Rust, and their marginalisation within current debates over orthographic reform (for example Kopke, 1995a; Birken-Bertsch & Markner, 2000), the claim that the 1996 reform constitute the 'first' of its kind simultaneously undermines the status of the Rust proposals as legitimate guidelines in their own right. As Kopke (1995a; 370–71) demonstrates, however, the key issue here seems to have revolved around the fact that the 1944 rules would not have constituted a *fundamental* shift in orthographic norms given that, in those cases where structural interventions were proposed (notably, in the case of foreign loans), a system of optional variants would have simultaneously obtained, thereby leaving the 'original' structures of German orthography intact.

17. For precise details of those invited to comment on the guidelines, see sections IV and V of the ruling. For a discussion and general impressions of the hearing, see also Mentrup (1998).

18. For details of individual politicians from the main political parties speaking out against the reform, see www.raytec.de/rechtschreibreform. For a broader overview of participants in the reform debate, see Stenschke (2002: 138–47).

19. For a discussion of teachers' (primarily negative) responses to the situation in Schleswig-Holstein, see Lüthgens (2002: 160–62).

20. German original: 'In den Schulen wird die allgemein übliche Rechtschreibung unterrichtet. Als allgemein üblich gilt die Rechtschreibung, wie sie in der Bevölkerung seit langem anerkannt ist und in der Mehrzahl der lieferbaren Büchern verwendet wird.'

21. For an interesting historical comparison with the situation in Prussia following Bismarck's 'ban' on the use of the Prussian School Orthography by the civil service in the late 19th century, see Meder (1997: 192).

22. There was one further hearing in relation to the reform – originally postponed due to the long-term illness of one of the judges involved. This took place in June 2001 when the upper administrative court in Lüneburg, Lower Saxony, ruled that the 12-year-old daughter of Gabriele Ahrens (the latter, one of the key figures in the national citizens' initiative against the reform) should no longer be taught the old orthography in accordance with a previous ruling of the administrative court in Hanover but should, like all other pupils, now learn the new rules of spelling and punctuation. It was a ruling, however, which was barely reported in the press and therefore went largely unnoticed (see 'Ministerium siegt mit Rechtschreibreform' in *Hannoversche Allgemeine*, 22.6.2001).

Chapter 5
The 1996 Reform as Language Ideological Debate

Chapter 4 of this book explored the various ways in which the 1996 reform of German orthography was publicly contested, focussing primarily on the legal disputes that obtained between 1996 and 1999. Within what I have characterised throughout as this 'language ideological debate', three broad groups of ideological brokers can be identified: the linguists, the complainants, and the judges of the Constitutional Court, each in pursuit of 'authoritative entextualisation' with regard to their own ideas about the re-standardisation of German spelling and punctuation.

In the context of the adversarial legal battle that ensued, the 'winners' and 'losers' of this debate are easily identified insofar as the Constitutional Court overruled the objections of the complainants. In doing so, the judges upheld the right of the state (or, more specifically, the 16 *Länder*) to participate in the regulation of orthography. In this way the guidelines proposed by the linguists, and described in Chapter 3, were confirmed as the rules of the new standard orthography, thereby achieving their own form of 'authoritative entextualisation'. However, the debate was, of course, much more complex than this. Even though the reformers managed to achieve their main aim, this was not without considerable opposition – opposition that did not end with the 1998 ruling. Moreover, if one of the key measures of 'success' where language planning is concerned is the criterion of public acceptance (Fishman, 1977), then the 1996 reform can hardly be seen as a particularly successful instance of policy implementation – even allowing for the fact that it is by no means atypical for spelling reforms to incite such vociferous public opposition (e.g. Coulmas, 1989; Fishman, 1977; Smalley, 1964).[1] Yet, it is precisely the *nature* of this opposition that can itself reveal much about the ideological perspectives characteristic of each of the three groups involved. At this juncture, it is worth therefore recalling Blommaert's (1999: 10) point that *unsuccessful* 'bids' for authoritative entextualisation, that is, those that ultimately *fail* in terms of the desired outcome, are as apposite a focus for sociolinguistic analysis as *successful* ones, even though the latter may well have a more formative influence on language ideologies in the longer term. Moreover, as Blommaert (1999: 10) notes: 'The difference between formative and inconsequential ideologies often does not lie in the nature and structure of the ideologies themselves, but rather in what kind of *reproduction* they are subject to' (emphasis in original).

Of course, the boundaries between the three groups of ideological brokers involved in this particular dispute were by no means fixed. Thus not all of those responsible for the reform were linguists (many were politicians and senior civil servants), and some of the most vehement opponents of the reform were themselves academic linguists such as Theodor Ickler and/or teachers of German such as Friedrich Denk. Moreover, in the course of the dispute some linguists involved in the general process of reform, such as Peter Eisenberg and Horst Haider Munske, left the group in the light of their dissatisfaction with certain aspects of the new guidelines and/or the implementation process.[2] Similarly, the boundaries between the complainants and the judges of the Constitutional Court were often fuzzy in terms of professional identity and expertise. For example, two of the key complainants in the cases described in Chapter 4 were, as we have seen, either legal scholars (Rolf Gröschner) or legal practitioners (Thomas Elsner).[3] However, even allowing for the fluidity of the boundaries between them, each of the three groups can none the less be considered as *broadly* homogeneous in terms of their respective views on language. And as Wolfgang Mentrup (1998), the IDS linguist himself present at the Karlsruhe hearing in May 1998, points out, what was particularly intriguing about that hearing was the way in which these groups were summoned together, for the first and quite possibly last time, and given the opportunity to air their disparate assessments of the reform face-to-face.

The aim of this chapter is now to try to unpack those assessments in order to discover what each of the three groups perceived to be 'at stake' where the 1996 reform was concerned. In order to do this, the chapter begins with an overview of what I see as the much broader relationship between the standardisation of orthography, ideology, and the nation-state. Against this backdrop, I then re-examine perceptions of the reform from the perspective of each of the three groups beginning with the complainants, then the judges, and finally the linguists.

Language Planning as a Modernist Project

As a branch of language planning and/or policy, language standardisation is closely connected to the rise of nation-states and the concomitant project of modernity (e.g. Blommaert, 1996). The sociologist Glyn Williams (1992: 128) describes how, as part of that project, language becomes tied into an evolutionary view of progress that is itself central to modernist thinking (see also Apter, 1982). This is insofar as, throughout the planning process, languages – and specific *varieties* of language – are objectified and dichotomised into 'modern' versus 'traditional' and 'developed' versus 'less developed'. And as Williams (1992: 128) concludes: 'The most important of the diacritica of such a typology are literacy and writing, and what is referred to as graphisation is essential before a language can be "modernised".'

German, with its long history of standardisation and explicit language cultivation (*Sprachpflege*), was no exception in this regard.[4] Indeed Martin Durrell (1999) has noted how the history of standard German is probably best characterised as the standardisation of the *written* language (or *Schriftdeutsch*), whereas standard forms in English tended to derive from both written *and* spoken usage.[5] Underpinning the comparatively greater emphasis on written German were a number of factors, not least the considerable diversity between the regional/national varieties of the spoken language that, even today, can render communication between its speakers difficult and, on occasion, impossible (Barbour, 2000: 153). In the specific case of pre-19th-century Germany, such diversity was combined with the lack of an obvious single metropolis or region that might have afforded a canonical model for a national spoken standard, such as London or Paris in the case of English and French, respectively.[6] These are then factors that relate to the fractured political histories of the German-speaking areas more generally. At the same time, it is precisely this *political* fragmentation that partly accounts for the significance attached to *language* in the 18th and 19th centuries within the overall process of 'imagining' the German *Kulturnation* – a nation based on a common cultural heritage as opposed to a shared political history (see, *inter alia*, Anderson, 1983; Barbour, 2000: 159; Coulmas, 1995: 57; Stevenson, 2002). It also helps to explain why, following the relatively 'late' political unification of Germany in 1871 – itself consolidating Germany's own identity as an independent *Staatsnation* and its concomitant dominance over Austria and Switzerland – the authorities of the newly-formed nation-state would have a comparatively more active role to play than, say, their British counterparts in the standardisation of the national language (see Durrell, 1999: 291). Against this backdrop, as we saw in Chapter 2, written German, and specifically *orthography*, was to take on a particularly important indexical function within the nation-state building process. This is not least as the form of language that lends itself most readily to the kind of explicit codification and control that typifies official policy geared towards standardisation (see Milroy & Milroy, 1999: 56).[7]

Even allowing for the fact that a degree of explicit standardisation may well help to secure the functional efficacy of a given language variety, for Williams (1992: 20–35), all official policy geared towards standardisation remains none the less an inherently ideological project. This is insofar as language is simultaneously invoked by, or on behalf of, the state as an instrument for the socialisation of its subjects (see also Blommaert, 1996). As a symbol of both unity and division, any national standard thereby acquires a crucial gate-keeping function through which membership of the nation-state is not only afforded but also denied (see also Lippi-Green, 1997; Woolard, 1998). At an *inter*national level, this operates via the specification of those individuals and groups who do, or do not, have a native command of the national language, a process that is grounded in the Herderian conflation of language, culture and nation, that Jan Blommaert and Jef Verschueren (1998a,b) refer to as 'homogeneism' (see also Bauman & Briggs, 2000). At an *intra*national level, by contrast, such linguistic gate-keeping works via the setting of a national *standard*, whereby the specification of that which is 'modern' (*viz.* arbitrary standard) becomes tantamount to a prescription of that which is 'correct' (*viz.* minimum standard). Moreover, because the initial selection of the standard variety is itself interest-driven – it is no coincidence that the 1901 guidelines on orthography were themselves based on usage in the largest and most influential German-speaking areas at the time – standardisation becomes a useful means with which to shore up the privileges of already powerful social, regional, and economic groups, thereby legitimising inequality. As Williams points out (1992: 25), a central role in the naturalisation of this 'disciplinary discourse' of language is then accorded to *education*. Here the inculcation of the values associated not just with the usage, but notably the *correct* usage, of the national language itself becomes 'a pedagogical exercise' (see also Foucault, 1984). In this way education serves as a key domain in which standard language practices can be ritualised, thereby underpinning both the disciplinary dimension of authority and control as well as the unificatory function that are indexed via the notion of a shared language (see Stevenson, 2002: 71).

However all processes of modernisation and the concomitant standardisation of any area of social life, raise a fundamental philosophical dilemma with regard to the authority of the state over its subjects. Central to this dilemma, according to Williams (1992: 9), is the distinction between what Ferdinand Tönnies (1887) referred to as *Gemeinschaft* or community, on the one hand, and *Gesellschaft* or society, on the other. Tönnies argued how, following the Renaissance, processes of urbanisation and industrialisation had meant that the *Gemeinschaft*, with its primordial ties of friendship and kinship within a so-called 'community of fate', had gradually been forced to give way to the *Gesellschaft* with its complex regulatory frameworks superimposed by the state. There are, of course, many objections to this view. Ralf Dahrendorf (1968: 146–47), for example, not only describes the community–society dichotomy as 'historically misleading, sociologically uninformed and politically illiberal' (my translation), he also doubts the very existence of the idealised version of community posited by Tönnies, which romanticises the pre-modern era together with the purportedly organic origins of its regulatory social practices.[8] As Williams (1992: 10–11) notes, however, such objections render the ideological purchase of the *Gemeinschaft–Gesellschaft* distinction no less valuable for the emergent nation-state. This is because: 'The superimposition of time upon society in such a way that social change proceeds in a unilinear direction with a degree of inevitability means that *Gemeinschaft* MUST give way to *Gesellschaft*, thereby implementing and justifying the state in society' (1992: 10, my emphasis). In other words, it is the purported *inevitability* of the transition from community to society that is itself invoked by the state in order to legitimise its own intervention into hitherto unregulated areas of social life (see also Bauman & Briggs, 2000: 193).

According to this view, the interests of the state might well appear to be in direct conflict with those of the community. However, although this would arguably underline the state's need to divert the individual *away* from a dependency on community ties, the dilemma then becomes one of how to conserve any kind of moral imperative – or sense of right and wrong – not least against a backdrop of rising secularity. The problem is especially vexing given that the very concept of the nation-state is rooted in an Enlightenment tradition that necessarily puts a premium on the rights and freedom of the individual. As Williams notes: 'In this sense it is not the state and the *community* which are in opposition but the state and the *individual*' (1992: 11, my emphasis). The 'solution', it seems, lies once again in the invocation by the state of the concept of *Gemeinschaft*, this time with its idealised notions of consensus and solidarity as a source from which individuals derive their moral imperative. As Williams (1992: 11) concludes, the objective of the state then becomes that of teaching its subjects to '"respect the sacred bond" of community' for it is precisely in order to consolidate its own interests that the state must compel the individual to *act as a member of the community.*[9]

The Complainants

The constitutional challenge to the 1996 reform of German orthography provides what is in my view a fascinating illustration of this ideological process in action. Here the various brokers – the complainants, the judges of the Federal Constitutional Court and the reformers themselves – were engaged in a dispute over the ownership of orthography as part of the German language. And in their respective pursuit of 'authoritative entextualisation', many questions arose with regard to the nature, function, and origin of orthographic norms. Do such norms originate 'organically' as a result of a moral imperative from within the speech community or *Sprachgemeinschaft*? Is it desirable, not to mention legitimate, for the state to actively intervene in the definition and prescription of such norms? And what are the implications for, and rights of, the individual language user within this complex?

The roots of this particular debate lie, as we saw in Chapter 2, in the historical development of the German language and the decision by the newly-founded nation-state (or, more specifically, its constituent *Länder*) to engage in the official prescription of orthographic norms at the end of the 19th century. But having laid down a set of standardised guidelines in 1901 for the nation as a whole (as well as for Austria and Switzerland), the German state then found itself in the classic modernist dilemma: how to reconcile the static quality of a fixed standard with the dynamics of language change? For not only had the 1901 rules crystallised an inevitably imperfect snapshot of a standard orthography, itself subject to much dispute at the time, orthographic norms and practices would continue to evolve throughout the 20th century. This would gradually increase the need for *re*-modernisation on the part of the state for which crucially, indeed fatefully, no provision had been made. This need was particularly acute if the efficacy of orthography was to be maintained as a means of inculcating the value of standard language more generally, especially via the school system. By the end of the 20th century a range of discrepancies had arisen between the official 1901 guidelines and what was considered to be 'current usage'. This was due in no small part to the 'interventionism' of the Duden, even though its editors consistently claimed to be engaging in a process of orthographic *de*scriptivism as opposed to *pre*scriptivism. However, whatever their origin or intent, partly as a result of such changes, together with the state-sanctioned authority conferred upon the Duden, many school-teachers were finding the instruction and evaluation of spelling and punctuation increasingly frustrating and time-consuming (Lüthgens, 2002). This was particularly so in the early years of schooling where dictation-based exercises were (and still are) central to the teaching of literacy.

But reaching agreement on the *linguistic* aspects of the reform would by no means be the only problem with which the reformers would have to contend (Augst *et al.*, 1997). Once a new set of guidelines had been agreed by 1995, a process that was itself fraught with difficulties (see Chapters 2 and 3), it was their *political* implementation that would pose a major obstacle. And although it is important not to overlook the political controversies surrounding the normification of orthography one hundred years previously, it was clearly not just orthography that had evolved in the intervening century. Following World War II, the constitutional arrangement of the West German state (and, from 1990, that of the newly unified Germany) meant that the rights of the individual citizen, including both minors and servants of the state, were now much more firmly anchored in the constitution. This, together with a range of political developments such as the student protest movement of the 1960s and 1970s, and the rise of citizens' action groups or *Bürgerinitiativen* in the 1980s, meant that German citizens were not only more constitutionally able, but perhaps more fundamentally willing, to challenge the authority of the state on a plethora of issues and from a broad spectrum of political standpoints (Beck, 1992, 1995, 1997). To this, one might add the increased expression of scepticism toward scientific expertise that is generally thought to characterise the period now referred to as 'late' or 'high' modernity (Giddens, 1991) together with the potentially greater access of such counter-discourses to information networks, including, and especially, the World Wide Web.[10] As Gerd Antos (1996: 238–49) has convincingly argued, the state was faced with a very different sociopolitical context in which to instigate the *re*-standardisation of German orthography than had been the case for its initial modernisation in 1901 (see also Kohrt, 1997: 301). Indeed, we might reasonably see the debate surrounding the reform as a classic manifestation of what Jürgen Habermas (1976) refers to as a crisis of legitimation that occurs as the state increasingly attempts to take control over matters of, *inter alia*, culture previously fixed by tradition (1976: 47–48). This then takes place against the backdrop of a 'transformed' public sphere (Habermas, 1962 [1989]), in which the state struggles to reconcile a range of competing interests while simultaneously presenting, and thereby legitimising, its own actions as in the greater *public* interest (see Johnson, forthcoming).

As became clear in Chapter 4, the dispute over orthographic reform that was brought before the Federal Constitutional Court has also to be seen in terms of a much broader tradition of liberal individualism, according to which citizens contest the role of the state to take action that is perceived to impinge upon their own basic freedoms. We then saw how the purported infringement of 'personality rights' as enshrined in Article 2 of the Basic Law accorded a key role to *language* in the context of such freedoms via the notion of 'linguistic integrity'. This is because language, it was argued, underpins all human acts of cognition together with the ability to transform 'intellectual concepts' into 'concrete actions'. Any attempt to intervene in that transformative process (via explicit acts of linguistic regulation, for example) could therefore be construed as an attack on the individual's right to freedom of speech and/or thought. Against this backdrop it comes as little surprise to find the protest against orthographic reform frequently framed in terms of an Orwellian dystopia in which the state was attempting to curtail individual freedom via language manipulation in the form of 'New-write' (*Neuschreib*), something that at least partly accounts for the considerable emotionality that permeated the disputes throughout (see Stenschke, 2002). For some commentators, such as the conservative legal expert Bernd Rüthers (2002), the 1996 reform was then seen as the brainchild of a generation of 1960s radicals who, having finally completed their 'long march through the institutions', were intent on imposing not so much orthographical, but systematic, *structural* change on a society allegedly incapable of reform.[11]

However, whereas the notion of 'personality rights' draws primarily on an Enlightenment view of language as central to the cognitive integrity of the autonomous individual, issues of *dignity* as enshrined in Article 1 appear to depend more heavily upon the views on orthographical correctness held by others within the speech community. At this juncture, it is crucial to distinguish between what Manfred Kohrt (1987, 1997) refers to as 'norm' versus 'usage', on the one hand, and 'external' versus 'internal' norms, on the other. Thus it is important to acknowledge that the orthographic *norm* (i.e. what users believe they are supposed to do) is unlikely to be consistently identical with orthographic *usage* (i.e. what users actually do). Moreover, the *external* norm (i.e. that which has been formally codified) is unlikely to equate in its entirety to the *internal* norm (i.e. users' own internalised variant of that external norm). This is not least since no one individual is likely to be able to reproduce the external norm in its entirety without a constant deferral to works of reference that would itself be communicatively prohibitive. At the level of the individual, we can therefore see the internalised norm as consisting to some extent in an 'imperfect reproduction' of the external norm – a kind of orthographical 'idiolect'. At the level of the speech community, such internalised norms then consist in an accumulation of such idiolects. However, even though the norms internalised by the speech community will always be influenced to a greater or lesser extent by the external norm, central to Kohrt's argument is that internal norms still constitute norms in their own right. Moreover, as Kohrt is at pains to point out (1997: 298), it would be erroneous to see the internalisation of any external norm as deriving *exclusively* from the imposition of state will. This is because language users do enjoy a degree of individual agency such that they may determine the extent to which their usage will (or will not) conform to that norm. Of particular interest from a language ideological perspective, however, is: (1) the scope for individual/speech community agency *per se* in an area of language where usage is almost entirely determined by external norms (cf the latitude where pronunciation is concerned); and (2) the extent of any coercion that might then be employed by the state in order to *constrain* such agency on the part of the speech community (see also Hymes, 1974: 196; Tollefson, 1991: 12–14).

To return to the 1996 reform, the dispute over the question of *dignity* centred on the right of the state to take action that upset the purported balance of consensus within the speech community, thereby impinging on the dignity of the individual. In other words, the complainants were contesting the right of the state to impose an external norm that was alleged to be fundamentally different from the internal norms characteristic of speech community usage. It was a line of argumentation that somewhat oversimplified, however, the dialectical relationship between external and internal norms more generally. So, for example, given their familiarity with the historical complexities surrounding the reform, the complainants ought to have been aware that the *internal* norms characteristic of speech community usage *prior* to 1996 had never developed entirely 'of their own accord'. Instead such norms and usages had been to some extent the product of *external* interventions on the part of the state, at least from the mid-19th century onwards. Such interventions consisted not only in the regulations drawn up for schools at *Länder* level that culminated in the 1901 guidelines, they also comprised the state-sanctioned codification carried out by the Duden from the 1950s onwards (see also Menzel, 1998a: 1179). Indeed, as we saw in Chapter 4, the role of the state in creating and upholding the Duden monopoly was central to Gröschner's complaint against the reform.

Moreover, familiar with the discussions in Kopke's doctoral thesis (1995a: 294–371), the complainants (or Gröschner at the very least) ought to have been aware that, at the root of the debate over orthographic reform, is the use of spelling and punctuation by schools as a means of 'disciplining' pupils via the teaching and evaluation of literacy. As Kopke (1995a: 321) himself shows, one way of countering the use of orthography as an 'instrument of social selection' would in fact have been to *reduce* the overall significance attributed to spelling and punctuation within the education system. Yet it is important to note how at no point in the cases brought before the Constitutional Court was this disciplinary dimension of orthography under dispute. On the contrary, a cornerstone of the argument put forward by Gröschner was his claim that the reform would actually *undermine* his own authority *vis à vis* both his daughter and the students whose examinations he marked. In the case of the Diercks-Elsners, this claim was somewhat modified, being expressed more in terms of the threat presented by the reform to parents' ability to *complement* the school-based acquisition of literacy with reference to their own knowledge of standard orthography. Either way, it is possible to characterise the complainants' views as very much in accordance with the model outlined by Williams (1992) as discussed above. As individuals they were convinced that they should be taking their moral (or, at least, orthographical) imperative not *explicitly* from the state, but *implicitly* from within the speech community. Underpinning that imperative, they believed, should therefore be an external norm imposed by the state that is itself limited to the prescription of only those usages already accepted by the speech community. Yet the complainants were in no way contesting the involvement of the state in the regulation of orthography *per se*. Subject to dispute was merely the basis of any external norm that might be imposed. Thus in their roles as parents and members of the speech community, the complainants could be seen to be actively, and willingly, participating in the dissemination of what might none the less be characterised as a 'state-sanctioned ideology of standard orthography' via the education of those in their charge.[12]

Of course it was precisely in order to maintain the disciplinary efficacy of the standard orthography that the state was in one sense obliged to re-modernise the guidelines of 1901, but whereas processes of modernisation typically serve to consolidate the economic, cultural, linguistic and/or academic 'capital' of already powerful groups (Bourdieu, 1991), this particular process was one in which the complainants feared they stood to lose out. Accepting (and through their actions *reinforcing*) the belief that spelling errors are commonly taken to be an indicator of low intelligence by the speech community at large, the complainants now considered the capital acquired in the form of the pre-1996 orthography to be vulnerable. In the case of their children, the potential risks were even more acute. The shift to a revised external norm not only represented a departure from the previously internalised standard, thereby potentially undermining much of the academic capital already accumulated in this regard, it also threatened to diminish, on a symbolic level, their overall educational achievement and hence future life chances (*viz.* economic capital). And even allowing for the fact that, as Kohrt (1997: 310) reminds us, language users are naturally predisposed to that which is familiar, it is a view that accords with what Deborah Cameron (1995: 14) refers to as the 'circle of intimidation' that surrounds literacy more generally. In this sense, the very fact of having invested so much time and effort into mastering the complexities of the previous standard generates an in-built incentive to defend the cultural significance of such expertise.

While the complainants therefore proceeded to argue that the 1996 changes constituted a lowering of the overall standard of German orthography (*viz.* minimum standard), such changes might be more fruitfully conceptualised as a lowering of the symbolic *value* accorded to the pre-1996 standard (*viz.* arbitrary standard). Such prestige is linked, moreover, to the broader historical concept of the German language as *Kulturgut*, a 'cultural asset' with its origins very much in the tradition of the *Kulturnation* of the late 18th and early 19th centuries (Munske, 1997c). It was an asset embodied not least in the canon of classical literature that afforded the model for the emergent national written standard at that time, familiarity with both the linguistic and philosophical facets of which remain to this day key components of the cultural capital of the educated middle classes or *Bildungsbürgertum*. From the perspective of the complainants, the external norm underpinning the 1901 guidelines had merely resulted from the documentation of norms that had been generated organically from within the speech community over time, hence the frequent reference to the 1996 reform as the 'first of its kind'. Accordingly, we see how the re-standardisation process was perceived as potentially disrupting the transmission to the next generation of a literary canon that had evolved historically, by undermining the value of classical literary works not only in a figurative, but also a material sense. And it was both dimensions of the literary canon that the complainants wished to bequeath to their children, unfettered by state interference.[13]

The extent to which the reform did indeed constitute a fundamental threat to the rights of the individual complainants and their offspring was, of course, for the judges of the Constitutional Court to decide, and is a question to which I shall return below. But either way, from the point of view of the complainants, the reform symbolised a potential loss of status that they were willing to contest with all the constitutional force they could muster. Yet however radical the form of protest might appear (certainly from a British perspective), there was little that was radical in its motivation, for this was a protest that in no way challenged the broader ideological functions underpinning the standardisation process. This was a defence of tradition, albeit a tradition that was itself once modern. It was, moreover, a defence that invoked and romanticised the organic solidarity of the speech community and pitted this against what was perceived to be a more mechanical form of regulation imposed by the state upon the collective free will of the individuals who make up that community. Against this backdrop, the complainants' objections represent much more than what might readily be dismissed in debates such as these as a straightforward case of linguistic purism or a more general 'unwillingness to reform' (e.g. Geerts *et al.*, 1977: 202–203; Langer, 2000). Such objections need to be seen as part of a long tradition of debate within the bourgeois public sphere according to which citizens resist what they see as absolutist forms of authority exercised on the part of the state (Calhoun, 1992; Habermas, [1962] 1989; Habermas [1973], 1976). However, what appears to constitute an identification of the interests of the educated middle classes with those of the public *as a whole* is indicative of a rhetorical move that, as Benjamin Lee (2001: 173) points out, is 'at the heart of modern ideology'.

The Judges

Throughout Chapter 4 we saw how wherever German citizens consider actions by third parties, in this case, the state, to have disproportionately impinged upon their individual rights as laid down in the Basic Law, it is their constitutionally guaranteed prerogative to contest those actions, first via the administrative courts and then, if necessary, via the Federal Constitutional Court. In such cases, it is the remit of the Constitutional Court to mediate between the various parties and, as Günter Dürig (1998: xvi–xvii) describes in his introduction to the text of the Basic Law, there are three important elements to that process. First, it is the fundamental task of the Court to protect the constitutional order on which the state is founded. Secondly, the protection of that order is to be achieved by allowing conflicts to surface rather than by repressing them. Thirdly, the Court aims to resolve such conflicts via a process of *de*-politicisation (my emphasis).

The impossibility of de-politicising what is an inherently *political* conflict should by now be clear for, as we have seen throughout, the legal controversies surrounding the reform were not only a question of the relative freedom of the individual *vis à vis* the state, but also of the instrumentalisation of written language to broader ideological ends. Upholding the right of the executive to prescribe orthographic norms by ministerial decree, the judges went on none the less to declare the rights of the state and its schools (in accordance with Article 7) to be greater than those of parents (in accordance with Article 6). Against this backdrop, the Court dismissed the significance of the reform for the wider speech community by noting how individuals outside of schools and state authorities could continue to write as they pleased, both during the interim period up to 2005 and in the years to follow.

It is in this context, however, that we see how the ability of the state to take normative action in relation to orthography is itself heavily dependent upon a division of the public sphere along the lines of 'community' and 'society' as described by Williams (1992). For whereas the executive has the power to regulate the practices of those institutions of the *Gesellschaft* such as schools and official authorities, it has no jurisdiction over the practices of the *Gemeinschaft*.[14] Accordingly, language users outside of state institutions cannot be compelled in any legal way to comply with the new norm. In this juridical–technical sense, the Court was therefore correct in its judgement that individuals within the speech community are free to continue writing as they please. However, not only is it important to highlight how the ability to impose and maintain such a division of the public sphere is itself ideological insofar as the judiciary is invested *by the state* with the power to do so, the crux of the matter concerns the nature of the relationship between the *Gesellschaft*, on the one hand, and the *Gemeinschaft*, on the other. In other words, what will be the impact of the orthographical norm imposed by the state on practices within the wider speech community? Or seen in Kohrt's terms (1987, 1997), to what extent will the new *external* norm impact upon those norms already internalised within speech community usage?

This question of the reform's so-called *Breiten-* or *Außenwirkung* is especially relevant when one considers that Article III of the Vienna Declaration explicitly declared the role of the Mannheim-based International Commission as one of working towards the longer-term preservation of orthographic unity in the whole of the German-speaking area. As Heller states in his widely publicised edition of *Sprachreport* containing the new guidelines:

> [The new orthography] is a model for all other fields in which language users wish to orientate themselves to an orthography that, as far as possible, is universally valid. This is especially true for printers, publishing houses and editorial boards, but also for private individuals. (Heller, 1998: 2)[15]

Seen in these terms, the reform is a clear attempt to bring about a shift in speech community usage via a revision of the external norm that is none the less formally valid for schools and official authorities only. And, as noted by Rüthers (2002), individuals and institutions within the wider speech community, not least creative writers and their printers, publishers, and editorial boards, were soon being coerced by the state into adopting the 1996 norm (see also Munske, 1997a: 154). This was insofar as any writer or publisher who wished to see their works licensed for use in the classroom quickly found themselves working within a recontextualised publishing practice, where the dominant expectation was that texts be produced in the new orthography (a situation which the writer and long-term opponent of the reform Reiner Kunze (2002) compared to the 'deprivation of citizenship' he had previously experienced in the former German Democratic Republic). From the perspective of the Court, none the less, any decision to adopt the new orthography on the part of a writer or publisher is one that merely derives from an assessment of 'prevailing market conditions'. In this sense, and as we shall see again below, the Court accords a high degree of individual agency to social actors within the wider speech community or *Sprachgemeinschaft*.

At this juncture, it is crucial to emphasise how the Constitutional Court was in no way obliged to side with the state on this or any other matter. Yet it was here that the judges engaged in a classic piece of ideological brokerage on behalf of the state, itself very much in line with the process characterised by Williams (1992) and discussed above. In the case of Gröschner, the Court did not accept that his individual constitutional rights were disproportionately infringed by the reform. However, the judges then tried to offer him some measure of reassurance by noting how the *speech community* would not in fact think less highly of him for his continued use of the pre-1996 orthography. This was because the speech community bases its understanding of orthographic correctness not on norms prescribed *de jure* by the state, but on those norms that are acknowledged *de facto* by the speech community. Moreover, the judges suggested that those members of the speech community who had already learned to read and write would not conclude that Gröschner was writing *incorrectly* should he continue to use the old spellings. Instead, they would simply assume that he was adhering to the traditional, as opposed to the revised, orthography.

However, even allowing for the fact that, from Gröschner's perspective, the ruling of the Court somewhat missed the point (since it was precisely his fear that an adherence to the traditional, pre-reform spellings would mark him out as conservative against the backdrop of the social stratification of orthography that would subsequently obtain), what is of particular theoretical interest is the distinction made by the Court between rulings on orthographical correctness by the *state* and perceptions of correctness within the *speech community* – whereby precedence was clearly given to the latter. Seen in Kohrt's (1987, 1997) terms, the judges were implicitly distinguishing between external and internal norms, acknowledging (correctly) that speech community usage was unlikely to equate in its entirety with any externally imposed norm. This is not least because the speech community consists in language users with a degree of individual agency to reject or modify the external norm. In the context of Gröschner's complaint, greater priority was therefore accorded by the judges to the internal norms characteristic of speech community usage than to any external norm imposed by the state.[16] And it is precisely here that we see how the judges, just like Gröschner and the other complainants, were invoking the idealised solidarity of the speech community as the source of the individual's moral (or orthographical) imperative. As predicted by Williams (1992), in an attempt to offset the tension between the will of the individual, on the one hand, and that of the state, on the other, the judges tried to compel the individual, in this case Gröschner, *to act as a member of the (speech) community.*

In the early days of the disputes, it was precisely such comments from the judges of the Constitutional Court that continued to fuel the legal debates surrounding the reform (see Menzel, 1998a,b). Initially it seemed that, while the Court was downplaying the relevance of the reform for the wider speech community, on the one hand, its paradoxical emphasis on the primacy of speech community practices and values, on the other, merely appeared to lend credence to Gröschner's original assertion that the reform might indeed be of *fundamental* significance for individuals within that community. So by the time the complaints were returned to the Court in 1998, a fuller exploration of the reform's wider impact was necessary. This time the comments of the judges were somewhat more differentiated with regard to the role of schools *vis à vis* the speech community. Not only were the rights of the educational authorities deemed to be greater than those of parents where the teaching of orthography was concerned, the judges noted how it was inevitable that what was taught in the classroom would eventually filter through to the wider community. Besides, parents could not expect to keep pace with everything their children learned at school. In this sense, it was implicitly acknowledged that the *internal* norms of speech community usage are indeed likely to be influenced by any *external* norm imposed by the state on those institutions under its jurisdiction.

However, a further source of controversy in this regard was the extent to which the state was actually permitted under the terms of the Basic Law to participate in the regulation of language *per se*, and, by implication, orthography. From the perspective of the complainants, language belongs to 'the people' (*das Volk*). Any external norm imposed by the state should therefore be rooted in those internal norms that have established themselves as such within speech community usage (see Kopke, 1995a: 372–411). The judges, however, disagreed. Even though the Basic Law itself has nothing to say on orthography (or language specifically), at the same time there is nothing that actually prevents the state from attempting to regulate related practices. In this regard, the judges argued, language is no different from any other 'rule-governed area of social life' – the state is restricted only by the type and extent of any regulation it may wish to perform, not by the ability to take normative action *per se*.[17] In accordance with Article 7 of the Basic Law the state may therefore regulate written language in ways that help to clarify and/or simplify problematical areas of usage, since teachers and pupils need clear guidance on such matters.

The extent to which the judges did in fact address the overall aims of the reform is a point to which I shall return below and in Chapter 6. However, it is interesting to highlight the views of language change that are contained either explicitly or implicitly in the comments of both the opponents and the judges. From the opponents' point of view, language change is a naturally occurring organic process in which the state should not interfere. Although such beliefs are by no means restricted to discourses of German orthography or, indeed, to Germany generally, they are, as Ingo Reiffenstein (1999: 232) argues, rooted in a well-established tradition within German thought. This has its origins in the late 18th-century writings of philosophers that were then incorporated into theories of language by early Romantics such Friedrich Schlegel and Wilhelm von Humboldt. Such ideas, which posit language as an autonomous organism with an innate capacity for self-regulation, to be protected as far as possible from the machinations of the state, themselves form the backdrop to a long (and typically conservative) tradition of language criticism (*Sprachkritik*) and language cultivation (*Sprachpflege*) that has enjoyed something of a renaissance in post-unification Germany (see, *inter alia*, Klein, 2001; Law, 2002; Wiechers, 2001).[18]

On one level, it is to their credit that the judges of the Constitutional Court saw through the language idealism professed by the complainants, which downplays the role of human agency and interest in relation to change and normification within the speech community itself. The judges noted, for instance, how even though language change might well be in some sense 'self-regulating', this does not, and historically has not, prevented the state and state-sanctioned institutions such as the Duden from intervening in its development (or, indeed, the many other individuals and organisations across the centuries motivated by particular interests).[19] In this sense, the judges correctly acknowledged a broad typology of the processes underpinning both change and codification. This ranges from processes that can occur within the speech community and/or from 'below' the level of individual consciousness, through to explicit intervention on the part of clearly identifiable agents such as the state, linguists and/or dictionary publishers. Accordingly, the judges implicitly acknowledged Kohrt's (1987, 1997) assertion that the internal norms characteristic of speech community usage are indeed norms in their own right. And it was against this backdrop that they went on to argue how, following the end of the interim period in 2005, it was clear that speech community usage would *continue* to develop to some extent 'of its own accord'. Given, however, that any further changes to the external norm on the part of the state would be relatively minimal (and would in all likelihood be limited to norms already acknowledged internally within the speech community) the judges could not see how the 1996 reform would *disproportionately* impinge upon the rights of individuals within that community, even after 2005.

While this is intuitively correct, it is none the less central to an understanding of the dispute to unpack this particular set of claims put forward by the judges. First, the fact that the state has engaged in the codification of an external norm *in the past* does not of itself justify such intervention in either the *present* or the *future*. Secondly, the fact that any future revisions to the external norm would be 'minimal' is not in itself tantamount to a justification for state codification *per se*. And thirdly, the fact that speech community usage might well be governed by a degree of internal codification (that may be to some extent independent of the external norm) does not, in itself, justify the imposition of such a norm on the part of the state. All in all, what appears to be happening here is that the judges were themselves invoking the same romantic ideal of the speech community as the locus of an autonomous and disinterested form of codification and change as that which characterises the arguments of the complainants. And in a *non sequitur* of considerable ideological import – very much in accordance with the process described by Williams (1992: 10) – the judges were invoking the very *inevitability* of change to speech community usage as a means of justifying the state regulation of orthography for those institutions specifically under its jurisdiction, namely schools and official authorities.

In a legal and linguistic assessment of the 1998 ruling, Julian Rivers and Christopher Young (2001: 176–77) noted how the decision of the Constitutional Court to allow the reform to proceed might well be seen as a sensible and pragmatic attempt to avoid an excessive juridification of matters orthographic, combined with a healthy degree of agnosticism regarding the vexed question as to who exactly controls the German language. Moreover, the verdict was entirely consistent with previous rulings on a range of issues in the post-war period where judges have similarly resisted citizens' attempts to challenge executive action in ways that would lead only to an enhancement of state power via a monopoly for the legislature. As the constitutional theorist Fritz Ossenbühl (1989: 326–27) points out, judges are only too aware that such a monopoly could never really serve to consolidate the democratic rights of the individual. On the contrary, it could only weaken such rights by undermining the very structures designed to guarantee them, namely the separation of legislative, executive, and judicial powers. It is a political and constitutional tension that is well illustrated by the dispute over orthographic reform. For while the complainants, in their pursuit of a more deregulated version of orthography along the lines of English in the UK, were ultimately resisting orthographic regulation on the part of the executive, they were by no means resisting state regulation *per se*. And as part of their challenge to *executive* action, they then turned to the *judiciary* in order to demand intervention on the part of the *legislature*, thereby paradoxically according an even greater role for the state overall (Menzel, 1998a: 1184). However, in addition to such constitutional–theoretical considerations, the judges were also well aware of the potential practical consequences of not allowing the reform to proceed at such a late stage. Not only would any further modifications of the 1996 guidelines have in all probability led to another round of litigation along the lines of that already experienced, it was also likely that publishers of school books and many other businesses affected by a possible collapse of the reform would attempt to sue the state for damages (see Wagner, 1998a).

However, even allowing for such considerations, the 1998 verdict remains in many ways unsatisfactory. For whereas the Court was clear in its ruling concerning the rights of parents and pupils *vis à vis* schools in accordance with Article 5 of the Basic Law, the issues raised by the complainants in relation to Articles 1 and 2 on the dignity and personality rights of individuals within the wider speech community received only cursory attention. Yet as Rivers and Young (2001: 177) point out, once the Court admitted consequences *of a sort* for the rights of such individuals, the tradition of constitutional jurisprudence in the Federal Republic dictates that the judges should at least have addressed the issues thereby raised. As Kopke (1995a: 296–331) shows, this would normally involve a detailed assessment of two overarching points: (1) were the proposed measures of sufficient benefit to the community as a whole (*Gemeinwohl*) so as to outweigh any potential infringements on the rights of individuals within that community? and (2) were the measures in question (a) characterised by necessity (*Erforderlichkeit*) and (b) subject to the most appropriate form of implementation (*Geeignetheit*)? In the context of the 1996 reform this amounted to three basic questions: was the reform strictly necessary, would German orthography be easier to learn as a result, and was the reform, and its method of introduction, the most appropriate manner of achieving any such pedagogic benefits? Only once these questions were comprehensively addressed, would it have been possible to assess the overall 'fitness for purpose' (*Zweckmäßigkeit*) of the reform *vis à vis* schools and official authorities, and then evaluate this against the potential 'disproportionality' (*Unverhältnismäßigkeit*) of any impact on the dignity and personality rights of individuals within the wider speech community. However, the Court did not address these issues in any great detail, merely claiming to be satisfied that the state had acted in the best interests of pupils and their education. In doing so, the judges avoided the key questions central to an adequate resolution of the dispute, claiming that constitutional means could not in any case be used to assess the necessity, content, value and purpose of the reform since the Basic Law itself has nothing to say on orthography.

I would argue, however, that there is good reason for the inadequate resolution of this debate on the part of the Constitutional Court. For while the success of the reform *in the long term* clearly depends upon the cooperation of the wider speech community, its implementation *in the short term* was equally dependent on the marginalisation of that role. This is because, as we have seen throughout, while schools and state authorities are under the jurisdiction of the executive, the wider speech community is not. Yet once the judges seriously began to explore the extent to which the constitutional rights of those *outside* of schools and state authorities were infringed by the reform, they would have been under an even greater obligation to address the crucial question of the reform's overall purpose *vis à vis* language users within the speech community more generally. However, it is difficult to see how this could have been achieved within the Court's own remit of *de-politicising* conflict situations, and without unpacking the broader ideological dimensions of the standardisation process. And, as the opening statement of the 1998 ruling makes clear, this was never seriously going to be on the agenda:

> The purpose of orthography, the embodiment of the rules for correct writing, is to guarantee the unity of writing in the interests of communication. In schools, it is the object of instruction and a measure for the evaluation of achievement. (*Bunderverfassungsgericht*, 12 May 1998)[20]

This statement, with its *explicit* commitment to the instrumentalisation of orthography for both unificatory and disciplinary purposes, reveals the discursive boundaries within which the legal debate was to be conducted. And it is in this context that the judges were always going to (or going to have to) sideline what were arguably the more fundamental sociolinguistic and juridical questions surrounding the reform. But the fact that the judges were in a position to do just that was ultimately contingent on the power with which the Federal Constitutional Court is itself invested by the state. And therein, no doubt, lies the ability of many an ideological broker to authoritatively entextualise its particular standpoint within a language ideological debate.

The Linguists

So far, this chapter has explored the dispute over the 1996 reform from the perspective of the complainants, on the one hand, and the judges of the Constitutional Court, on the other. While this was a dispute that was ultimately triggered by the actions of the *linguists* (in conjunction with politicians and senior civil servants), I have deferred the discussion of this particular group of ideological brokers until last. This is because the actions of the linguists require careful examination not only in terms of the ideas about language and language planning/policy underpinning them, but because they will also provide the basis for exploring alternative ways in which the reform might itself have been handled, a key theme to be taken up in the final chapter.

As we saw in Chapter 3, the theoretical backdrop for the 1996 reform was a view of spelling and punctuation based on a *structuralist* approach to the study of language. As we also saw, however, the reformers were by no means unaware of the potential shortcomings of such an approach. Rooted in the notion of the 'primacy of speech', structuralism inevitably accords a secondary function to writing whose task is then to *re*-represent objective, real-world meanings that have been previously encoded at the level of spoken language. It is a view that has itself been widely challenged, not least in the second half of the 20th century during which time theories of written language developed that saw reading, writing, and orthography as more than just attempts to encode *speech*, but as linguistic/communicative systems in their own right (e.g. Derrida, 1978; Prieto, 1968, 1986; Stetter, 1990, 1997; Vachek, 1945–1949, 1973). Moreover, as became clear in Chapter 2, reformers' attempts throughout the 1980s and early 1990s to revise orthographic structures in ways that largely prioritised phonological and/or phonemic principles, in areas such as vowel length and foreign loans, continued to meet with such widespread opposition that they were in many cases abandoned. As the linguists and reform critics Hanno Birken-Bertsch and Reinhard Markner (2000: 122–25) propose, it was in this context that the reformers moved towards a hybrid view of orthography that emphasised the contingency of reading and writing on not only phonological, but also *semantic*, principles.

It is not within the scope of this discussion to say whether, as the German language historian Peter von Polenz (1999: 246) has suggested, the shift towards this compromise view was little more than an opportunistic attempt on the part of the reformers to restore their own academic reputation in the light of their previous failures to secure more radical revisions. Either way, as we saw in Chapter 3, it was clear that any attempt to marry such potentially conflicting views of orthography was always liable to create new tensions and attract further criticism. As Birken-Bertsch and Markner (2000: 122–25) point out, the broader acknowledgement of semantic principles certainly resulted in what they consider to be a number of more 'sensible' decisions in relation to sound–letter correspondences, according to which unity of spelling across related word groups was enhanced. But even here, the prioritisation of synchronic over diachronic considerations led to what they see as a number of rather unconventional 'pseudo-etymological folk' spellings, such as *belemmert*→ *belämmert* ('miserable', as in *Lamm* in current usage) or *Quentchen*→ *Quäntchen* ('scrap' as in *Quantum*) (Birken-Bertsch & Markner, 2000: 125). Even more problematic from their point of view, however, was the way in which the phonological principle continued to dominate many areas of the reform. This was the case, for example, in relation to [ss] and [ß], where vowel length as opposed to morpheme boundaries afforded the main criterion for the new guidelines, leading to such visually problematic changes as *Meßergebnis→ Messergebnis* (measurement).[21] The same applied to the new rules on hyphenation and word division that largely prioritised phonology over morphology, as in *Teenager→ Tee-nager.*[22] Such examples could then be adduced as evidence for what Birken-Bertsch and Markner (2000: 123) see as the reformers' continued adherence to a theoretically outdated, phonocentric view of orthography.

From the perspective of the *complainants*, any change that involved the creation of previously non-existent forms, thereby impinging on existing orthographic structure, could be considered 'fundamental'. The judges did not agree, working as they did with a much broader concept of fundamentality that presupposed an impact upon the rights of individuals that was disproportionate to the measures in question. That said, neither the judges nor the linguists denied that the 1996 reform involved changes at the level of orthographic structure. Indeed, as one of the reformers Horst Haider Munske (1997a) himself emphasises, any attempt to systematise German spelling and punctuation in ways that would hopefully improve both the communicative and pedagogic efficacy of the written language would necessarily involve intervention at a structural level. And even allowing for the relatively minimal impact on existing usage overall, it is clear that the extent of such intervention in 1996 by far exceeded that of 1901 in both quantitative and qualitative terms. However, while the *structural* pros and cons of the 1996 guidelines were widely and heatedly discussed by linguists on both sides of the reform debate (see, *inter alia*, Augst *et al.*, 1997, Eroms & Munske, 1997), as Rosina Lippi-Green (1997: 9) points out: 'The irony is that where linguists settle down to an uneasy truce, non-linguists take up the battle cry. The least disputed issues around language structure and function [...] are those which are most often challenged by non-linguists, and with the greatest vehemence and emotion.' (See also Pinker, 1994: 17–18.) And as noted by Munske (1997a: 143), the extent to which the reform might be seen as infringing the democratic and constitutional rights of language users, although central to the process of *legitimation*, was of little more than peripheral interest to the linguists behind the 1996 guidelines.

Of particular concern to the complainants were the various ways in which the reform led to changes in the appearance of written German or so-called *Schriftbild*. Thus, even allowing for the fact that phonologically-motivated changes generally lead to a greater degree of modification to the appearance of individual words, it was not directly relevant whether the theoretical motivation for change was, for example, phonological/phonemic (*daß→dass*), morphological–semantic (*Stengel→Stängel*) or syntactic–semantic (*in bezug auf→in Bezug auf*): what counted was that the fact that the items in question *looked* different. The same applied to those changes that prioritised users' 'current' perceptions of the etymological links between word groups. The complainants were seemingly less concerned with the linguistic-theoretical distinction between synchronic and diachronic approaches to orthographic structure. Of greater importance was the fact that changes prioritising the synchronic dimension often led to spellings that breached the visual, aesthetic, and historical continuity of the language. Moreover, in some cases visual alterations were perceived to impact upon the overall *referential* potential of German. This was the case regarding the much-contested changes to compound spellings such as *sitzenbleiben→sitzen bleiben*, where the ability to distinguish between one meaning ('to remain seated') and another ('to repeat a school year') was felt to have been lost. In terms of the complaints brought before the Constitutional Court, *pre*-1996 spellings were then deemed to be part of the mental lexicon of those individuals who had already learned to read and write. Since such items must be visually identified and retrieved from that lexicon, any changes that altered their appearance could be construed as impacting upon the retrieval process, hence as a form of external interference in the cognitive transformation of 'intellectual concepts' (thought) into 'concrete actions' (here: writing). And it was this interference, as constituted by the reform that was perceived to infringe personality and dignity rights as guaranteed by the German Basic Law.

As we have seen throughout, however, the complainants' concerns were by no means as politically disinterested as might appear in view of their apparent emphasis on the psycholinguistic, or *mentalistic*, dimensions of language processing. This was partly because the process of external interference was itself seen as an 'act of will' on the part of the state (*viz.* external norm) that was felt to breach the 'linguistic integrity' of the autonomous individual (*viz.* internal norm). However, it was also because the complainants' apparent emphasis on 'competence' as opposed to 'performance' in a Chomskyan sense was closely tied up with their own particular prioritisation of the needs of experienced writers over young learners, on the one hand, and readers over writers, on the other. This, in turn, amounts to a view of orthographic processing that goes beyond a narrowly psycholinguistic definition of competence.

In addition, it draws, albeit implicitly, on a broader sociolinguistic under-standing of the term via the notion of *communicative* competence that consists not just in an innate, mentalistic ability to use language appropri-ately, but in an acquired, *cultural* ability to do so (Hymes, 1972). And as Jack Sidnell (2001: 35–36) points out, this is a view that, in practice, turns the *langue* = competence and *parole* = performance dichotomy on its head. This is insofar as competence is no longer seen solely in terms of an inherent ability to process language in the sense of *langue*, but as an accumulated history of performances in the sense of *parole* (see also Vološinov, 1973 [1986]). And once we see orthography in these terms, that is, as *cultural* competence that has been acquired as a result of repeated performances over time – whether by individuals, communities, or nations – then it is clear how and why any process of reform might be construed as a threat to the value of the previous standard as cultural *capital*.

Objections to the reform need, then, to be interpreted in terms of the complainants' implicit perception of orthography as a form of compe-tence that draws not only on psycholinguistic, but also cultural and com-municative, dimensions. It is particularly striking, therefore, that such perspectives appear to have been precisely those that were *excluded* from the linguistic–theoretical model of orthography underpinning the reform. Indeed, as highlighted by Dieter Nerius (2000a: 96), the linguists considered, only to explicitly reject, approaches to orthography that drew on visual, aesthetic, and historical factors since these did not lend them-selves to 'generalisable and systematic explanatory schemata' ([. . .] *verall-gemeinerbares und systematisches Erklärungsmuster*).

Against this backdrop, it starts to become clear how, at the heart of the dispute over the reform, were the differing views of orthography held by the linguists, on the one hand, and the complainants, on the other. Here we encounter an epistemological conflict according to which the linguists were explicitly motivated by a desire for generalisability, systematicity and objectivity of orthography at a *structural* level (with instrumental–functional outcomes) that was diametrically opposed to the *specificity, con-tingency and subjectivity* underpinning the complainants' implicit notion of orthographic competence (with its emphasis on the integrative function of orthography/language as a link to the social group/community). In this sense, the dispute has to be seen as part of a much broader philosophical conflict over the very nature of language that pitches the empiricism of the linguists, on the one hand, against the rationalism of the complainants, on the other (see Chapman, 2000). For the linguists, working within a structural–theoretical paradigm, language constitutes an *a posteriori* means with which to represent a reality that is itself external to language: to alter the form of the language (here: its orthography) in no way impinges upon the nature of that reality. For the complainants, on the other hand, there is no access to reality without the internalised *a priori* knowledge that is constituted by language itself: to alter the form of the language is therefore to distort the perception of that reality.[23] As such, we see how the dispute was not only centred on the very nature of linguistic *expertise* (see Johnson, 2001a), but also embodied the key epistemological conflicts between modernist and post-modernist approaches to the relationship between language and real-world phenomena (e.g. Lash, 1990).

From a language policy perspective, one is immediately left to ponder the value of an orthographic model underpinning such a monumental undertaking as the 1996 reform that appears to marginalise so explicitly the real-world concerns of language users – or certain groups thereof. This is particularly so when one considers that the rationalism underlying the complainants' approach to language has a much longer philosophical tradition in Germany (*viz.* Leibniz/Kant) than the empiricism of the linguists. However, it would be an over-simplification, I believe, to dismiss the linguists as an intellectual élite conspiring to manipulate German orthography from the sublime heights of their academic ivory towers, as was so frequently imputed by the opponents' characterisation of the reformers as 'an anonymous group of experts'. This is partly because, as evidenced throughout the recent history of the reform process, most linguists were acutely aware of the potential for popular resistance to their own expert views on orthography, even if they did not always accept the validity of their opponents' arguments (e.g. Augst & Schaeder, 1997b; Heller, 1999: 79; Zabel, 1989, 1996, 1997a). However, it is also because the reformers' attempts were motivated by a genuine desire to liberalise what they considered to be the *over-normification* of the 1901 guidelines that had ensued throughout the 20th century. This was, not least, with a view to improving both the communicative and pedagogic efficacy of German punctuation and spelling, with particular regard for the needs of younger and/or less experienced users of the written language (Augst & Schaeder, 1997b: 4–6). And seen in these terms, many of the decisions made by the reformers turn out to be rather less a case of malicious intent on the part of an intellectually disengaged élite, than indicative of a liberal *anti*-élitism that was in fact at the heart of the reform project.

It was in this context that the linguists were especially concerned to prioritise the needs of younger and/or inexperienced users of the written language, who must arguably draw upon their knowledge of the *spoken* language as a means of mastering orthography as a secondary representation of speech. By the same token, the reformers were at pains to address the needs of those users of German who were *not* steeped in the traditions of the literary–philosophical canon. Such users would not, for example, be able to call upon an appreciation of historical–linguistic developments when making judgements about the correctness of certain spellings, only upon their knowledge of language in its current form. In this regard, the reformers' ideas were a welcome corrective to the opponents' implicit understanding of cultural knowledge as an *a priori* component of communicative competence. Instead, the linguists were clear that such competence exists only as an *a posteriori* expertise that is itself acquired as the product of acculturation. So whereas reform opponent Hans Krieger (1997: 124) dismissed many aspects of the reform, such as the liberalisation of commas, as a 'cheap concession to schoolchildren', for reformers, such as Gerhard Augst and Burkhard Schaeder (1997b), the objections of *experienced* writers (who must undergo a process of 're-learning' that is almost universally disliked) had none the less to take second place behind the needs of younger and generally less practised users of the written language.

Nevertheless, one of the key problems surrounding the reform process was the need to establish the precise extent to which any given structural change would, in fact, render a particular orthographical item easier to learn and/or improve the overall communicative efficacy of the written language (Meder, 1997: 193). The problem here was that no real baseline data were ever available against which to evaluate the purported benefits of those spellings that were altered. This is explicitly conceded by Augst and Schaeder (1997b: 6–7) who note, however, that it is simply not always possible to know exactly which orthographic features render a given word (or text) easier to write or read (see also Hinney, 1997). Nor is it possible to estimate the extent to which a language user will draw upon such potential cognitive cues at any one time (Heller, 1999: 78). Although it is not atypical for reforms of this kind to proceed without such empirical evidence (Bird, 2001: 151) – and it is not entirely clear how sufficiently exhaustive data could ever be acquired *prior* to a reform's introduction – this was inevitably grist to the mill of the complainants. In this sense the complainants were justified in their disputation of the extent to which the reform had been truly *necessary* in accordance with the constitutional criteria as defined by Kopke (1995a). And it was precisely this issue that the judges of the Constitutional Court failed to address in any satisfactory way.

However, it is in this context that we also see how, despite specific claims to the objectivity of the linguistic–theoretical model underpinning the reform (Nerius, 2000a: 96), the actions of the reformers were themselves no less characterised by a position of interest than those of their opponents. This is partly because the autonomous view of language characteristic of structuralism, that is, one that sees language as governed by its own internal logic and therefore excludes all that is deemed to be external to the language system, is no longer tenable once language problems are applied to real-world situations. Any orthographic reform will be more than merely a question of corpus planning: it will always involve a degree of status planning that has inherently social effects. However, what is particular interesting here is the way in which the purportedly objective underpinnings of a structuralist approach to *orthography* – the in-built preference for phonological over semantic principles, and synchronic over diachronic factors – were themselves co-opted within the reform process to expressly political ends. These include the desire to improve both the communicative and pedagogic efficacy of German orthography, with a particular emphasis on the needs of certain social groups, namely younger learners and/or inexperienced users of written German. And for these reasons alone, the opponents were right to see the reform as an inherently *political* act with tangible consequences for individual language users.

It is beyond the scope of this discussion to establish the extent to which such interest-laden co-option of structuralist principles on the part of the reformers was ultimately *implicit* or *explicit* (see Woolard, 1998). None the less, it is worth recalling how the structuralist project is itself rooted in a philosophy of liberalism that posits all languages – and, by implication, language users – as fundamentally equal (Pennycook, 2001). Such egalitarianism has its *linguistic* origins in a Saussurean view of language that sees all meanings as generated internally, and self-referentially, within the sign system of language itself. As such, notions of inequality in relation to language are typically dismissed as *social* rather than linguistic effects, thereby erasing the potential for language itself to function as a site for the production and/or contestation of power relations. But while, as Alastair Pennycook (2002: 14–19) emphasises, the marginalisation of the social from the linguistic is itself a thoroughly ideological move, what we appear to be encountering here is a somewhat different type of ideological brokerage. For it is the very claim to scientificity of the structuralist approach that is itself invoked as a means of justifying the reform *vis à vis* the speech community at large. It is in this sense that the reformers' actions can be located within a much longer historical tradition in linguistic thinking where, as Susan Gal (2001: 33) points out, correctness in language is not modelled on any one particular social group within the speech community, but derived from the inherent laws of language to be identified via 'the disinterested expertise of linguistic science.'

Notwithstanding, it is important to question the extent to which modifying the spellings of a relatively small number of linguistic items can genuinely contribute to a redistribution of cultural and/or economic capital in, and amongst, disparate social groups in the longer term. In this sense, we might see the reformers' approach as indicative of an equally questionable facet of linguistic autonomy that *over*-estimates the value of change to linguistic structure (here: via corpus planning) as a socially emancipatory force in its own right (e.g. Blommaert, 1996; Tollefson, 1991). However, once we see the 1996 reform in this light, that is, not just a piece of corpus planning, but a clear attempt to bring about a change in the behaviour of the real social actors who read and write in German, then the whole approach to the question of the reform's *implementation* must necessarily shift. It is to the possibilities for such a shift that we now turn in the final chapter.

Notes

1. See also, *inter alia*, Haugen (1966) and Gundersen (1977) on Norwegian; Rabin (1977) on Hebrew; Geerts *et al.* (1977) on Dutch; Murchú (1977) on Irish; Rothstein (1977) on Polish; Ager (1996: 199–225) on French.
2. Both left the International Commission for German Orthography (Munske in September 1997 and Eisenberg in March 1998) amidst disputes over the reform's content and implementation (for further discussion see Eisenberg, 1997a,b, 1999; Eisenberg in Lønnum, 2003; Munske, 1997a,b,c, 2002).
3. For a broader discussion and attempt to characterise participants in the debate according to their *linguistic* expertise, see Stenschke (2002: 138–47).
4. See, *inter alia*, Berthele *et al.* (2002), von Polenz (1978, 1991, 1994, 1999), Reiffenstein (1999) and Wells (1985).
5. On English, see, *inter alia*, Crowley (1989), Joseph (1987), Milroy and Milroy (1999) and Parakrama (1995).
6. For this reason German constitutes a classic case of what Kloss (1978: 66–67) defines as a pluricentric language, in other words a language with several centres each characterised by its own codified norms (e.g. Clyne, 1995; Ammon, 1991). However, it is a status that is by no means acknowledged in everyday language practices within the German-speaking areas, nor in the specific case of orthography where the pursuit of standardisation has, at least since the 19th century, been primarily on a supra-national level.

7. Note how, while the norms of standard German speech were similarly formalised in the late 19th century in the form of Theodor Siebs' *Deutsche Bühnensprache* ('The Language of the German Stage') of 1898 (Wells, 1985: 353–55), the success of a standardised pronunciation in superseding traditional regional varieties cannot be compared to that of the standard orthography as formulated in 1901 (see Reiffenstein, 1999: 234). For a concise historical survey of the standardisation of spoken German, see von Polenz (1999: 257–63).

8. Dahrendorf (1968: 145) goes on to describe the threat of the demise of the 'community' by the artificially imposed structures of the 'state' as part of the 'folklore of German political consciousness' (my translation), which has been drawn upon at several key points in German history – Hitler, for example, promised to bring to an end the political upheavals of the Weimar era by appealing to the idea of the German-speaking peoples as members of a 'community of fate' or *Schicksalsgemeinschaft*.

9. From a methodological perspective, such a view accords with Duranti's proposal that analysts abandon the notion of the community (or, specifically, the speech community) as 'an already constituted object of enquiry' (1997: 82), in favour of an exploration of the ways in which the notion of the speech community might itself be constructed in the course of communicative activity (cited in Patrick, 2001: 574).

10. For a broader discussion of the use of the World Wide Web in the context of public language awareness in Germany recently, see Klein (2001).

11. Rüthers is by no means alone in his assertions. For further discussion of reform debates in the broader context of Germany's purported overall incapacity for reform, see Johnson (2000: 122–23; see also Bertram, 1997).

12. In the case of Gröschner, this paradox is particularly marked given his dual identity as both a servant of the state (in his capacity as a university professor) and as a member of the speech community (as both an individual and a parent) (see Kopke, 1995a: 277–93).

13. Against this backdrop it is unsurprising to find that literary writers should themselves have been so vehement in their protests against the reform (see especially Kunze, 2002).

14. In this sense, the concept of *Gemeinschaft* and *Gesellschaft* correspond broadly to the Gramscian division of 'civil' versus 'political' society, respectively (Gramsci, 1978). For a discussion of literacy in this context, see Clark and Ivanič (1997: 23–26).

15. German original: '[Die neue Regelung] hat... Vorbildcharakter für alle anderen Bereiche, in denen die Sprachteilhaber an einer möglichst allgemein gültigen Rechtschreibung orientieren möchten. Das gilt speziell für Druckereien, Verlage und Redaktionen, aber auch für Privatpersonen.'

16. Note how the same argument was employed *vis à vis* the possibility that the state of Schleswig-Holstein would opt out of the new guidelines following the referendum insofar as absolute unity of norms internalised within the

speech community was not itself a prerequisite for the success of the newly-imposed external norm.

17. In this regard, the spelling reform exemplified the classic dilemma in federal constitutional jurisprudence, namely to what extent is the state 'permitted' to act (*darf*) versus the extent to which it is 'obliged' to act (*muss*) – see Ossenbühl (1989: 342–43) for further discussion.

18. See Klein (2001: 5–6) for a discussion of the increased public interest in language-related issues, and the concomitant founding of a number of new (and mostly private) organisations since the mid-1990s such as the *Arbeitsgemeinschaft für Deutsche Sprache, der Verein für deutsche Rechtschreibung und Sprachpflege e.V., der Verein für Sprachpflege* and, most significantly, the Dortmund-based *Verein der Deutschen Sprache*. Klein situates such developments both in their broader historical context of language cultivation and purism, as well as the more recent public debates over national identity against the backdrop of unification in 1990. However, while public disputes over orthographic reform certainly accord with such developments, it would be erroneous, I believe, to over-interpret the role of political unification in those disputes given that attempts to reform German orthography considerably pre-dated 1990.

19. While it is not within the scope of this work to trace such historical processes in the development of German orthography prior to the 19th century, see Reiffenstein (1999) for a useful survey in the context of the reform debate.

20. German original: 'Die Rechtschreibung, der Inbegriff der Regeln über die richtige Schreibung, dient dem Ziel, im Interesse der Kommunikation die Einheitlichkeit des Schreibens sicherzustellen. In der Schule ist sie Gegenstand des Unterrichts und Maßstab der Leistungsbewertung.'

21. The problem here is that *Messergebnis* is likely to be read as *Messer-gebnis* as opposed to *Mess-ergebnis*, given the existence of the lexical item *Messer* (knife).

22. This example is problematic given that it might be misread as a compound form of *Tee* (tea) and *Nager* (rodent) . . .

23. This also accounts for the vehement response to the reform on the part of creative writers. For them, language is the primary tool with which to make sense of reality. To interfere in the shape of the language, at whatever level, is to impinge upon the very process of sense-making, thereby distorting the reality that is to be captured.

Chapter 6
The Trouble with Spelling?
Discussion and Conclusions

The key premise underlying the study of any language ideological debate is the need to explore the processes by which ideologies are produced, reproduced and/or contested, and to situate those processes in the historical contexts in which they are embedded (Blommaert, 1999; Kroskrity, 2000a). In their volume, *Languages and Publics*, Susan Gal and Kathryn Woolard (2001a) are similarly concerned with the hegemonic struggles that surround what they refer to as the 'making of authority' in language. And central to the process by which particular ideological viewpoints are authoritatively entextualised, they argue, is the manner in which social actors must systematically exclude the 'personal' from the object of their concern (Gal & Woolard, 2001a: 4). There are two main ways in which this is typically achieved. The first involves the definition of the object in question as 'independent of human will'. This is closely linked to the second, namely the invocation of a so-called 'aperspectival objectivity' or 'view from nowhere' (Nagel, 1986). It is on this basis that ideological brokers attempt to claim authority for their particular viewpoints on the grounds that these do not represent the concerns of an interested party as such, but those of the 'public at large' (see also Habermas, [1962], 1989; Lee, 2001).

The legal dispute surrounding the 1996 reform of German orthography shows how each of the three main groups of ideological brokers engaged in the dispute positioned themselves, implicitly or explicitly, in accordance with the principles identified by Gal and Woolard. The linguists, for example, saw themselves as the proponents of a scientific view of orthography based on a structuralist approach to language. This is an approach that formally excludes the relevance of human will – both on the part of lay users within the speech community and linguists themselves in their role as language experts – from its object of enquiry. And it was on this basis that the reformers could view themselves as

149

acting (albeit somewhat paradoxically) in the interests of the wider public insofar as the reform would improve the functional efficacy of German spelling and punctuation for all concerned. This 'expert' view was one that was rejected as élitist and esoteric, however, by the reform's opponents. This group was at pains to invoke a (literally) common-sense view of orthography that sees spelling and punctuation not just as tools for reading and writing that can be modified in terms of 'efficiency gains', but as more broadly indexical of German language, culture, and history. While purporting to represent the interests of a wider public, however, such a view revealed itself to be fuelled largely by the desire to maintain the status quo for educated language users for whom know-ledge of the pre-1996 standard functioned as cultural and academic capital. Meanwhile, the judges of the Constitutional Court, in an attempt to mediate between the linguists and their opponents, were similarly con-cerned to position themselves as occupying the 'view from nowhere'. Indeed, their treatment of the dispute was explicitly framed within the remit of the Court that formally demands the *de*-politicisation of any con-flict brought to its attention. And it was against this backdrop that the judges presented their ruling as independent of their own will as social actors (and representatives of the state), as well as drawing in part on an autonomous view of language characterised by an agentless process of normification and change. As became clear in Chapters 4 and 5, however, such claims to objectivity could only be maintained in the context of a ruling that ultimately circumvented the truly political issues at the heart of the dispute, namely the overall necessity, value and purpose of the reform.

In sum, we see then how each of the three groups of ideological brokers tried to position itself as the 'voice of reason', thereby purporting to re-present the interests of the public at large (Lee, 2001). Yet it is not only the basic strategies of argumentation by which each group pursued the nor-malisation of its particular viewpoint that was common to all concerned. Upon closer inspection, we see how in terms of a range of further presup-positions about the role of the speech community in the normification process, the three groups had more in common than initially apparent.

Orthography, Authority and the Paradox of Legitimation

The debate surrounding the 1996 reform of German orthography represents a classic dispute over who controls the German language. As Julian Rivers and Christopher Young (2001: 177) have suggested, this then revolved around the adjudication of what Renate Bartsch (1987) refers to as primary and secondary norms of language. *Primary* norms, in Bartsch's terms, are those that govern correct linguistic practice and behaviour, while *secondary* norms determine the authority to specify and/or modify the primary norms, together with the adjudication of disagreements surrounding their application. In practice, disputes over the two types of norm are routinely conflated, as in the case of the 1996 reform, with its concern for the specification and adjudication of orthographical norms 'from above' (i.e. the state) or 'from below' (i.e. the speech community). Yet what was intriguing about this dispute was the way in which at key points all three groups of ideological brokers, while disagreeing on the nature and extent of permissible *state* involvement in the specification of orthographic norms, drew on seemingly shared presuppositions regarding the role of the *speech community*. For the opponents, the only authentic basis for a state-codified standard consisted in speech community usage, itself seen a product of an organic and consensual process of normification over time. Meanwhile, the judges, while clearly upholding state involvement, similarly prioritised the views of the *speech community* regarding evaluations of the relative 'correctness' of the old versus the revised orthography. In this sense both groups were drawing on what Peter Patrick describes as a long historical tradition of positing the speech community as the ultimate 'tribunal' in matters linguistic (e.g. Whitney, 1875 cited in Patrick, 2001: 578). Moreover, the judges even proceeded to invoke the *inevitability* of change within the speech community as a means of shoring up the state's involvement in the process of orthographic regulation.

As we saw in Chapter 5, however, such invocation of the concept of 'community' is redolent of a paradox that goes far beyond the specific dispute over orthography. As highlighted by Glyn Williams (1992), it is tied to a much broader debate over the historical relationship between 'community' (*Gemeinschaft*), on the one hand, and 'society' (*Gesellschaft*), on the other. As Benjamin Lee (2001: 174–80) shows, this is a relationship closely linked to what Hannah Arendt (1963) saw as the fundamental legitimation paradox at the heart of modern constitutional democracies. According to Arendt, any group of individuals that comes together to form the constitution of a democratic state is, by definition, *pre*-constitutional and, hence, politically illegitimate. As Lee (2001: 175) then suggests: 'The modern notion of "we, the people" solves this problem by attributing foundational legitimacy to a *non-political collective agency* that creates itself through its own actions in secular time' (my emphasis). In other words, it is the invocation of the 'people' or 'community' on the part of the state that is central to the state's own attempts to

regulate social practice. In the context of the dispute over German orthography, we can see how such a paradox, and its proposed resolution,
works in two main ways. First, the state appeared to have no *a priori* authority with which to regulate orthography, even within schools and official
authorities – a point that was formally acknowledged by the Constitutional Court. In order to justify the right of the state to intervene in
such matters, the judges were therefore paradoxically obliged to invoke
the concept of the speech community as a 'non-political collective
agency' and, hence, ultimate arbiter in matters orthographic. Secondly,
the reform was in any case intended to act as a blueprint for orthographic
practices within the wider speech community. This further bolstered the
need to invoke the speech community as 'popular collective' in order to
uphold state involvement in the regulatory process. Moreover, it is at this
juncture that we see how the views of the judges melded on one level
with those of the opponents, the latter having similarly invoked the idea
of the apolitical collective, not least, via their citizens' initiative 'WE [the
people] against the spelling reform' or '*WIR gegen die Rechtschreibreform*'.

However, it was not only the complainants and the judges who drew
on this notion of speech community agency but also the linguists
behind the reform. Following the 1998 ruling of the Constitutional
Court, for example, the long-term reformer and Chair of the International
Commission for German Orthography, Gerhard Augst, noted how:

> The official orthography is compulsory for schools and state authorities
> only. In all other circumstances people are free to write as they please,
> and as they think they will be understood. [...] The Federal Consti-
> tutional Court has noted with absolute clarity that anyone who con-
> tinues to use the old orthography will not be considered to be writing
> incorrectly, but in the 'traditional' way. (Augst, 1998: 3–4)[1]

This would appear to run counter to the idea of the reform as a model for
speech community usage more widely, as declared in Article 2 of the
Vienna Declaration:

> The [International] Commission [for German Orthography] will work
> with the aim of securing a unified orthography in the German-speaking
> areas. It will accompany the introduction of the new guidelines and
> monitor the future development of the language. Where necessary, it
> will formulate suggestions for the adaptation of the regulations.[2]

While these aims might appear irreconcilable, in a technical–legal sense
they are not. Thus whereas the right is claimed for the state to directly
involve itself in the standardisation of orthography in relation to

schools and official authorities, agency is none the less accorded to the *speech community,* which can ultimately choose whether or not to accept the new norms. In this sense, 'the people', as a non-political collective, are once again invoked as the arbiters of the overall success or failure of the regulatory process. Using the example of the relaxation of certain comma rules, Augst notes how the Mannheim-based Commission will simply have to wait and see to what extent the new rules are acknowledged within the wider community:

> There can be no talk of compulsion. Schools will put into practice the revised rules of Germany orthography but will subsequently delete from the syllabus that which is not accepted by the speech community. This was also the case after the decree of 1902. (Augst, 1998: 4)[3]

On one level, Augst's claim holds true. This is insofar as the Commission is implicitly committed to 'taking into account' speech community practices and values when deliberating upon possible further modifications to the 1996 standard. As such, one can feasibly imagine situations where certain areas of the guidelines will be re-considered, and *possibly* even repealed, should they fail to be adopted by the wider speech community.[4] A key site of such community agency could well be those sectors of the press and various publishing houses who have forged their own 'house styles' (and, not least, manufacturers of computer software such as spell-checkers). As we saw in Chapter 3, such styles occasionally run counter to the 1996 recommendations, notably in those areas of the guidelines characterised by optional variability such as foreign loans, punctuation, hyphenation, and syllabification/word division at the end of lines (Rivers & Young, 2001).

Where *schools* are concerned, however, the feasibility of Augst's claim is less apparent. This is because the 1996 guidelines comprise the (minimum) standard according to which pupils' work will be formally evaluated. In a specifically educational context, the extent to which speech community usage will be able to function as a 'corrective' to the 1996 guidelines is therefore questionable. What Augst's claim downplays is the coercive power of the education system to enforce the new guidelines given the role of schools as the long arm of the state in matters orthographic – as opposed to merely representative of (speech) community interests. Thus, teachers (and, in many cases, their pupils) may well feel that certain orthographic revisions do not make good sense, perhaps, for example, because they have failed to improve pedagogic and/or communicative efficiency.[5] However, even allowing for the inevitably imperfect internalisation of the new external norm on the part of teachers themselves, the supreme authority of the state in matters educational will severely constrain any agency that such teachers (or their pupils) might have in this regard – a constraint shored up by the state-sanctioned use in the classroom of only those dictionaries that have been revised according to the new guidelines. Besides, as Rivers and Young (2001: 177) have highlighted, while the location of orthographic authority was certainly at the crux of the dispute surrounding the reform, one thing made clear by the Federal Constitutional Court in its 1998 ruling was that such authority did *not* lie with schools (see also Bärnthaler, 2000).

We see then how the linguists, just like the opponents and the judges of the Constitutional Court, placed considerable emphasis on the views of the *speech community* with regard to the acceptability of the 1996 guidelines. Indeed, a central purpose of the reform, from the linguists' point of view, was that of improving the overall efficiency of German orthography for members of that community. Yet the linguists, literally as servants of the state, were inevitably caught up in the same legitimation paradox as the judges. Given that the German Basic Law afforded linguists no *a priori* constitutional right to participate in the regulation of German orthography, this group was similarly obliged to appeal to the authority of 'the people' as the ultimate arbiter of state action. This, in turn, presupposed the invocation of the speech community as characterised by a shared competence not only at a strictly *communicative* level, that is, knowledge of standard orthographic norms with a view to correct usage. It also assumed some level of agreement *vis à vis* the '*organisation* and *interpretation* of sociolinguistic norms', that is, the ways in which those norms are collectively evaluated (Patrick, 2001: 580, my emphasis). And this came remarkably close to the notion of *cultural* competence characteristic of the opponents' view of language as highlighted in Chapter 5.

Once again, therefore, the question arises as to why the linguists should have attempted to appeal to a sense of *cultural* competence on the part of the speech community, while having underpinned the reform with a linguistic–theoretical paradigm that so explicitly marginalised all notion of 'culture' (Nerius, 2000a). The answer, I believe, lies in the way in which the linguists, as representatives of the state, were not only caught up in a legitimation paradox *vis à vis* the speech community. Their actions were simultaneously bounded by the need for legitimation with regard to their own academic community (Johnson, 2001a). Given the dominance of the autonomous, structuralist approach to language study within mainstream linguistics in Germany (as in much of Western academe), peer disapproval of the reform was inevitable for two main reasons. First, as we saw in Chapter 3, structuralism is itself grounded in a view of the primacy of speech that traditionally failed to recognise written language, let alone orthography, as a legitimate object of linguistic enquiry. Secondly, the descriptivist stance underpinning structuralism renders its advocates necessarily sceptical of the explicitly *pre*scriptivist nature of a reform such as this. Against this backdrop, we might see the linguistic–theoretical grounding of the 1996 reform as part of an overall attempt to bestow credibility upon the reform *vis à vis* an academic community of practice that would be (understandably) disinclined to associate itself with a formal policy of telling people how to spell.[6]

It might be argued that the price to be paid for an unwillingness and/or inability to engage on a theoretical level with the social, cultural, and political dimensions of such a hugely ambitious undertaking as the 1996 reform has become clear in the course of this book. Yet this would constitute an over-simplification of the dispute. This is because the protests could not, I believe, have been circumvented via the mere 'bolting-on' of a more explicitly *socio*linguistic dimension to the planning and implementation process. Moreover, such a potential theoretical shortcoming is by no means limited to the example of the German reform. As Dennis Ager has noted in the context of the difficulties surrounding the implementation of orthographic reform in France in the late 1980s and early 1990s:

> [...] the negotiation inside the advisory groups [...] had clearly not taken sufficient account of the warnings, nor of the previous history of attempts at reform, nor had it realised that formal consultation of such groups as publishers and proofreaders needed to go farther than meetings of their leaders and representative committees. Nor, indeed, had it anticipated the political connotations of reform and the strength of the opposition of traditionalists and conservatives to what could be – and was – interpreted as an attack on the fabric of (traditional) society and the identity of France. It looks very much as though the advisory group assumed that *the logic of reform and the authority of its collective view* would be sufficiently persuasive to enable the reform to go ahead, and that if the policy community was agreed then the policy would be successful. (Ager, 1996: 125, my emphasis)

What the French, German, and many other disputes over the creation and revision of standard orthographies highlight is the latter-day sociolinguistic truism, already noted in Chapter 5, that questions of *corpus* planning can never be entirely separated from those of *status* planning (see, *inter alia*, Bird, 2001; Eira, 1998; Schieffelin & Doucet, 1994). This is not simply because issues of corpus planning are likely to be 'of consequence' for social actors in the 'real world', but because such linguistic engineering is from the very outset geared towards modifying the behaviour of such actors (Blommaert, 1996; Cooper, 1989; Tollefson, 1991). In this sense, *all* instances of language planning and/or policy are part of a broader social agenda that Susan Gal and Kathryn Woolard (2001b: 8) refer to as the 'strategic recontextualisation' of publics. In other words, the semiotic properties of language (here: spelling and punctuation) are specifically invoked within the planning process in ways that will help to 'create images of continuity (and discontinuity) with times, places, and people not present in the immediate interaction' (Gal & Woolard, 2001b: 8).

Notwithstanding, the motives on the part of language planners might be well intentioned in a liberal sense, as I believe they were in the case of the 1996 reform. This was insofar as the reform was characterised, on one level, by an attempt to invoke a degree of *dis*continuity in matters orthographic via a reconfiguration of the privileges traditionally accorded to those with a high level of competence in standard orthography. That said, in practice, the reform served only to exacerbate orthographic 'insecurity' within the education system as well as the wider speech community, as opposed to reducing the significance traditionally attached to notions of correctness. Either way, once we acknowledge the explicitly social motivation of an act of language planning such as this, it becomes clear how any attempt to frame such an act within an autonomous, asocial view of orthography is likely to be misplaced. This, in turn, presupposes the need for a rather different approach to the organisation and implementation of the reform process, that is, one that *formally* acknowledged language users as individuals and groups whose concerns must be explicitly addressed. How this might be achieved and on what basis, however, is subject to differing interpretations.

The Reform, Public Relations, and Knowledge Transfer

From the point of view of the reformer and one-time member of the International Commission for German Orthography, Hans-Werner Eroms (1997: 56), the most immediate lesson to be learned from the 1996 reform is that more attention should have been paid to the question of *publicity*. Given the historical difficulties surrounding the standardisation and *re*-standardisation of German orthography, there was clearly a need for a sustained campaign of public relations (PR) with a view to communicating to the wider public the overall necessity, content, value, and purpose of the reform. In this sense, as Eroms (1997: 56) notes, the reform might usefully be compared to another example of 'change man-agement' in post-unification Germany: the introduction of a common system of postal codes in eastern and western Germany in the early 1990s.[7] As with the spelling reform, such changes were characterised by a form of structural intervention with an ostensibly minimal impact on everyday practice. Given, however, the semiotic dimension of post codes as indices of a cultural/geographical sense of rootedness, the poten-tial for popular protest and/or non-compliance was equally prescient. However, while the introduction of the new post codes was preceded by a formidable campaign of publicity and passed relatively smoothly (all German households received leaflets outlining the details and purpose of the changes), as Eroms highlights (1997: 56), this compared noticeably with the lack of any concerted effort to persuade the wider public of the need for orthographic reform (see also Munske, 1997c: 289). While the reformer Klaus Heller similarly concedes the lack of pub-licity to have been an overall weakness of the implementation process, he points out how there was neither sufficient time nor means with which to undertake the necessary PR work (see Heller in Lønnum, 2003: 51). Yet leaving aside the question of the adequacy of the public consultation process *prior* to the reform, one thing remains clear: it was unwise to effec-tively devolve the task of PR to the media, large sectors of which were from the outset seemingly hostile to the very concept of orthographic re-standardisation (e.g. Ledig, 1999; Zabel, 1989, 1996, 1997a).[8]

Although it is not within the scope of this book to explore in detail the role played by the media in the reform debate overall, it is feasible to suggest that more could have been done on the part of the reformers in order to facilitate the implementation process. This is one conclusion reached by Oliver Stenschke (2002) in his in-depth survey of the reform's coverage in a purpose-built corpus of print media texts.[9] Using a discourse–analytical approach to the study of such texts, Stenschke (2002: 285–88) shows how the media's representation of the reform was 'distorted' in two main ways. On the one hand, the process of *selectivity* was partial insofar as there was a disproportionate emphasis on individ-ual cases of sound–letter correspondences such as the use of umlaut, the digraph <ss>, and foreign loans. These sub-areas of the reform were then repeatedly indexed with recourse to a small set of key examples such as *belämmert* (miserable/awful), *dass* (that) and *Spagetti* (see also Kohrt, 1997: 310–11). In this way, the reform was essentially reduced, via a process of iconisation (Irvine & Gal, 2000), to a cluster of seemingly trivial lexical items that acquired a *pars pro toto* function with regard to the reform (Stenschke, 2002: 293–94). Such selectivity then combined with the recurrent use of a number of fixed phrases that shored up what Stenschke sees as the second main characteristic of print media discourse on the reform, namely its *emotionalism*. This was insofar as the changes were repeatedly dismissed as, in the words of the former Federal President, 'about as much use as a hole in the head' (*überflüssig wie ein Kropf*), while protests against the reform were typically construed as a 'crusade' (*Glaubenskrieg*). Here we encounter, however, the contradiction inherent in so much popular discourse on language: the trivialisation of language-related issues, on the one hand, a process that is none the less diametrically opposed to the intensity and vehemence of concern, on the other (Cameron, 1995).

Approaching the reform's media representation as an example of 'knowledge transfer' (*Wissenstransfer*),[10] it is Stenschke's contention that the linguists involved might have done more to circumvent the inherent potential for *mis*representation and/or distortion of the reform's content and purpose. Given, for example, that the main text drawn upon in most media commentaries was the 1994 version of Klaus Heller's reform summary in the journal *Sprachreport*, one practical suggestion is that greater attention might have been paid to the selection of examples within that text, given that these would quickly emerge as keywords within media discourse on the reform (Stenschke, 2002: 295–97). At the same time, however, it is not entirely clear to what extent considerations of PR could genuinely have brought about a shift in perspective on the part of a media that, as Stenschke (2002: 298–99) acknowledges, is informed by rather different agendas to those of language experts (see also Heller, 1999: 80–81). This is insofar as the print media, for example, are inescapably driven by the economic prerogative to sell newspapers, not least in the so-called *Sommerloch* or 'silly season', that is, the period of parliamentary recess during the summer months where 'hard' news stories tend to be thin on the ground and where spelling reform stories typically flourished (see also Jansen-Tang, 1988; Küppers, 1984; Ledig, 1999; Zabel, 1989, 1996, 1997a). Added to this, one should not underestimate the extent to which the hard-won expertise of journalists as language professionals in their own right was potentially undermined by the 'new' orthography. As Stenschke (2002: 296–97) concludes, discourses of orthographic reform could hardly be expected to conform to the Habermasian ideal of the media as a site of rational debate, characterised by mutual respect and tolerance, eventually resulting in an enlightened public consensus. In many cases, such discourses might even appear to demonstrate precisely the opposite: the inherent instrumentalisation of the reform on the part of large sectors of the media with the underlying aim of generating disinformation and dissent *vis à vis* the new guidelines.

As noted in Chapter 1, there is much that can be learned in this regard from analogous debates on public understandings of *science* and, in particular, the role of the media in the representation and construction of scientific expertise as problematised within the field of Science Studies (see also Johnson, 2001a). As Alan Irwin and Brian Wynne (1996), for example, have argued in their seminal volume *Misunderstanding Science?*, mainstream views of the so-called transfer of scientific knowledge were for many years similarly framed in terms of a deficit model of public expertise. For this reason, public ignorance of scientific endeavour was to be combated primarily via the delivery of an increased volume of expert information in forms that were felt to be more widely accessible to the lay public. This was an approach that was itself rooted in a canonical sender–receiver model of communication based on a linear process of information exchange, according to which messages flow unidirectionally from one social actor to another (Scollon, 1998: 149–52). It is a view that presupposes, moreover, the *a priori* existence of objective scientific facts – a monopoly on which is held by experts – that can then be relayed accurately (or inaccurately) by mediating institutions to the intended recipients, that is, a non-expert public.

However, as Ian Hargreaves (2000) has argued on the basis of in-depth analyses of media debates in the UK over, *inter alia*, 'mad cow disease' (BSE) and the production of genetically modified foodstuffs, while accessible information is clearly an important component of public understandings of science, a more fruitful approach to the question of knowledge transfer presupposes a shift away from the idea of an uncontested expert 'truth' to be communicated to a single, non-expert public. While by no means refuting the potential for empirically verifiable, scientific truths *per se*, what is needed instead, Hargreaves suggests, is an exploration of the processes whereby a multiplicity of *competing* truth claims are generated and mediated on both sides of the expert–lay divide. This is partly because the sheer volume of information available in the multimedia age, together with the manifold opportunities for its (re-)production and dissemination, mean that more than ever before knowledge producers are unable to guarantee the reception of information in a pre-intended manner to previously specified publics, or even its reception *per se*. Moreover, public understandings of science need to be set against the more general backdrop of the increased expression of scientific scepticism on the part of such publics that is itself widely considered to be a key feature of late modernity (e.g. Beck, 1992, 1994, 1995, 1997; Giddens, 1991;

Wynne, 1996a,b). To sum up: what has to be acknowledged is not only the inherent ability of the general public, but ultimately its democratic *right*, to question the expert knowledge with which it is presented. In this sense, an increase in the volume and/or 'quality' of information available in the public domain is, in itself, no guarantor of either an enhanced understanding of scientific endeavour on the part of the lay public, nor of a greater acceptance thereof.

Acknowledgement of the potential validity of public scepticism towards scientific endeavour inevitably demands of experts a reflexive stance with regard to their own role as knowledge producers. Rather than present the fruits of their endeavours as the product of disinterested scientific processes that are then *mis*represented and/or *mis*understood (not least by the media), it is widely argued within Science Studies that experts must themselves address the potential for critical reflexivity on the part of the public and its mediating institutions (e.g. Irwin & Wynne, 1996; Hargreaves, 2000). In this sense we are back to the idea of the 'pursuit of symmetry' raised in Chapter 1. Here the aim of critical research is to avoid the facile dismissal of lay understandings of science as inherently irrational, in favour of an exploration of the moral and epistemological conflicts in which competing truth claims are themselves embedded. And in the context of the debate over the 1996 reform of German orthography, this shift in perspective has the following concrete implications, not only for the way in which the changes were purportedly *mis*represented by the media, but also for an understanding of the reform debate *per se*.

To begin, it is doubtful whether there is much to be gained from the lamentations of many linguists (however justified) regarding the purported lack of meta-linguistic awareness on the part of the lay public exemplified in the course of the reform debate. For Rudolf Hoberg (1997), a member of the International Commission, for example, such knowledge deficit was manifest not least in the widespread inability on the part of 'lay' language users (including many politicians, writers, and journalists) to disentangle issues of orthography, specifically, from written language, language *per se*, culture, and even national identity, more generally (see also Langer, 2000). This was a deficit that went hand in hand, it was proposed, with a general tendency to conflate the expressive and reflexive dimensions of language, that is, to confuse the ability to *use* language (however, competently), on the one hand, with a scientific understanding *of* language, on the other. What Klaus Heller (1999: 79) similarly refers to as lay users' 'linguistic semi-literacy' (*linguistische Halbbildung*) has many possible origins. In Hoberg's view, these include, not least, the overall failure of the education system to achieve greater public enlightenment in matters linguistic, without which there could be little chance of securing a rational and objective debate over the reform. However, until such time as such enlightenment was forth-coming, or at least until the lay public had made at least some effort to comprehend the issues at hand, it was Hoberg's contention that non-experts (who, as he paradoxically acknowledged, have no means with which to be aware of their own ignorance) should quite simply have refrained from articulating their views (Hoberg, 1997: 98–99).

Of course, this immediately raises the question of what constitutes a 'proper' understanding of language and/or orthography in the eyes of expert linguists. By implication, such an understanding is one based on a scientific view of orthography, that is, one that systematically distinguishes between (1) the diachronic and the synchronic levels of analysis, (2) factors that are internal and external to the language system, and (3) the various internal levels of linguistic analysis – in sum: an autonomous, structuralist view. Only within this framework is it seemingly possible to disentangle the disparate levels of language analysis, thereby avoiding the *subjective* conflation of matters that are *objectively* distinct.

Yet if the public debates over the 1996 reform of German orthography illustrate just one thing, it is that, in the 'real world', language phenomena are not always compartmentalised in the manner demanded by many experts. On the contrary, nonlinguists' views are much more likely to be characterised by an *holistic* approach to language, that is, one where speech, writing, language, culture, and even national identity, are con-flated within the discursive complex that, in its totality, comprises language (see also Aitchison, 1997; Antos, 1996; Bauer & Trudgill, 1998; Cameron, 1995; Heller, 1999; Niedzielski & Preston, 2000). As Gunther Kress (2000: ix–x) reminds us: 'language has, throughout the history of human kind, furnished potent metaphors for social and political life, and spelling is, in this regard, the quintessence of language. [. . .] Spelling is that bit of linguistic practice where issues of authority, of control, of conformity can be most sharply focused'. Seen in this way, any attempt to re-configure orthography, however ostensibly minimal, is always liable to be perceived as more than a mere technical adjustment of the arbitrary semiotic relationship between phonemes/morphemes, on the one hand, and graphemes, on the other. Such attempts are *indeed* symbolic attacks on the written language, the language as a whole and, by extension, the fabric of German cultural, historical, and even political tradition. To dismiss such suggestions as redolent of a theoretically deficient, 'lay' approach to language is perfectly possible, indeed, from an autonomous linguistic perspective, entirely accurate. But to do so amounts to an abject failure to grasp what was so inherently objectionable about the re-standardisation process from the perspective of its opponents. Nor does it help us to begin to understand, *as linguists*, why otherwise highly educated and articulate individuals might genuinely consider the reform to constitute a breach of their fundamental freedoms as guaranteed by the German Basic Law.[11]

Notwithstanding, the prospect that oppositional voices in the reform debate might be accorded validity, or that a rejection of the re-standardisation process might itself constitute a legitimate standpoint, would not appear to have been on the linguists' discursive agenda (see, *inter alia*, Augst, 1998; Augst & Schaeder, 1997b). It is in this context that we see how the expert–lay divide itself functioned as a means with which to banish from the discursive arena those participants who were either unable, or *unwilling*, to enter into the debate over orthography within the parameters set by the experts. Seen in these terms, moreover, it becomes clear how expert calls for a 'rational' debate on orthographic reform leading to an 'enlightened' public consensus amounted, in practice, to little more than a scenario whereby the expert view was itself to be authoritatively entextualised. And it was in this context that opposition to the reform was routinely dismissed under the epithet of *emotionalism*, the very antithesis of the rationality that is itself axiomatic to the modernist project of language standardisation.[12]

Competing Discourses of Orthography

Rather than posit the disputes surrounding the 1996 reform in terms of the opposing poles of rationalism and emotionalism, a potentially more fruitful approach would be to see the various groups of ideological brokers as drawing on, and/or re-producing, competing *discourses* of orthography. This is an approach adopted by Christina Eira (1998) in her analysis of the selection of an orthographic system for Hmong, a language spoken by descendants of Chinese migrants, in Coolaroo, near Melbourne, Australia (see also Stebbins, 2001). In this work, Eira (1998: 172–73) proposes how, when trying to unravel the complex disputes that typically ensue in debates over the creation and/or revision of orthographic systems, it can be useful to explore the manner in which social actors draw upon disparate discourses as competing *sites of authority*. Working with a concept of discourse as 'an underlying set of cultural belief frameworks', she then argues how 'the basis for orthography selection is fundamentally a question of the location of authority, which is in turn a function of the prevailing discourse' (Eira, 1998: 172). Accordingly, disputes over orthography can to a considerable extent be explained in terms of 'disagreement on discourse allegiance', whereby she sketches a number of potential discourses as follows.

(1)   The **Scientific Discourse** is the one that is traditionally drawn upon by professional linguists working on orthography selection and revision, and is characterised by an overriding concern with the representation of sound and/or meaning. Within this discourse, the optimal writing system is typically posited as one characterised by phoneme–grapheme correspondence and/or the systematic representation of morphemes (see also Stebbins, 2001: 186–87). As we have seen in the debate over German, and as Eira (1998: 176) herself notes: 'whether or not one can propose principles for a linguistically optimal writing system, it does not at all follow that linguistic efficacy is the only or the most significant factor in the creation of orthography, defined as the accepted standard for writer/readers of the language'. That said, the Scientific Discourse has traditionally enjoyed a privileged and dominant status in Western academic debates over orthography, a status that, as Eira notes (1998: 177), has typically masked its nature as *discourse*, thereby allowing (or even encouraging) its exponents 'to pass off any motivation other than the scientific as "superstitious" or "unenlightened"'.

(2)   The **Political Discourse** is rooted in the principle whereby the social inclusion and exclusion of individuals and groups are symbolically embedded in orthographic practices and values in such a way that national and/or cultural boundaries are constructed and/or maintained (see also Stebbins, 2001: 187–89). Here Eira (1998: 177) points out how orthographies come to 'symbolise the validity or supremacy of the relevant cultural group [whose] usage must therefore reflect the nationalist/culturalist position at hand.' For example, while the Chinese character script serves the crucial purpose of unifying a number of otherwise diverse language communities, both British and American users of English can often be seen fiercely defending the small number of differences between their respective orthographies as indices of their own, arguably superior, cultural identities. As Eira (1998: 178) concludes: 'Unification and differentiation, assimilation and repression, language/culture maintenance, and official recognition are all functions of the Political Discourse,

and therefore have ramifications for ensuring lasting relevance of an orthography for a given language/culture group.'

(3) The **Historical Discourse**, according to Eira (1998: 175), typically manifests itself as a conservative, perhaps even nativist, movement dedicated to the resistance of change, and is therefore likely to be of greater relevance in debates over the *revision* as opposed to *selection* of orthographic systems. Within this discourse considerable emphasis is placed on the cultural continuity of the language with a concomitant concern for historical, visual and aesthetic factors as embodied, not least, in the literary heritage. In this regard, there may be an overlap with the **Religious Discourse**, whereby orthographies and/or writing scripts have over time been 'endowed with sacred status', not least in view of the traditional links between the use of a given script (especially the Roman alphabet) and canonical renderings of the Bible (Eira, 1998: 178). However, in the case of highly standardised languages, the perception of a 'spiritual' relationship between not only the original content but also the *form* of sacred works may be so thoroughly naturalised that a deity is no longer called upon as the source of legitimation. Here, Eira notes how 'the *status quo* of the orthography may be regarded as sacred, i.e. as something in which change is perceivable only as degradation' (1998: 180, my emphasis).

(4) The **Pedagogical Discourse** revolves primarily around a concern for the ease with which a given orthography can be acquired by potential learners, and as such may be linked to debates over literacy more generally. As Tonya Stebbins (2001: 184–85) explains in the context of her study of Sm'algyax, the endangered language of the Tsimshian Nation in British Columbia, Canada, exponents of this discourse, typically teachers, tend to view the consistency and uniformity of orthographies as a pre-condition for ease of acquisition. In this sense there are overlapping concerns with the Scientific and Historical Discourses, although there may be less emphasis on phoneme–grapheme equivalence as the key to systematicity together with a general hostility towards variant spellings, which are widely considered a burden to learners.

This taxonomy of the potential discourses that may be invoked by participants in debates over orthography is by no means exhaustive. Eira (1998: 175) herself refers further to a **Technological Discourse**, according to which the efficacy of an orthography in the context of global electronic communication may be foreground in conjunction with the more general pursuit of linguistic and/or political modernity. Meanwhile, Stebbins (2001: 189–90) identifies a so-called **Community Discourse** where the cultural values of a community (as opposed to a nation) are inscribed in orthographic practices and values. Moreover, as Eira (1998: 175) notes: 'in real-world circumstances, these fields are never neatly separate, but occur in layers and hierarchies which reflect the belief system structure of the culture(s) concerned.' In this sense, it is not simply the case that different groups of social actors draw exclusively on disparate discourses, what is of interest is the way in which such discourses are variously assembled by those groups when presenting a case for, or against, a particular orthography.

Eira's notion of competing discourses as sites of *authority* in disputes over orthography melds well with Blommaert's (1999) concept of a language ideological debate together with Hargreaves' (2000) vision of competing truth claims within debates over the public understanding of science. In this sense, while it is clear that social actors are differently positioned in terms of the power to secure the normalisation of their par-ticular viewpoints, the notion of competing discourses allows us to explore the possibility that disparate groups of ideological brokers may in fact be *differently rationalising* the question of orthography. It is an approach that would appear to account well for the disputes over German described throughout this book. To simplify, we might see the reformers as drawing on (and re-producing) a Scientific Discourse of orthography. Meanwhile, the opponents' arguments were primarily couched in terms of an Historical Discourse with its emphasis on ortho-graphy as a symbol of cultural continuity, combined with the secular dimensions of the Religious Discourse according to which the written language is viewed as sacred and immutable. But as Eira (1998: 174) emphasises, it is not only an allegiance to *conflicting* discourses that can account for disputes over orthography. A further source of disagreement can be the manner in which social actors might draw upon the *same basic discourse* albeit in different ways. And it is in relation to the Political Dis-course, with its focus on the unificatory and disciplinary functions of orthography, that we encounter some of the more complex dimensions of the debate over German orthographic reform.

At this juncture it is useful to return to the stated aim of the reform as articulated in the 1996 guidelines in full:

[...] to regulate spelling within those institutions (schools, official authorities) for which the state has jurisdiction with regard to orthogra-phy [*sic*]. In addition, the guidelines will function as a model, thereby securing a unified orthography, for all those who wish to orientate themselves toward an orthography with general validity (i.e. businesses, especially printers, publishers, editorial boards – but also private individuals). The new rules replace those of 1902 and all subsequent modifications.

The new guidelines are based on the following principles:

- An attempt to achieve a modest simplification of orthographic content with the aim of removing a series of exceptions, thereby extending the validity of the basic rules.
- A commitment to a re-formulation of the rules according to a unified concept [of orthography].[13]

(*Deutsche Rechtschreibung*, 1996: 10).

Here we encounter a commitment on the part of the reformers to the *unificatory* function of the Political Discourse in relation to German orthography. And, as we have seen throughout, from the perspective of the linguists such unity was optimally indexed via the kind of *linguistic* systematicity that could be achieved with recourse to the Scientific Discourse. Undoubtedly, the maintenance of orthographic coherence was one that was shared by the reform's opponents. However, their protest was fuelled largely by a concern that it was the re-standardisation process *itself* that posed a threat to such unity. A further difference was that whereas the opponents' concept of unity was allied to an Historical Discourse that explicitly foregrounded the historical, visual and aesthetic dimensions of German orthography, these were the very factors formally excluded by the Scientific Discourse of the linguists (Nerius, 2000a).

These competing rationalisations of the unificatory function of the Political Discourse have, in turn, repercussions for its *disciplinary* dimension. Here orthographic practices and values function as a symbolic means of constructing and maintaining not only in-/out-group boundaries *vis à vis horizontal* social relations. They also help to consolidate such boundaries in relation to *vertical* social relations, a function that is then especially closely tied to the Pedagogical Discourse. Thus whereas the reformers saw the re-standardisation process to some extent as a means of re-configuring the vertical social relations typically indexed by orthographic practices, their opponents were primarily concerned with the maintenance of the extant social order. Moreover, the linguists viewed the reform as an opportunity to enhance the pedagogic efficacy of what they knew to be an *arbitrary* standard, optimal access to which is afforded to users of the written language by means of a re-standardisation process justified in terms of the internal logic of the language system itself. This compared to the opponents, who were not only concerned that the reform failed to achieve its basic aim of improving the teachability and learnability of German orthography. For them, the standard was not arbitrary, but a *minimum* standard that was itself the product of an historical–cultural tradition of writing to have evolved over many centuries. In this sense any re-configuration of the guidelines not only constituted a *lowering of* that standard – it implicitly threatened to relativise notions of correctness, thereby diminishing both the disciplinary and unificatory value of orthography for future generations of language users.

We see therefore how the reformers and their opponents differently interpreted the functions of the Political Discourse in relation to German orthography. However, it is not only the differences in their respective standpoints that are of interest here, but also the similarities. For what united the two groups throughout this dispute was their concomitant *marginalisation* of the political dimensions of the reform with recourse to the other discourses on which they drew as potential sites of authority. In other words, it was the Scientific Discourse, with its autonomous view of the orthographic system as structurally self-referential, that functioned for the linguists as a means of disaggregating the (re-)standardisation process from all notion of the polity. Meanwhile, for the opponents, it was the invocation of the Historical Discourse, with its emphasis on orthography as indexical of an organic culture and aesthetic, that was similarly invoked as a means of de-politicising their objections to the reform. In sum, while both groups subscribed (at least implicitly) to the functions of the Political Discourse, each attempted to legitimise its own particular standpoint via a process of *de*-politicisation that was underpinned by the other discourses upon which it drew. It was in this way that each of the two groups attempted to project itself as occupying the 'view from nowhere', thereby representing the interests, not of any particular group of social actors (least of all themselves), but of the *public at large*.[14]

In spite of their invocation of competing discourses of orthography, on the one hand, and/or disparate interpretations of the same basic discourse, on the other, it is crucial to note how none of the ideological brokers involved in the legal dispute was at any point *contesting* the need for a standard orthography *per se*, nor indeed the state's explicit involvement in that process. As such, we see how no group called into question the political instrumentalisation of orthography that was implicit in the (re-)standardisation project. This was insofar as no group challenged the underlying *unificatory* purpose of orthographic standardisation in relation to a much longer-term attempt on the part of the German state to modernise the language as an index of the purported homogeneity of its community of users (and dominance over users of the language elsewhere). Nor was the basic *disciplinary* function of a standard orthography questioned in any tangible way, such that even the revised guidelines of 1996 will continue to act as a means of benchmarking the educational achievement and/or intellectual standing of language users, not least that of school-pupils. Accordingly, we see how both of the two main groups of ideological brokers operated throughout this dispute within an overarching 'ideology of standardisation' (e.g. Lippi-Green, 1997: 53–62). And it was in this way that a standardised variant of German orthography was able to retain its status as a seemingly normal, natural and inevitable fact of language – a view, moreover, that was *re*-produced in the course of the legal dispute, not least with the help of the third group of ideological brokers, the judges of the Constitutional Court.

While the authority of the state in relation to German orthography was left firmly intact in the course of this dispute, we might none the less see the language ideological debate that ensued as a relatively predictable challenge to the *legitimacy* of that authority. It was in many ways 'predictable' because, as Blommaert (1999: 8) reminds us, in any situation where language is seized upon as a symbolic resource: 'What counts for power also counts for its results: conflict, inequality, injustice, oppression, or delicate and fragile status-quo.' In other words, the dispute can be viewed as a public re-articulation of the self-same social conflicts that are semiotically inscribed in the practices and values of the orthographic standard. And in this sense, we might see the dispute over the 1996 reform as a case of the state merely reaping the fruits of such conflicts, the seeds of which were sown when it first embarked on the formal codification of German orthography one hundred years earlier.

Concluding Remarks

We might, then, see the disputes surrounding the 1996 reform as a fairly inevitable, perhaps even democratic, challenge to the fragile status quo underpinning the orthographic standardisation process more generally. That said, it is worth returning, by way of conclusion, to the key question of how the organisation and implementation of the reform might have been differently handled.

In relation to the reform's publicity, it is certainly possible that some individuals and groups might have been more favourably disposed to the revised orthography had they been afforded a greater volume of accessible information on the changes to be implemented. Here, for example, the linguists might indeed have differently presented the *content* of the new guidelines with a view to alleviating the trivialisation and emotionalisation of media coverage as highlighted by Stenschke (2002). However, this presupposes not only a model of public enlightenment according to which the linguists, as knowledge producers, were able to retain control over the reform's re-presentation. It also assumes an ability to provide a convincing account of not just the content of the new guidelines, but also the key issues that remained so crucially unresolved throughout the legal dispute: the overall necessity, value and purpose of the reform. And here we encounter the central paradox surrounding the reform for, as the discussion throughout this book has highlighted, it appears that the very success of the implementation process depended to some extent on the need to *avoid* an explication of precisely those issues. However, this is hardly surprising, given that we encounter here the very essence of ideological actions, namely that they work best when remaining at the level of the *implicit*, thereby helping to shore up their status as common sense.

For this reason, it is difficult to see how the *explicit* articulation of the underlying political aims of orthographic (re-)standardisation could in practice have been squared with a process of legitimation that itself depended upon their *de*-politicisation. This relates not least to the use of decree as opposed to parliamentary law as a means of implementing the reform. For if we see the standardisation process as informed by the unificatory and disciplinary functions of a Political Discourse of orthography, then it is also possible to argue that the reform was indeed *fundamental* in the sense defined by the German Basic Law. This is insofar as the instrumentalisation of language inherent in any policy geared towards standardisation on the part of the state might well be construed as a breach of citizens' right to the very human dignity that is specifically enshrined in Article 1 of the German Basic Law, the *protection* of which is the 'duty of all state authority'. Seen in these (admittedly highly idealistic) terms, the reform might well have required the formal involvement of the democratic legislature, that is, a parliamentary law as opposed to an executive decree. So while it is crucial not to lose sight of the fact that the protests against the reform were voiced by a *minority* of German citizens only, we might reasonably speculate that a more visible and sustained campaign of publicity might even have resulted in a greater, rather than lesser degree, of public opposition . . .

Even allowing for the liberal motivations of the linguists behind the 1996 reform, we see how the re-standardisation process constituted a fairly typical example of what James Tollefson (1991) refers to as a 'neo-classical' approach to language planning. This is an approach where efforts are almost exclusively directed towards language structure and the individual language user in ways that largely 'insulate language planners from any evaluation which is "external" to the planning process' (Tollefson, 1991: 28). It is in this way that language planners are seemingly extricated from the need to pose the key moral questions underpinning the planning act, that is, not simply how the policy might be configured in linguistic terms, but the extent to which it might in fact be *appropriate* to the needs of language users. And an obvious context in which to consider the appropriateness of the 1996 reform would have been in relation to the teaching and learning of literacy more generally.

In 2000, Germany was one of 32 countries world-wide to participate in a longitudinal survey of educational performance among 15-year-old pupils, focussing on the three key areas of reading, mathematical, and scientific literacy (Baumert *et al.*, 2001). The report of the first cycle of PISA (Programme for International Student Assessment), published in 2002, sent shock waves through German society (Baumert *et al.*, 2002; Stanat *et al.*, 2002). For the results showed Germany's level of attainment in reading to be significantly below the international average, with the poor overall results attributable to the wide disparity in the performance of pupils from different social class backgrounds (Stanat *et al.*, 2002: 7–8). Of course, the findings of PISA came too late so as to provide a productive context in which to think about orthographic reform. Moreover, orthography is not co-terminous with literacy, low 'performance' in reading/writing has many (primarily social) causes, and students in Austria (which shares the same orthographic standard) fared considerably better than their German counterparts. However, quite apart from highlighting the hierarchical structure of the German school system relative to other participating countries (Stanat *et al.*, 2002: 13), the PISA report raised some interesting issues with regard to the teaching of reading and writing more generally. Especially noted was the finding that German pupils scored comparatively low on tasks requiring them to reflect on, and critically evaluate, written texts, faring better on information retrieval and textual interpretation (Stanat *et al.*, 2002: 15).

It is in this context that one cannot extricate the emphasis placed within the German educational system on the declarative knowledge associated with a standard orthography from the considerable attention devoted by the state to the formal codification of that standard. Of course, the German education system is not alone in the significance it attaches to correct spelling and punctuation. Moreover, there may even be democratic

advantages to the kind of explicit state-sanctioned codification of orthography characteristic of German insofar as all language users have at
least the possibility to inform themselves of its nature and content. But
as Gunter Kress has highlighted in his discussion of the teaching and
learning of spelling in the context of the broader challenges now facing
the education system in the UK:

> Whereas the former economic situation was marked by the stability of
> practices, of structures and of identities, this new situation is the antith-
> esis of all these, and is likely to be so for a considerable time to come. So,
> rather than the need to acquire stable skills and knowledges in the form
> of conventional speech and writing-based skills, what is now required
> is to develop skills and knowledges of an entirely flexible kind. The
> identities and personal dispositions that will be most highly valued,
> and most essential, will be those of flexibility, creativity and innovation.
> *This is the defining context in which to think about spelling and the teaching of
> spelling.* (2000: 13–14, my emphasis)

For Kress, it is in the context of the new information-based economies,
where computers can perform many of the mundane tasks in relation
to orthography, that one ought to be questioning the rigid emphasis
on conformity, convention and correctness. For while such values –
metaphorically inscribed in any language standard – may well have
fulfilled the needs of an earlier economic era, it remains doubtful that
they will continue to meet the demands of late-modern polities with
their overriding emphasis on contingency and creativity.

Kress is by no means dismissing the value of teaching young people
how to spell *per se* as part of an overall process of literacy acquisition.
Moreover, the instrumentalisation of orthography within education has
been questioned by pedagogues for many years now, forming, as we
saw in Chapter 2, a significant component of social and educational critiques in (West) Germany in the 1960s and 1970s. However, despite the
efforts of the reformers behind the 1996 guidelines to improve the communicative and pedagogic efficacy of German orthography with recourse
to a scientific approach to language structure, these were not ultimately
problems whose solutions were to be found in the internal logic of the
language system. On the contrary, the problems surrounding orthography have always been, and will continue to be, not simply questions of
language, but of language in relation to political, social and educational
problems. These are problems that require not only linguistic, but also
political, social and educational solutions.

One alternative to the 1996 reform, proposed by Elisabeth and Johann Leiss (1997), would have been to work towards the de-hegemonisation of standard orthography, not least by uncoupling the normification process from state intervention and returning to a scenario similar to that prior to 1901. However, as we have seen throughout, this so-called 'English way' itself rests on the problematic assumption of the speech community as a site of normification governed by regulatory social practices that are somehow less motivated by interest than those of the state. Ironically, perhaps, it is therefore the legal scholar whose theoretical arguments triggered the judicial dispute, who summarises what were arguably the most apposite solutions to the 'problem of orthography'. While exploring the overall necessity of the 1996 reform, Wolfgang Kopke (1995a: 315–24) considers three main alternatives to re-standardisation. The first would have involved the liberalisation of existing regulations, freeing up the state-approved orthography to include more acceptable variant spellings, without none the less abandoning extant forms. The second would have been to consider alternative methodologies for the teaching and learning of orthography, an approach traditionally favoured by pedagogues (e.g. Hinney, 1997). And, finally, possibly the simplest solution of all, would have been to re-consider the level of emphasis placed on correctness in spelling and punctuation within the education system, not least via a re-think of the testing procedures used to evaluate pupils' performance in the written language.

The need to give explicit consideration to these alternatives was, as we have seen throughout, central to the adequate resolution of the judicial dispute surrounding the 1996 reform. For if it could be demonstrated that any of these suggestions might have afforded the same, if not greater, benefits to pupils as the reform itself, then this might indeed have negated the necessity for a revised orthography. But leaving aside the fact that such alternatives might not in themselves have been entirely unproblematic, the crucial questions of the reform's overall necessity, purpose and value were to remain unresolved by the Constitutional Court. And this, perhaps, is symptomatic of the dispute surrounding the reform in general. For whether one sees the 'solution' to the 'problem' of German orthography as lying in its liberalisation, de-regulation, de-hegemonisation or otherwise, one thing is clear: the language ideological debate over the 1996 reform constituted a missed opportunity to re-think a number of important political, social and educational issues in relation to the spelling and punctuation of German. Only time will tell whether a further hundred years must elapse before that opportunity will present itself once more.

Notes

1. German original: 'Die amtlichen Rechtschreibregeln sind nur für Schulen und Behörden bindend. Sonst kann jeder schreiben, wie er will und wie er denkt, dass er verstanden wird. [...] Das Bundesverfassungsgericht hat mit aller Klarheit darauf hingewiesen: Wer noch die alte Rechtschreibung schreibt, schreibt nicht falsch, sondern "traditionell".'

2. German original: 'Die Kommission wirkt auf die Wahrung einer einheitlichen Rechtschreibung im deutschen Sprachraum hin. Sie begleitet die Einführung der Neuregelung und beobachtet die künftige Sprachentwicklung. Soweit erforderlich erarbeitet sie Vorschläge zur Anpassung des Regelwerks.'

3. German original: 'Von Zwang kann also keine Rede sein. Die Schule setzt die Neuregelung der deutschen Rechtschreibung in die Praxis um. Was aber die Schreibgemeinschaft nicht annimmt, wird die Schule wieder aus ihrem Lehrplan streichen. So war es auch nach dem Erlass von 1902.' (I would like to acknowledge the assembling of the three above quotations to Rob Neal, a student on the MA in Language Teaching at Lancaster University, 2002–2003, in an assignment written on language ideologies in relation to the 1996 reform.)

4. This again raises the question of the empirical verification of speech community usage that was central to the dispute. Moreover, as Eisenberg points out (in Lønnum, 2003: 63), the Commission itself has no formal mandate to modify the 1996 guidelines such that further changes would in any case be subject to political approval. Ironically, no mechanism for the achievement of such approval exists. For this reason, the 1996 reform has not entirely resolved the shortcomings of 1901 *vis à vis* the problem of ongoing orthographic change within the speech community.

5. On the basis of an empirical survey of teachers' responses to the reform following its introduction in 1998, Lüthgens (2002) shows how the key areas of dissatisfaction relate to the spelling of *daß/dass* and the retention of the grapheme <ß>, which many teachers wished to see abolished, thereby bringing Germany and Austria in line with Swiss usage. There is also a continued preference for the option of moderate minisculisation and a general concern about the lack of systematicity of the new rules, especially where optional variability is concerned.

6. See Eisenberg (2000) who, like many linguists, believes that the reform and its surrounding conflicts have considerably damaged the professional credibility of linguistics as a discipline in the German-speaking countries (see also interview with Eisenberg in Lønnum, 2003: 68).

7. A more recent comparison might even be Germany's adoption of the Euro in 1999.

8. See, however, Klaus Heller (1999: 79), who considers the discussions surrounding the 1996 reform on the part of the linguists to have been characterised more than ever before it by an awareness of the feasibility and acceptability of the proposals.

9. The corpus was built on a selection of 733 texts from *Der Spiegel*, *Focus*, and *Süddeutsche Zeitung* appearing between 1994 and 1999.

10. See, for example, Antos (1996), Munske, (1997c: 283–90), Niederhauser (1997, 1999), Stenschke (2001, 2002), Stenschke and Busch (2004), Wichter (1999) and Wichter and Stenschke (2004).

11. As Peter Eisenberg (2000: 120) argued following his own resignation from the International Commission for German Orthography in 1999: 'Even those linguists who have an understanding of their object of study as inherently apolitical, must have noticed throughout the many years of dispute surrounding the debate over orthography, that this was a question of both the science of linguistics **and** politics' (emphasis in original). [German original: 'Auch wer seine Wissenschaft als vollkommen unpolitisch versteht, muß doch in den vielen Jahren öffentlicher Orthographiedebatte gemerkt haben, daß Wissenschaft **und** Politik verhandelt wurde.' (bold in original).] For a more general discussion on the relationship between language criticism in the public domain and the discipline of linguistics more generally, see Lanthaler *et al.* (2003).

12. This does not, of course, exclude the potential for contestation on *scientific* grounds, hence the huge disputes among professional linguists themselves regarding the most appropriate format of the new guidelines.

13. German original: 'Das folgende amtliche Regelwerk [...] regelt die Rechtschreibung innerhalb derjenigen Institutionen (Schule, Verwaltung), für die der Staat Regelungskompetenz hinsichtlich der Rechtschreibung hat. Darüber hinaus hat es zur Sicherung einer einheitlichen Rechtschreibung Vorbildcharakter für alle, die sich an einer allgemein gültigen Rechtschreibung orientieren möchten (das heißt Firmen, speziell Druckereien, Verlage, Redaktionenen – aber auch Privatpersonen). Diese Regelung ersetzt jene von 1902 und alle anschließenden Ergänzungsverordnungen.

    Die neue Regelung ist folgenden Grundsätzen verpflichtet:

    • Sie bemüht sich um eine behutsame inhaltliche Vereinfachung der Rechtschreibung mit dem Ziel, eine Reihe von Ausnahmen und Besonderheiten abzuschaffen, so dass der Geltungsbereich der Grundregeln ausgedehnt wird.
    • Sie verfolgt eine Neuformulierung der Regeln nach einem einheitlichen Konzept.

14. Seen in these terms we can more readily account for the basic conflict that permeated the legal dispute described in Chapter 5: is orthographic unity optimally achieved 'top–down' (via the co-option of the Scientific Discourse on the part of the state) or 'bottom–up' (in accordance with an Historical Discourse invoked on the part of the community)? Here we might also see the opponents' arguments as simultaneously framed within what Stebbins (2001: 189–90) describes as a Community Discourse, whereby the cultural values of the purportedly non-political collective of 'the people' (as opposed to the nation) are to be inscribed within the standardisation process, itself underpinning a key tension that has permeated attempts to secure a *state-*sanctioned standardisation of orthography since the mid-19th century.

Bibliography

Legal sources

Bundesverfassungsgericht (21 June 1996) *BVerfG, 1 BvR 1057/96 – Rechtschreibreform. Beschluß der 3. Kammer des Ersten Senats.* On WWW at www.bundesverfassungsgericht/entscheidungen.

Bundesverfassungsgericht (30 December 1997) *1 BvR 2264/97* and *1 BvR 2368/ 97.* On WWW at www.bundesverfassungsgericht/entscheidungen.

Bundesverfassungsgericht (27 August 1997) *Pressemitteilung des Bundesverfassungsgerichts. No. 77/97. BVerfG: Verfassungsbeschwerde im Zusammenhang mit der Rechtschreibreform.*

Bundesverfassungsgericht (12 May 1998) *BVerfG, 1 BvR 1640/97 – Rechtschreibreform. Urteil des Ersten Senats vom 14. Juli 1998.* (Reprinted in *Entscheidungen des Bundesverfassungsgerichts. 98. Band* (1999) (pp. 218–64). Tübingen: J.C.B. Mohr. On WWW at http://www.bundesverfassungsgericht.de/entscheidungen.)

Bundesverfassungsgericht (20 July 1999) *1 BvQ 10/99.* On WWW at http:// www.bundesverfassungsgericht.de/entscheidungen.

Bundesverfassungsgericht (25 November 1999) *2 BvR 1958/99.* On WWW at http://www.bundesverfassungsgericht.de/entscheidungen.

Bundesverwaltungsgericht (24 March 1999) *BVerwG, C9/98, VR 2000.*

Bürgerliches Gesetzbuch (2000) Munich: dtv. 47th edition.

Gemeinsame Absichtserklärung zur Neuregelung der deutschen Rechtschreibung (1 July 1996) (Reprinted in G. Augst *et al.* (eds) 1997. *Zur Neuregelung der deutschen Orthographie. Begründung und Kritik* (p. 69). Tübingen: Niemeyer.)

Grundgesetz (1998) 35th edition. Munich: dtv.

Dictionaries and reference works

Bertelsmann (1996) Verfasst von Ursula Hermann. *Die neue deutsche Rechtschreibung.* Völlig neu bearbeitet und erweitert von Lutz Götze.

Mit einem Geleitwort von Klaus Heller. Gütersloh: Bertelsmann Lexikon Verlag.

Bertelsmann (1999) Verfasst von Ursula Hermann. *Die deutsche Rechtschreibung*. Völlig neu bearbeitet und erweitert von Lutz Götze. Mit einem Geleitwort von Klaus Heller. Gütersloh: Bertelsmann Lexikon Verlag.

de Saussure, F. (1915, [1959]) *Course in General Linguistics*. New York: McGraw Hill.

Deutsche Rechtschreibung (1996) *Regeln und Wörterverzeichnis. Text der amtlichen Regelung*. Tübingen: Gunter Narr Verlag.

Duden, K. (1880) *Vollständiges Orthographisches Wörterbuch der deutschen Sprache. Nach den neuen preußischen und bayrischen Regeln*. Leipzig.

Duden, K. (1902) *Vollständiges Orthographisches Wörterbuch der deutschen Sprache. Nach den für Deutschland, Österreich und die Schweiz gültigen amtlichen Regeln*. Leipzig.

Duden, K. (1907 [1903]) *Rechtschreibung der Buchdruckereien deutscher Sprache*, 2nd edition. Leipzig.

Duden (1915) *Rechtschreibung der deutschen Sprache und der Fremdwörter*, 11th edition. Leipzig.

Duden (1986) *Rechtschreibung der deutschen Sprache und der Fremdwörter*. Hrsg. von der Dudenredaktion. Auf der Grundlage der amtlichen Rechtschreibregeln. 19., neu bearbeitete und erweiterte Auflage. Mannheim, Vienna, Zürich: Bibliographisches Institut.

Duden (1991) *Rechtschreibung der deutschen Sprache*. Hrsg. von der Dudenredaktion. Auf der Grundlage der neuen amtlichen Rechtschreibregeln. 20., völlig neu bearbeitete und erweiterte Auflage. Mannheim: Dudenverlag.

Duden, K. and Sitta, H. (1994) *Informationen zur neuen deutschen Rechtschreibung. Nach den Beschlüssen der Wiener Orthographiekonferenz vom 22. bis 24. 11. 1994 für Deutschland, Österreich und die Schweiz*. Mannheim: Dudenverlag.

Duden (1996) *Rechtschreibung der deutschen Sprache*. Hrsg. von der Dudenredaktion. Auf der Grundlage der neuen amtlichen Rechtschreibregeln. 21., völlig neu bearbeitete und erweiterte Auflage. Mannheim: Dudenverlag.

Duden, K. and Scholze-Stubenrecht, W. (1999) *Duden. Das große Wörterbuch der deutschen Sprache*. Hrsg. vom Wissenschaftlichen Rat der Dudenredaktion. 3., völlig neu bearbeitete und erweiterte Auflage. Mannheim: Dudenverlag.

Duden (2000) *Die deutsche Rechtschreibung*. Hrsg. von der Dudenredaktion. Auf der Grundlage der neuen amtlichen Rechtschreibregeln. 22., völlig neu bearbeitete und erweiterte Auflage. Mannheim, Vienna, Zürich: Dudenverlag.

Protokoll (1901). [*Protokoll der*] *Beratungen über die Einheitlichkeit der deutschen Rechtschreibung.* Reprinted in D. Nerius and J. Scharnhorst (eds) (1980) *Theoretische Probleme der deutschen Orthographie* (pp. 330–50). Berlin.

Siebs, T. (1969) *Deutsche Aussprache. Reine und gemäßigte Hochlautung mit Aussprachewörterbuch*, 19th edition. Berlin.

Press releases

Bulletin der Bundesregierung (20 December 1955) No. 238, p. 2048.

Bundesverfassungsgericht (14 July 1998) Press release: BVerfG: Erfolglose Verfassungsbeschwerde gegen 'Rechtschreibreform'. No. 79/98.

Initiative WIR gegen die Rechtschreibreform (25 April 1997) Münchner Erklärung zur Rechtschreibreform. On WWW at http://staff-www. uni-marburg.de/rechtschreib.htm.

Institut für Deutsche Sprache (IDS) (9 November 1995) *Richtigstellungen zur Rechtschreibreform.*

Institut für Deutsche Sprache (IDS) (22 November 1995) *Korrekturen bei Beratungen zur Rechtschreibreform.*

Kultusministerkonferenz (KMK) (30 November 1995) *Beschluß zur Neuregelung der deutschen Rechtschreibung.*

Kultusministerkonferenz (KMK) (1 July 1996) *Präsident der Kultusminister-konferenz unterzeichnet 'Gemeinsame Absichtserklärung' von Vertretern aus den deutschsprachigen Staaten und Gemeinschaften zur Neuregelung der deutschen Rechtschreibung.*

Kultusministerkonferenz (KMK) (25 Oct 1996) *Dresdner Erklärung zur Neuregelung der deutschen Sprache.*

Kultusministerkonferenz (KMK) (31 July 1998) *Neuregelung der deutschen Rechtschreibung ab 1. August wirksam.* Präsidentin der Kultusminister-konferenz zur Einführung der Rechtschreibreform.

Kultusministerkonferenz (KMK) (25 September 1998) *Kein Stopp der neuen Rechtschreibung in den anderen Ländern.*

Ministerpräsidentenkonferenz (MPK) (14 December 1995) *Ergebnisproto-koll. Neuregelung der deutschen Rechtschreibung.*

WIR gegen die Rechtschreibreform (15 July 1998) *Zur Urteilsbegründung des Bundesverfassungsgerichtes über die Rechtschreibreform.*

WIR gegen die Rechtschreibreform (30 July 1998) *Zur Einführung der sog. Rechtschreibreform am 1. August 1998 – ein Appell an die Öffentlichkeit.*

WIR gegen die Rechtschreibreform (26 August 1998) Initiativen appellieren an Ministerpräsident und Kanzlerkandidat Gerhard Schröder.

Newspaper/magazine articles

Bertram, C. (8 August 1997) 'Nicht nur die Politik, auch die Gesellschaft ist reformunwillig – die neue deutsche Lethargie.' *Die Zeit.*

Bildzeitung (30 July 1997) 'Rechtschreibreform – jetzt ist das Chaos perfekt.'

BZ-Berlin (30 July 1997) 'Bildungsminister Rüttgers: Rechtschreibreform gescheitert!'

Christen, U.B. (28 September 1998) 'Zurück zu den alten Regeln. Schleswig-Holsteiner ändern das Schulgesetz.' *Lübecker Nachrichten.*

Ewald, R. (28 September 1998) 'Sonderweg bei Schreibreform.' *Die Welt.*

Focus (6 July 1998) 'Das Hin und Her um die Klage von Karlsruhe.' *Focus Online.* On WWW at www.focus.de.

Focus (4 August 1997) 'Auf dem Weg nach Karlsruhe.'

Guratzsch, D. (19 March 2002) 'Wir müssen manches zurücknehmen.' Interview: Die hessische Wissenschaftsministerin Ruth Wagner (FDP) hält die Rechtschreibreform für gescheitert und plädiert für eine Umkehr. *Die Welt.*

Hannoversche Allgemeine (22 June 2001) 'Ministerium siegt mit Rechtschreibreform.'

Hörzu (23 August 2002) 'Ein Quäntchen Katastrofe.'

Ickler, T. (25 July 2000) 'Die "wohl durchdachte" Reform stirbt. Die Rechtschreibreform kehrt stillschweigend zur alten Orthografie zurück.' *Die Welt.*

Martenstein, H. (20 October 1996) 'Meister der Kampagne.' *Der Tagesspiegel.*

Moench, R. (19 August 1996) 'Viele Schüler reagieren begeistert auf die Rechtschreibreform.' *Der Tagesspiegel.*

Munske, H.H. (19 March 2002) 'Scheitern oder weiterwursteln? Die Halbzeitbilanz der Rechtschreibreform.' *Frankfurter Allgemeine Zeitung.*

Nerius, D. (17/18 May 2003) 'Ein Reförmchen setzt sich durch.' *Ostsee-Zeitung.*

Rüthers, B. (23 December 2002) 'Willkür in den Worten: Die Rechtschreibreform und das Recht.' *Frankfurter Allgemeine Zeitung.*

Der Spiegel (19 June 1995) 'Packet, Rytmus, Tron? Günther Drosdowski über die Reform der Rechtschreibung.'

Der Spiegel (11 November 1995) 'Viele werden erschrecken: Interview mit Bayerns Kultusminister Hans Zehetmair über die Rechtschreibreform.'

Der Spiegel (14 October 1996) 'Der Aufstand der Dichter: Rettet die deutsche Sprache!'

Der Spiegel (4 August 1997) 'Die wollen durch die Wand.'

Der Spiegel (27 October 1997) 'Belämmerter Tollpatsch.'

Der Spiegel (5 October 1998) 'Ihr spinnt ja.'

Der Spiegel (2 August 1999) 'Hausmitteilung.'

Der Spiegel (27 May 2002) 'Mit den Eltern Klartext reden'.

Stock, U. (12 September 1997) 'fff: Ein Frontbericht aus dem Rechtschreibkrieg'. *Die Zeit.*

Der Tagesspiegel (21 October 1997) 'Niedersachsen setzt als erstes Bundesland Rechtschreibreform aus.'

Zemb, J.-M. (2 September 1995) 'Alles gleich ist alles anders.' *Frankfurter Allgemeine Zeitung.*

Zimmer, D.E. (29 September 1996) 'Rechtschreibung: Der Kampf Duden gegen Bertelsmann.' *Die Zeit.*

Secondary literature

(1997) Abschlusserklärung der 3. Wiener Gespräche zur Neuregelung der Deutschen Rechtschreibung Vom 22. bis zum 24.11.1994. In G. Augst, K. Blüml, D. Nerius and H. Sitta (eds) (1997). *Zur Neuregelung der deutschen Orthographie. Begründung und Kritik.* (p. 67). Tübingen: Niemeyer.

Ager, D. (1996) *Language Policy in Britain and France: The Processes of Policy.* London: Cassell.

Aitchison, J. (1997) *The Language Web: The Power and Problem of Words.* Cambridge: CUP.

Ammon, U. (1991) *Die Internationale Stellung der deutschen Sprache.* Berlin: de Gruyter.

Anderson, B. (1991 [1983]) *Imagined Communities: Reflections on the Origin and Spread of Nationalism.* London: Verso.

Androutsopoulos, J.K. (2000) Non-standard spellings in media texts: The case of German fanzines. *Journal of Sociolinguistics* 4(4), 514–33.

Antos, G. (1996) *Laien-Linguistik: Studien zu Sprach- und Kommunikationsproblemen im Alltag. Am Beispiel von Sprachratgebern und Kommunikationstrainings.* Tübingen: Niemeyer.

Apter, A. (1982) National language planning in plural societies: The search for a framework. *Language Problems and Language Planning* 6(3), 219–40.

Arendt, H. (1963 [1973]) *On Revolution.* London: Penguin.

Augst, G. (ed.) (1985) *Graphemik und Orthographie.* Frankfurt/M.: Peter Lang.

Augst, G. (ed.) (1986) *New Trends in Graphemics and Orthography.* Berlin: de Gruyter.

Augst, G. (1997a) Das Problem des Regelaufbaus und der Regeloperationalisierung am Beispiel der Großschreibung von Substantiven und Substantivierungen. In G. Augst, K. Blüml, D. Nerius and H. Sitta (eds) (1997). *Zur Neuregelung der deutschen Orthographie. Begründung und Kritik.* (pp. 379–96). Tübingen: Niemeyer.

Augst, G. (1997b) Die Worttrennung. In G. Augst, K. Blüml, D. Nerius and H. Sitta (eds) (1997). *Zur Neuregelung der deutschen Orthographie. Begründung und Kritik* (pp. 259–68). Tübingen: Niemeyer.

Augst, G. (1998) Die Gegner der Reform behaupten – Richtig ist... On WWW at http://www.ids-mannheim.de/reform/Diskussionsbeiträge_richtig.html.

Augst, G. and Schaeder, B. (1997a) Die Architektur des amtlichen Regelwerks. In G. Augst, K. Blüml, D. Nerius and H. Sitta (eds) (1997). *Zur Neuregelung der deutschen Orthographie. Begründung und Kritik.* (pp. 73–92). Tübingen: Niemeyer.

Augst, G. and Schaeder, B. (1997b) *Rechtschreibreform. Eine Antwort an die Kritiker.* Stuttgart: Klett.

Augst, G. and Stock, E. (1997) Laut-Buchstaben-Zuordnung. In G. Augst, K. Blüml, D. Nerius and H. Sitta (eds) (1997). *Zur Neuregelung der deutschen Orthographie. Begründung und Kritik* (pp. 113–34). Tübingen: Niemeyer.

Augst, G. and Strunk, H. (1988) Wie der Rechtschreibduden quasi amtlich wurde. *Muttersprache* 98, 329–44.

Augst, G. and Strunk, H. (1989) Dokumente zur Einführung der amtlichen Rechtschreibung in den deutschsprachigen Ländern 1901–1903. *Muttersprache* 99, 231–35.

Augst, G., Blüml, K., Nerius, D. and Sitta, H. (eds) (1997) *Zur Neuregelung der deutschen Orthographie. Begründung und Kritik.* Tübingen: Niemeyer.

Barbour, S. (2000) 'Deutsch' as a linguistic, ethnic and national label: cultural and political consequences of a multiple ambiguity. In G. Hogan-Brun (ed.) *National Varieties of German Outside Germany: A European Perspective* (pp. 33–48). Oxford: Peter Lang.

Barbour, S. and Stevenson, P. (1990) *Variation in German. A Critical Approach to German Sociolinguistics.* Cambridge: CUP.

Bärnthaler, G. (2000) Die Rechtschreibreform 1996 und die Schule. In S. Schmidt *et al.* (eds) *Specht und Gämse: Beiträge zur Rechtschreibung des Deutschen* (pp. 139–54). Göppingen: Kümmerle.

Barton, D. (1994) *Literacy. An Introduction to the Ecology of Written Language.* Oxford: Blackwell.

Barton, D. (1995) Some problems with an evolutionary view of written language. In S. Puppel (ed.) *The Biology of Language* (pp. 19–32). Amsterdam: John Benjamins.

Barton, D. and Hamilton, M. (1996) Social and cognitive factors in the historical elaboration of writing. In A. Lock and C.R. Peters (eds) *Handbook of Human Symbolic Evolution* (pp. 793–858). Oxford: Clarendon.

Barton, D. and Hamilton, M. (1998) *Local Literacies.* London: Routledge.

Barton, D., Hamilton, M. and Ivanič, R. (eds) (2001) *Situated Literacies: Reading and Writing in Context.* London: Routledge.

Bartsch, R. (1987) *Norms of Language. Theoretical and Practical Aspects.* London: Longman.

Baudusch, R. (1997a) Zur Reform der Zeichensetzung – Begründung und Kommentar. In G. Augst *et al.* (eds) *Zur Neuregelung der deutschen Orthographie. Begründung und Kritik* (pp. 243–58). Tübingen: Niemeyer.

Baudusch, R. (1997b) Die unproblematischsten Vorschläge sind die zur Zeichensetzung. In G. Augst *et al.* (eds) *Zur Neuregelung der deutschen Orthographie. Begründung und Kritik* (pp. 489–95). Tübingen: Niemeyer.

Baudusch, R. (2001) Die Getrennt- und Zusammenschreibung als Problemschwerpunkt der deutschen Rechtschreibreform. *Muttersprache* 1, 36–45.

Bauer, L. and Trudgill, P. (eds) (1998) *Language Myths.* London: Penguin.

Bauman, R. and Briggs, C.L. (2000) Language philosophy as language ideology: John Locke and Johann Gottfried Herder. In P. Kroskrity (ed.) *Regimes of Language: Ideologies, Polities and Identities* (pp. 139–204). Santa Fe: School of American Research Press.

Baumert, J., Artelt, C., Klieme, E., Neubrand, M., Prenzel, M., Schiefele, U., Schneider, W., Schümer, G., Stanat, P., Tillmann, K.-J. and Weiss, M. (eds) (2002) *PISA 2000 – Die Länder der Bundesrepublik Deutschland im Vergleich. Zusammenfassung zentraler Befunde.* Berlin: Max-Planck-Institut für Bildungsforschung.

Baumert, J., Artelt, C., Klieme, E., Weiss, M. and Stanat, P. (eds) (2001) PISA – Programme for International Student Assessment: Zielsetzung, theoretische Konzeption und Entwicklung von Messverfahren. In F.E. Weinert (ed.) *Leistungsmessungen in Schulen* (pp. 285–310). Weinheim: Belz.

Baynham, M. (1994) *Literacy Practices: Investigating Literacy in Social Contexts.* London: Longman.

Beck, U. (1992) *Risk Society: Towards a New Modernity.* London: Sage. (German original: *Risikogesellschaft: Auf dem Weg in eine andere Moderne.* (1986) Frankfurt/M.: Suhrkamp. M. Ritter, trans.).

Beck, U. (1994) The reinvention of politics: Towards a theory of reflexive modernization. In U. Beck, A. Giddens and S. Lash (eds) *Reflexive Modernization: Politics, Tradition and Aesthetics in the Modern Social Order* (pp. 1–55). Oxford: Polity.

Beck, U. (1995) *Ecological Politics in an Age of Risk.* Cambridge: CUP.

Beck, U. (1997) *The Reinvention of Politics: Rethinking Modernity in the Global Social Order.* Oxford: Polity. (German original: *Die Erfindung des Politischen* (1993) Frankfurt/M.: Suhrkamp. M. Ritter, trans.).

Bernstein, B. (ed.) (1971) *Class, Codes and Control* (Vol. 1). London: Routledge & Kegan Paul.

Berschin, H. (1998) Laufenlassen oder nicht laufen lassen? Eine Zwischenbilanz zur Rechtschreibreform. *Zeitschrift für Dialektologie und Linguistik* 1, 43–49.

Berthele, R. (2000) Translating African-American vernacular English into German: the problem of 'Jim' in Mark Twain's *Huckleberry Finn. Journal of Sociolinguistics* 4(4), 588–613.

Berthele, R., Christen, H., Germann, S. and Hove, I. (eds) (2002) *Die deutsche Schriftsprache und die Regionen: Entstehungsgeschichtliche Fragen in neuer Sicht.* Berlin/New York: de Gruyter.

Bird, S. (2001) Orthography and identity in Cameroon. *Written Language and Literacy* 4(2), 131–62.

Birken-Bertsch, H. and Markner, R. (2000) *Rechtschreibreform und National-sozialismus: Ein Kapitel aus der politischen Geschichte der deutschen Sprache.* Göttingen: Wallstein-Verlag.

Blommaert, J. (1996) Language planning as a discourse on language and society: The linguistic ideology of a scholarly tradition. *Language Problems and Language Planning* 20(3), 199–222.

Blommaert, J. (ed.) (1999) *Language Ideological Debates.* Berlin: Mouton de Gruyter.

Blommaert, J. (2001) Context is/as critique. *Critique of Anthropology* 21(1), 13–32.

Blommaert, J. and Bulcaen, C. (2000) Critical discourse analysis. *Annual Review of Anthropology* 29, 447–66.

Blommaert, J. and Verschueren, J. (1998a) *Debating Diversity: Analysing the Discourse of Tolerance.* London: Routledge.

Blommaert, J. and Verschueren, J. (1998b) The role of language in European nationalist ideologies. In B. Schieffelin *et al.* (eds) *Language Ideologies: Practice and Theory* (pp. 189–210). Oxford: OUP.

Blommaert, J., Collins, J., Heller, M., Rampton, B., Slembrouck, S. and Verschueren, J. (2003) Introduction to special issue on ethnography, discourse and hegemony. *Pragmatics* 13(1), 1–10.

Bloomfield, L. (1933) *Language.* New York: Holt, Rinehart & Winston.

Bloomfield, L. (1944) Second and tertiary responses to language. *Language* 20, 45–55. (Reprinted in C.F. Hockett (1970) *Leonard Bloomfield Anthology* (pp. 284–96). Chicago: University of Chicago Press.)

Blüml, K. (1997a) Die Geschichte der Reformbemühungen von 1960 bis 1995 in Österreich. In G. Augst *et al.* (eds) *Zur Neuregelung der deutschen Orthographie. Begründung und Kritik.* (pp. 25–36). Tübingen: Niemeyer.

Böhme, G. (2001) *Zur Entwicklung des Dudens und seinem Verhältnis zu den amtlichen Regelwerken der deutschen Orthographie.* Frankfurt/M.: Peter Lang.

Bokhorst-Heng, W. (1999) Singapore's speak Mandarin campaign: language ideological debates in the imagining of the nation. In J. Blommaert (ed.) *Language Ideological Debates* (pp. 235–65). Berlin: de Gruyter.

Bourdieu, P. (1991) *Language and Symbolic Power.* Cambridge: Polity Press.

Braudel, F. (1958 [1969]) Histoire et sciences sociales: La longue durée. In F. Braudel (ed.) *Écrits sur l'Histoire* (pp. 41–83). Paris: Flammarion.

Brenner, O. (1902) *Die lautlichen und geschichtlichen Grundlagen unserer Rechtschreibung.* Leipzig.

Brown, B. (1993) The social consequences of writing Lousiana French. *Language in Society* 22(1), 67–102.

Bucholtz, M. (2000) The politics of transcription. *Journal of Pragmatics* 32, 1439–65.

Bünting, K.-D. and Timmler, W. (1997) Probleme bei der Umsetzung der neuen Rechtschreibung im Wörterbuch. In H.-W. Eroms and H.H. Munske (eds) *Die Rechtschreibreform: Pro und Kontra* (pp. 25–38). Berlin: Erich Schmidt Verlag.

Calhoun, C. (ed.) (1992) *Habermas and the Public Sphere.* Cambridge, MA: MIT Press.

Cameron, D. (1995) *Verbal Hygiene.* London: Routledge.

Chapman, S. (2000) *Philosophy for Linguists: An Introduction.* London: Routledge.

Clark, R. and Ivanič, R. (1997) *The Politics of Writing.* London: Routledge.

Clyne, M. (1995) *The German Language in a Changing Europe.* Cambridge: CUP.

Collins, J. (1999) The Ebonics controversy in context: Literacies, subjectivities, and language ideologies in the United States. In J. Blommaert (ed.) *Language Ideological Debates* (pp. 201–34). Berlin: Mouton de Gruyter.

Cooper, R.L. (1989) *Language Planning and Social Change.* Cambridge: CUP.

Coulmas, F. (1989) *The Writing Systems of the World.* Oxford: Blackwell.

Coulmas, F. (1995) Germanness: language and nation. In P. Stevenson (ed.) *The German Language and the Real World* (pp. 55–68). Oxford: Clarendon Press.

Crowley, T. (1989) *Standard English and the Politics of Language.* Urbana: University of Illinois Press.

Dahrendorf, R. (1968) *Gesellschaft und Demokratie in Deutschland.* Munich: dtv.

de Saussure, F. (1915, [1959]) *Course in General Linguistics.* New York: McGraw Hill.

Denk, F. (1997) Eine der größten Desinformationskampagnen. In H.-W. Eroms and H.H. Munske (eds) *Die Rechtschreibreform: Pro und Kontra.* (pp. 41–46). Berlin: Erich Schmidt Verlag.

Derrida, J. (1978) *Writing and Difference.* London: Routledge and Kegan Paul.

Deutsche Akademie für Sprache und Dichtung (eds) (2003) *Zur Reform der deutschen Rechtschreibung: Ein Kompromißvorschlag.* Göttingen: Wallstein.

DiGiacomo, S.M. (1999) Language ideological debates in an Olympic city: Barcelona 1992–1996. In J. Blommaert (ed.) *Language Ideological Debates* (pp. 105–42). Berlin: de Gruyter.

Dittmann, J. (1999) Die Nachrichtenagenturen und die neue Rechtschreibung. Die deutschsprachigen Nachrichtenagenturen haben am 1. August 1999 umgestellt – aber wie? *Sprachreport* 4, 17–19.

Drewnowska-Vargáné, E. and Földes, C. (1999) Überlegungen zur Umstellung auf die neue deutsche Orthographie aus der Perspektive von Deutsch als Fremdsprache und Auslandsgermanistik. *LernSprache Deutsch* 7, 99ff.

Dürig, G. (1998) Einführung zum Grundgesetz. In *Grundgesetz* (35th edn). Munich: dtv.

Durrell, M. (1999) Standardsprache in England und Deutschland. *Zeitschrift für germanistische Linguistik* 27, 285–308.

Eira, C. (1998) Authority and discourse: towards a model for orthography selection. *Written Language and Literacy* 1(2), 171–224.

Eisenberg, P. (1997a) Die besondere Kennzeichnung der kurzen Vokale – Vergleich und Bewertung der Neuregelung. In G. Augst *et al.* (eds) *Zur Neuregelung der deutschen Orthographie. Begründung und Kritik* (pp. 323–36). Tübingen: Niemeyer.

Eisenberg, P. (1997b) Das Versagen orthographischer Regeln: Über den Umgang mit dem Kuckuckssei. In H.-W. Eroms and H.H. Munske (eds) *Die Rechtschreibreform: Pro und Kontra* (pp. 47–50). Berlin: Erich Schmidt Verlag.

Eisenberg, P. (1999) Vokallängenbezeichnung als Problem. *Linguistische Berichte* 179, 343–49.

Eisenberg, P. (2000) Regeln und regeln lassen: Geminate und Politik. *Linguistische Berichte* 181, 119–21.

Eroms, H.-W. (1997) Die öffentliche Diskussion um die Rechtschreibreform. In H.-W. Eroms and H.H. Munske (eds) *Die Rechtschreibreform: Pro und Kontra* (pp. 51–56). Berlin: Erich-Schmidt-Verlag.

Eroms, H.-W. and Munske, H.H. (eds) (1997) *Die Rechtschreibreform: Pro und Kontra.* Berlin: Erich Schmidt Verlag.

Errington, J. (2001) Ideology. In A. Duranti (ed.) *Key Terms in Language and Culture* (pp. 110–12). Oxford: Blackwell.

Ewald, P. and Nerius, D. (1997) Die Alternative: gemäßigte Kleinschreibung. In G. Augst *et al.* (eds) *Zur Neuregelung der deutschen Orthographie. Begründung und Kritik* (pp. 419–34). Tübingen: Niemeyer.

Fairclough, N. (1992) *Discourse and Social Change.* Cambridge: Polity Press.

Fairclough, N. (2003) *Analysing Discourse: Textual Analysis for Social Research.* London: Routledge.

Fishman, J. (ed.) (1977) *Advances in the Creation and Revision of Writing Systems.* The Hague: Mouton.

Fix, M. (1994). *Geschichte und Praxis des Diktats im Rechtschreibunterricht – Aufgezeigt am Beispiel der Volksschule/Hauptschule in Württemberg bzw. Baden-Württemberg.* Frankfurt/M.: Peter Lang.

Földes, C. (2000) Rechtschreibunterricht in der Lernsprache Deutsch – nach der Orthographiereform. *Zielsprache Deutsch* 31(1), 15–30.

Foucault, M. (1984) The order of discourse. In M. Shapiro (ed.) *Language and Politics* (pp. 108–38). New York: New York University Press.

Frankfurter Allgemeine Zeitung (FAZ) (2000) *Die Reform als Diktat: Zur Auseinandersetzung über die deutsche Rechtschreibung.* Frankfurt/M.: Frankfurter Allgemeine Zeitung GmbH.

Fuhrhop, N., Steinitz, R. and Wenzel, W.U. (1995) Tut das wirklich Not oder: Aufwändiger Zierrat? Zur geplanten Rechtschreibreform. *Zeitschrift für germanistische Linguistik* 23, 202–206.

Gal, S. (2001) Linguistic theories and national images in nineteenth-century Hungary. In S. Gal and K. Woolard (eds) *Languages and Publics: The Making of Authority* (pp. 30–45). Manchester, UK & Northampton, MA: St. Jerome.

Gal, S. and Woolard, K. (eds) (2001a) *Languages and Publics: The Making of Authority.* Manchester, UK & Northampton, MA: St. Jerome.

Gal, S. and Woolard, K. (2001b) Constructing languages and publics: authority and representation. In S. Gal and K. Woolard (eds) *Languages and Publics: The Making of Authority* (pp. 1–12). Manchester, UK & Northampton, MA: St. Jerome.

Gallmann, P. (1997a) Warum die Schweizer weiterhin kein Eszett schreiben. Zugleich eine Anmerkung zu Eisenbergs Silbengelenk-Theorie. In G. Augst *et al.* (eds) *Zur Neuregelung der deutschen Orthographie. Begründung und Kritik* (pp. 135–40). Tübingen: Niemeyer.

Gallmann, P. (1997b) Konzepte der Nominalität. In G. Augst *et al.* (eds) *Zur Neuregelung der deutschen Orthographie. Begründung und Kritik* (pp. 209–42). Tübingen: Niemeyer.

Gallmann, P. (1997c) Zum Komma bei Infinitivgruppen. In G. Augst *et al.* (eds) *Zur Neuregelung der deutschen Orthographie. Begründung und Kritik* (pp. 435–62). Tübingen: Niemeyer.

Gallmann, P. and Sitta, H. (1997) Zum Begriff der orthographischen Regel. In G. Augst *et al.* (eds) *Zur Neuregelung der deutschen Orthographie. Begründung und Kritik.* (pp. 93–109). Tübingen: Niemeyer.

Garbe, B. (ed.) (1978) *Die deutsche Rechtschreibung und ihre Reform: 1722–1974.* Tübingen: Niemeyer.

Gee, J. (1999) *An Introduction to Discourse Analysis: Theory and Method.* London: Routledge.

Geerts, G., van den Broeck, J. and Verdoodt, A. (1977) Successes and failures in Dutch spelling reform. In J. Fishman (ed.) *Advances in the Creation and Revision of Writing Systems* (pp. 179–245). The Hague: Mouton.

Gelberg, H.-J. (1997) Konsequenzen der Rechtschreibreform. In H.-W. Eroms and H.H. Munske (eds) *Die Rechtschreibreform: Pro und Kontra* (pp. 57–58). Berlin: Erich-Schmidt-Verlag.

Gersdorf, H. (2000) *Verfassungsprozeßrecht und Verfassungsmäßigkeit.* Heidelberg: C.F. Müller Verlag.

Giddens, A. (1991) *Modernity and Self-Identity.* Cambridge: Polity Press.

Gramsci, A. (1978) *Selections from Political Writings 1910–1920.* Q. Hoare (ed.) London: Lawrence & Wishart.

Grebe, P. (ed.) (1963) *Akten zur Geschichte der deutschen Einheitsschreibung 1870–1880.* Mannheim: Duden.

Gröschner, R. (1982) *Dialogik und Jurisprudenz.* Tübingen: Mohr.

Gröschner, R. (1992) *Das Überwachungsrechtsverhältnis.* Tübingen: Mohr.

Gröschner, R. (1995) *Menschenwürde und Sepulkralkultur in der grundgesetzlichen Ordnung.* Stuttgart.

Gröschner, R. (1997) Zur Verfassungswidrigkeit der Rechtschreibreform. In H.-W. Eroms and H.H. Munske (eds) *Die Rechtschreibreform: Pro und Kontra* (pp. 69–80). Berlin: Erich Schmidt Verlag.

Gröschner, R. and Kopke, W. (1997) Die 'Jenenser Kritik' an der Rechtschreibreform. *Juristische Schulung* 4, 298–303.

Gundersen, G. (1977) Successes and failures in the reformation of Norwegian orthography. In J. Fishman (ed.) *Advances in the Creation and Revision of Writing Systems* (pp. 247–65). The Hague: Mouton.

Günther, H. (1997) Alles Getrennte findet sich wieder – zur Beurteilung der Neuregelung der deutschen Rechtschreibung. In H.-W. Eroms and H.H. Munske (eds) *Die Rechtschreibreform: Pro und Kontra* (pp. 81–94). Berlin: Erich Schmidt Verlag.

Güthert, K. and Heller, K. (1997) Das Märchen tausendundeiner Differenz. Vergleichsstudie zur Quantität und Qualität der Abweichungen zwischen den marktführenden Wörterbüchern – vor und nach Einführung der Neuregelung der deutschen Rechtschreibung. *Muttersprache* 4, 339–53.

Häberle, P. (1996) Review of Wolfgang Kopke 'Rechtschreibreform und Verfassungsrecht. Schulrechtliche, persönlichkeitsrechtliche und kulturverfassungsrechtliche Aspekte einer Reform der deutschen Orthographie.' *Juristenzeitung* 14, 719–20.

Habermas, J. (1989, [1962]) *The Structural Transformation of the Public Sphere.* Cambridge: Polity Press.

Habermas, J. (1976 [1973]) *Legitimation Crisis.* London: Heineman.

Hantke, I. (2001) Geschichte der Rechtschreibreform. *Verwaltungsrundschau* 7, 235–39.

Hargreaves, I. (2000) *Who's Misunderstanding Whom? An Inquiry into the Relationship between Science and the Media.* London: ESRC. On WWW at www.esrc.ac.uk.

Harris, R. (1986) *The Origin of Writing.* London: Duckworth.

Harris, R. (1990) *The Language Makers.* London: Duckworth.

Harris, R. (2000) *Rethinking Writing.* London: Athlone.

Haugen, E. (1966) *Language Conflict and Language Planning: The Case of Modern Norwegian.* Cambridge, MA: Harvard University Press.

Haugen, E. (1972) Dialect, language, nation. In J.B. Pride and J. Holmes (eds) *Sociolinguistics* (pp. 97–111). Harmondsworth: Penguin.

Heller, K. (1998) Rechtschreibreform. In special extended December edition of *Sprachreport. Informationen und Meinungen zur deutschen Sprache.* Mannheim: Institut für deutsche Sprache.

Heller, K. (1999) Die Last der Freiheit *oder* Von den engen Grenzen einer weit gedachten Norm. Erfahrungen bei der Neuregelung der deutschen Rechtschreibung. In H. Omdal (ed.) *Språkbrukeren – fri til å velge? Artikler om homogen og heterogen språknorm* (pp. 73–90). Kristiansand: Høgskolen i Agder.

Heller, K. and Scharnhorst, J. (1997) Kommentar zum Wörterverzeichnis. In G. Augst *et al.* (eds) *Zur Neuregelung der deutschen Orthographie. Begründung und Kritik* (pp. 269–90). Tübingen: Niemeyer.

Heller, K. and Walz, B. (1992) Zur Geschichte der Fremdwortschreibung im Deutschen. Beobachtungen von Campe bis Duden. In D. Nerius and J. Scharnhorst (eds) *Studien zur Geschichte der deutschen Orthographie* (pp. 277–338). Hildesheim.

Heller, M. (1994) *Crosswords: Language, Ethnicity and Education in French Ontario*. Berlin: Mouton de Gruyter.

Heller, M. (ed.) (1999) Sociolinguistics and public debate. *Journal of Sociolinguistics* 3(2), 260–88.

Herberg, D. (1997) Aussageabsicht als Schreibungskriterium – ein alternatives Reformkonzept für die Regelung der Getrennt- und Zusammenschreibung (GZS). In G. Augst *et al.* (eds) *Zur Neuregelung der deutschen Orthographie. Begründung und Kritik.* (pp. 365–78). Tübingen: Niemeyer.

Hering, W. (1990) *Das preußische Regelbuch (pRb) – Geschichte, Aufgabe und Leistung: Ein Beitrag zur Geschichte der neuhochdeutschen Orthographie seit 1876.* Doctoral dissertation submitted to the Technische Universität (TU) Berlin.

Hillinger, S. and Nerius, D. (1997) Die Geschichte der Reformbemühungen von 1965 bis 1990 in der DDR. In G. Augst *et al.* (eds) *Zur Neuregelung der deutschen Orthographie. Begründung und Kritik* (pp. 15–24). Tübingen: Niemeyer.

Hinney, G. (1997) *Neubestimmung von Lerninhalten für den Rechtschreibunterricht. Ein fachdidaktischer Beitrag zur Schriftaneignung als Problemlöseprozeß.* Frankfurt/M.: Peter Lang.

Hoberg, R. (1997) Orthographie, Rechtschreibreform und öffentliche Meinung. In H.-W. Eroms and H.H. Munske (eds) *Die Rechtschreibreform: Pro und Kontra* (pp. 95–100). Berlin: Erich Schmidt Verlag.

Hufeld, U. (1996) Verfassungswidrige Rechtschreibreform? BVerfG, NJW 1996, 2221. *Juristische Schulung* 12, 1072–76.

Hufen, F. (1997). Unzulässige Verfassungsbeschwerde gegen Rechtschreibreform. *Juristische Schulung* 2, 170–71.

Hutton, C. (1999) *Linguistics and the Third Reich: Mother-Tongue Fascism, Race and the Science of Language.* London: Routledge.

Hymes, D. (1974) *Foundations of Sociolinguistics.* Philadelphia: University of Pennsylvania Press.

Hymes, D. (1972) On communicative competence. In J.B. Pride and J. Holmes (eds) *Sociolinguistics: Selected Readings* (pp. 269–85). Harmondsworth: Penguin.

Ickler, T. (1997a) Woran scheitert die Rechtschreibreform? *Sprachwissenschaft* 22(1), 45–99.

Ickler, T. (1997b) Die verborgenen Regeln. In H.-W. Eroms and H.H. Munske (eds) *Die Rechtschreibreform: Pro und Kontra* (pp. 101–10). Berlin: Erich Schmidt Verlag.

Ickler, T. (1997c) *Die sogenannte Rechtschreibreform. Ein Schildbürgerstreich.* St. Goar: Leibniz Verlag.

Ickler, T. (1997e) Getrennt- und Zusammenschreibung. Ein Kommentar zu §34 und §36 der Neuregelung. *Muttersprache* 4, 257–79.

Ickler, T. (2000) *Das Rechtschreibwörterbuch: Sinnvoll schreiben, trennen, Zeichen setzen. (Die bewahrte deutsche Rechtschreibung in neuer Darstellung.)* St. Goar: Leibniz Verlag.

Ickler, T. (n.d.) *Die Rechtschreibreform – Propaganda und Wirklichkeit.* On WWW at http://www.rechtschreibreform.com.

Internationaler Arbeitskreis zur Rechtschreibreform (eds) (1992) *Deutsche Rechtschreibung – Vorschläge zu ihrer Neuregelung.* Tübingen: Narr.

Internationaler Arbeitskreis zur Rechtschreibreform (eds) (1995) *Deutsche Rechtschreibung – Regeln und Wörterverzeichnis. Vorlage für die amtliche Regelung.* Tübingen: Narr.

Irwin, A. and Wynne, B. (eds) (1996) *Misunderstanding Science? The Public Reconstruction of Science and Technology.* Cambridge: CUP.

Irvine, J.T. and Gal, S. (2000) Language ideology and linguistic differentiation. In P. Kroskrity (ed.) *Regimes of Language: Ideologies, Polities and Identities* (pp. 35–84). Santa Fe: School of American Research Press.

Jaffe, A. (1996) The second annual Corsican spelling contest: orthography and ideology. *American Ethnnologist* 23(4), 816–35.

Jaffe, A. (1999a) *Ideologies in Action: Language Politics on Corsica.* Berlin: Mouton de Gruyter.

Jaffe, A. (1999b) Locating power: Corsican translators and their critics. In J. Blommaert (ed.) *Language Ideological Debates* (pp. 39–66). Berlin: de Gruyter.

Jaffe, A. (2000) Introduction: Non-standard orthography and non-standard speech. *Journal of Sociolinguistics* 4(4), 497–513.

Jaffe, A. and Walton, S. (2000) The voices people read: Orthography and the representation of non-standard speech. *Journal of Sociolinguistics* 4(4), 561–88.

Jäger, S. (1974). Der gegensatz zwischen herrschender rechtschreibung und sprachrichtigkeit und seine folgen in schule, beruf und familie. In B. Garde (ed.) (1978) *Die deutsche Rechtschreibung und ihre Reform 1722–1974* (pp. 211–20). Tübingen: Max Niemeyer Verlag.

Jäkel, C. (1996) Zur Bewertung der Sprachreform. *Rechtstheorie* 27, 491–514.

Jansen-Tang, D. (1988) *Ziele und Möglichkeiten einer Reform der deutschen Orthographie seit 1901.* Frankfurt/M.: Peter Lang.

Johnson, S. (Forthcoming 2005) 'Sonst kann jeder schreiben, wie er will...'? Orthography, legitimation and the construction of publics. In S. Johnson and O. Stenschker (eds) 'After 2005.' Special issue of *German Life and Letters* on the German spelling reform.

Johnson, S. (2001a) Who's misunderstanding whom? (Socio)linguistics, public debate and the media. *Journal of Sociolinguistics* 5(4), 591–610.

Johnson, S. (2001b) Review of 'Language Ideological Debates' (1999) edited by J. Blommaert. *Journal of Sociolinguistics* 5(3), 433–38.

Johnson, S. (2000) The cultural politics of the 1998 reform of German orthography. *German Life and Letters* 53(1), 106–25.

Johnson, S. (1998) *Exploring the German Language*. London: Edward Arnold.

Joseph, J.E. (1987) *Eloquence and Power: The Rise of Language Standards and Standard Languages*. London: Frances Pinter.

Joseph, J.E. and Taylor, T. (eds) (1990) *Ideologies of Language*. London: Routledge.

Kataoka, K. (1997) Affect and letter writing: Unconventional conventions in casual writing by young Japanese women. *Language in Society* 26, 103–36.

Keller, R. (1978) *The German Language*. London: Faber and Faber.

Kissel, O.R. (1997) 'Der "neue" Duden und die richterliche unabhängigkeit.' *Neue Juristische Wochenschrift* 17, 1097–1106.

Klein, W.P. (2001) Fehlende Sprachloyalität? Tatsachen und Anmerkungen zur jüngsten Entwicklung des öffentlichen Sprachbewusstseins in Deutschland. *Linguistik online* 9, 2/01. On WWW at http://www.linguistik-online.de.

Kloss, H. (1978) *Die Entwicklung neuer germanischer Kultursprachen seit 1800*. Düsseldorf: Schwann.

Knobloch, C. (1998). Zu Christoph Jäkels Beitrag über die Rechtschreibreform. *Rechtstheorie* 28(3), 393–96.

Kohrt, M. (1983) *Grundlagenstudien zu einer Theorie der deutschen Orthographie*. 2 vols. Münster: Westfälische Wilhelms-Universität Münster.

Kohrt, M. (1985) *Problemgeschichte des Graphembegriffs und des frühen Phonembegriffs*. Tübingen: Niemeyer.

Kohrt, M. (1987) *Theoretische Aspekte der deutschen Orthographie*. Tübingen: Niemeyer.

Kohrt, M. (1997) Orthographische Normen in der demokratischen Gesellschaft. In G. Augst *et al.* (eds) *Zur Neuregelung der deutschen Orthographie. Begründung und Kritik* (pp. 295–316). Tübingen: Niemeyer.

Kolonovits, D. (1997). Staatssprache und Rechtschreibreform. *Journal für Rechtspolitik* 5(1), 6–14.

Kommission für Rechtschreibfragen (1985) *Die Rechtschreibung des Deutschen und ihre Neuregelung*. Düsseldorf: Schwann.

Kommission für Rechtschreibfragen (1989) *Zur Neuregelung der deutschen Sprache*. Düsseldorf: Schwann.

Königlich Preußisches Ministerium der geistlichen, Unterrichts- und Medizinal-Angelegenheiten (ed.) (1880) *Regeln und Wörterverzeichnis für die deutsche Rechtschreibung zum Gebrauch in den preußischen Schulen.* Berlin.

Königlich Preußisches Ministerium der geistlichen, Unterrichts- und Medizinal-Angelegenheiten (ed.) (1902) *Regeln für die deutsche Rechtschreibung nebst Wörterverzeichnis.* Berlin.

Kopke, W. (1995a) *Rechtschreibreform und Verfassungsrecht. Schulrechtliche, persönlichkeitsrechtliche und kulturverfassungsrechtliche Aspekte einer Reform der deutschen Orthographie.* Tübingen: Mohr.

Kopke, W. (1995b) Rechtschreibreform auf dem Erlaßwege? *Juristenzeitung* 18, 874–80.

Kopke, W. (1996) Die verfassungswidrige Rechtschreibreform. *Neue Juristische Wochenschrift* 17, 1081–87.

Kopke, W. (1997) Ist die Rechtschreibreform noch zu stoppen? In H.-W. Eroms and H.H. Munske (eds) *Die Rechtschreibreform: Pro und Kontra* (pp. 111–16). Berlin: Erich Schmidt Verlag.

Kranich-Hofbauer, K. (2000) Zum 'ß': Graphie und orthographiegeschichtliche Aspekte eines 'Sorgenkindes' der deutschen Rechtschreibung. In S. Schmidt *et al.* (eds) *Specht und Gämse: Beiträge zur Rechtschreibung des Deutschen* (pp. 51–74). Göppingen: Kümmerle.

Kranz, F. (1998) *Eine Schifffahrt mit drei f: Positives zur Rechtschreibreform.* Göttingen: Vandenhoeck & Ruprecht.

Kress, G. (2000) *Early Spelling: Between Convention and Creativity.* London: Routledge.

Krieger, H. (1997) Wachstumslogik und Regulierungswahn. In H.-W. Eroms and H.H. Munske (eds) *Die Rechtschreibreform: Pro und Kontra* (pp. 117–26). Berlin: Erich Schmidt Verlag.

Kroskrity, P. (ed.) (2000a) *Regimes of Language: Ideologies, Polities and Identities.* Santa Fe: School of American Research Press.

Kroskrity, P. (2000b) Regimenting Languages: Language ideological perpectives. In P. Kroskrity (ed.) (2000) *Regimes of Language: Ideologies, Polities and Identities* (pp. 1–34). Santa Fe: School of American Research Press.

Küppers, H.-G. (1984) *Orthographiereform und Öffentlichkeit. Zur Entwicklung und Diskussion der Rechtschreibreformbemühungen zwischen 1876 und 1982.* Düsseldorf: Schwann.

Langer, N. (2000) The 'Rechtschreibreform' – A lesson in linguistic purism. *German as a Foreign Language*, Issue 3. On WWW at http://www.gfl.-journal.de.

Lanthaler, F., Ortner, H., Schiewe, J., Schrodt, R. and Sitta, H. (2003) Sprachkritik und Sprachwissenschaft – Anmerkungen zu einer komplizierten Beziehung. *Sprachreport* 19(2), 2–5.

Lash, S. (1990) *Sociology of Postmodernism.* London: Routledge.

Latour, B. (1993) *We Have Never Been Modern.* Hemel Hempstead: Harvester Wheatsheaf.

Law, C. (2002) Das sprachliche Ringen um die nationale und kulturelle Identität Deutschlands. *Muttersprache* 1, 67–83.

Ledig, F. (1999) Die öffentliche Auseinandersetzung um die Rechtschreibreform von 1996. *Deutsche Sprache* 2, 97–117.

Lee, B. (2001) Circulating the People. In S. Gal and K. Woolard (eds) *Languages and Publics: The Making of Authority* (pp. 164–81). Manchester, UK & Northampton, MA: St. Jerome.

Leiss, E. and Leiss, J. (1997) *Die Regulierte schrift: Plädoyer für die Freigabe der Rechtschreibung.* Verlag Palm & Enke: Erlangen und Jena.

Lepsius, R. (1981 [1863, 1855]) *Standard Alphabet for Reducing Unwritten Languages and Foreign Graphic Systems to Uniform Orthography in European Letters.* J. Alan Kemp (ed.) Amsterdam: Benjamins.

Lippi-Green, R. (1997) *English with an Accent: Language, Ideology and Discrimination in the United States.* London: Routledge.

Lønnum, E. (2003) *Die Neuregelung der deutschen Rechtschreibung.* Unpublished dissertation, Germanistisches Institut, University of Oslo.

Looser, R. (1998) *Dokumentation zur neueren Geschichte der deutschen Orthographie in der Schweiz.* (Documenta Orthographica, Band 9.) Hildesheim: Georg Olms Verlag.

Looser, R. and Sitta, H. (1997) Die Geschichte der Reformbemühungen von 1970 bis 1995 in der Schweiz. In G. Augst *et al.* (eds) *Zur Neuregelung der deutschen Orthographie. Begründung und Kritik* (pp. 37–48). Tübingen: Niemeyer.

Lüthgens, S. (2002) *Rechtschreibreform und Schule: Die Reformen der deutschen Rechtschreibung aus der Sicht von Lehrerinnen und Lehrern.* Frankfurt/M.: Peter Lang.

Maas, U. (1997) Orthographische Regularitäten, Regeln und ihre Deregulierung. Am Beispiel der Dehnungszeichen im Deutschen. In G. Augst *et al.* (eds) *Zur Neuregelung der deutschen Orthographie. Begründung und Kritik* (pp. 337–64). Tübingen: Niemeyer.

Madumulla, J., Bertoncini, E. and Blommaert, J. (1999) Politics, ideology and poetic form: The literary debate in Tanzania. In J. Blommaert (ed.) *Language Ideological Debates* (pp. 307–42). Berlin: Mouton de Gruyter.

Marx, H. (1999) Rechtschreibleistung vor und nach der Rechtschreibreform: Was ändert sich bei Grundschulkindern? *Zeitschrift für Entwicklungspsychologie und Pädagogische Psychologie* 31(4), 180–89.

Meder, S. (1997) Der Streit um die Kodifikation von Recht und Schreibung. Seine Konsequenzen für die geplante Reform der Rechtschreibung. *Juristische Zeitung* 4, 190–93.

Mentrup, W. (1979) *Die Groß- und Kleinschreibung im Deutschen und ihre Regeln. Historische Entwicklung und Vorschlag zur Neuregelung.* Tübingen: Günter Narr.

Mentrup, W. (1983) *Zur Zeichensetzung im Deutschen – Die Regeln und ihre Reform. Oder: Müssen Duden-Regeln so sein, wie sie sind?* Tübingen: Günter Narr.

Mentrup, W. (1993) *Wo liegt eigentlich der Fehler? Zur Rechtschreibreform und zu ihren Hintergründen.* Stuttgart: Klett.

Mentrup, W. (1998) Neuregelung der Rechtschreibung. Zur Anhörung des Bundesverfassungsgerichtes (Karlsruhe 12. Mai 1998). Impressionen – Argumentationen. On WWW at http://www.ids-mannheim.de/Rechtschreibreform.

Menzel, J. (1998a) Von Richtern und anderen Sprachexperten – ist die Rechtschreibreform ein Verfassungsproblem? *Neue Juristische Wochenschrift* 51(17), 1177–84.

Menzel, J. (1998b) Sprachverständige Juristen. Eine Zwischenbilanz zum Rechtsstreit um die Rechtschreibreform. *Recht der Jugend und des Bildungswesens* 46(1), 36–61.

Miethaner, U. (2000) Orthographic transcription of non-standard varieties: The case of earlier African-American English. *Journal of Sociolinguistics* 4(4), 534–60.

Milroy, J. (2001) Language ideologies and the consequences of standardisation. *Journal of Sociolinguistics* 5(4), 53–55.

Milroy, J. and Milroy, L. (1999) *Authority in Language: Investigating Standard English*, 3rd edition. London: Routledge.

Munske, H.H. (1997a) Wie wesentlich ist die Rechtschreibreform? In H.-W. Eroms and H.H. Munske (eds) *Die Rechtschreibreform: Pro und Kontra* (pp. 143–56). Berlin: Erich Schmidt Verlag.

Munske, H.H. (1997b) Über den Sinn der Großschreibung – ein Alternativvorschlag zur Neuregelung. In G. Augst *et al.* (eds) *Zur Neuregelung der deutschen Orthographie. Begründung und Kritik* (pp. 397–418). Tübingen: Niemeyer.

Munske, H.H. (1997c) *Orthographie als Sprachkultur.* Frankfurt/M.: Peter Lang.

Murchú, M.O. (1977) Successes and failures in the modernization of Irish spelling. In J. Fishman (ed.) *Advances in the Creation and Revision of Writing Systems* (pp. 267–91). The Hague: Mouton.

Nagel, T. (1986) *The View from Nowhere.* New York: Oxford University Press.

Neef, M. and Primus, B. (2001) Stumme Zeugen der Autonomie – Eine Replik auf Ossner. *Linguistische Berichte* 187, 353–78.

Nerius, D. (1975) *Untersuchungen zu einer Reform der deutschen Orthographie.* Berlin.

Nerius, D. (ed.) (2000a) *Deutsche Orthographie,* 3rd edition. Mannheim: Duden.

Nerius, D. and Scharnhorst, J. (1977) 'Sprachwissenschaftliche Grundlagen einer Reform der deutschen Rechtschreibung.' In G. Ising (ed.) *Sprachkultur – Warum – Wozu?* (pp. 156–94). Berlin.

Niederhauser, J. (1997) Sprachliche Streifzüge. Populärwissenschaftliches Schreiben über sprachliche Fragen und linguistische Themen. In K. Adamcik, G. Antos and E.-M. Jakobs (eds) *Domänen- und kulturspezifisches Schreiben* (pp. 203–21). Frankfurt/M.: Peter Lang.

Niederhauser, J. (1999) Kaum präsente Linguistik – Zur Behandlung von Sprachfragen und sprachbezogenen Themen in der Öffentlichkeit. In M. Becker-Mrotzek and C. Doppler (eds) *Medium Sprache im Beruf. Eine Aufgabe für die Linguistik* (pp. 37–52). Tübingen: Narr.

Niederhauser, J. (2001) Rechtschreibwörterbücher. *Zeitschrift für germanistische Linguistik* 29(2), 261–73.

Niedzielski, N.A. and Preston, D.R. (2000) *Folk Linguistics.* Berlin/ New York: Mouton de Gruyter.

Nürnberger, A. (2000) *Arbeitsgruppe der deutschsprachigen Nachrichtenagenturen. Beschluss zur Umsetzung der Rechtschreibreform.* On WWW at http://www.dpa.info/rechtschr/beschluss.html.

Ossenbühl, F. (1989) Der Vorbehalt des Gesetzes. In J. Isensee and P. Kirchhof (eds) *Handbuch des Staatsrechts der Bundesrepublik Deutschland* (pp. 320–49). Heidelberg: Band VI.

Ossner, J. (2001a) Das ⟨h⟩ Graphem im Deutschen. *Linguistische Berichte* 187, 323–51.

Ossner, J. (2001b) Worum geht es eigentlich? Replik auf die Replik von Martin Neef und Beatrice Primus. *Linguistische Berichte* 187, 379–82.

Parakrama, A. (1995) *De-hegemonizing Language Standards: Learning from (Post)Colonial Englishes about 'English'.* London: Macmillan Press.

Pardoe, S. (2000) Respect and the pursuit of 'symmetry' in researching literacy and student writing. In D. Barton, M. Hamilton and R. Ivanič (eds) *Situated Literacies: Reading and Writing in Context* (pp. 149–66). London: Routledge.

Patrick, P.L. (2001) The speech community. In J.K. Chambers, P. Trudgill and N. Schilling-Estes (eds) *The Handbook of Language Variation and Change* (pp. 573–97). Oxford: Blackwell.

Pennycook, A. (2001) *Critical Applied Linguistics: A Critical Introduction.* London: Lawrence Erlbaum.

Pennycook, A. (2002) Prologue: Language and linguistics/discourse and disciplinarity. In C. Barron, N. Bruce and D. Nunan (eds) *Knowledge and Discourse: Towards an Ecology of Language* (pp. 13–27). London: Longman.

Phillips, S.U. (2000) Constructing a Tongan nation-state through language ideology in the courtroom. In P. Kroskrity (ed.) *Regimes of Language: Ideologies, Polities and Identities* (pp. 229–58). Santa Fe: School of American Research Press.

Pike, K.L. (1947) *Phonemics: A Technique for Reducing Language to Writing.* Ann Arbor: University of Michigan Press.

Pinker, S. (1994) *The Language Instinct.* London: Penguin.

Poschenrieder, T. (1997) S-Schreibung – Überlieferung oder Reform? In H.-W. Eroms and H.H. Munske (eds) *Die Rechtschreibreform: Pro und Kontra* (pp. 173–84). Berlin: Erich Schmidt Verlag.

Preston, D. (2000) Mowr and mowr bayud spellin': Confessions of a sociolinguist. *Journal of Sociolinguistics* 4(4), 614–21.

Prieto, L.J. (1968) La sémiologie. In A. Martinet (ed.) *Le Langage* (pp. 93–144). Paris.

Prieto, L.J. (1986) Semiotic approaches to writing. In T.A. Sebeok (ed.) *Encyclopedic Dictionary of Semiotics* (pp. 1169–76). Berlin.

Primus, B. (1997) Satzbegriffe und Interpunktion. In G. Augst *et al.* (eds) *Zur Neuregelung der deutschen Orthographie. Begründung und Kritik.* (pp. 463–88). Tübingen: Niemeyer.

Primus, B. (2000) Suprasegmentale Graphematik und Phonologie: Die Dehnungszeichen im Deutschen. *Linguistische Berichte* 181, 9–34.

Rabin, C. (1977) Spelling reform – Israel 1968. In J. Fishman (ed.) *Advances in the Creation and Revision of Writing Systems* (pp. 149–76). The Hague: Mouton.

Ramers, K.H. (1999a) Vokalquantität als orthographisches Problem: Zur Funktion der Doppelkonsonanzschreibung im Deutschen. *Linguistische Berichte* 177, 52–64.

Ramers, K.H. (1999b) Zur Doppenkonsonanzschreibung im Deutschen: Eine Rereplik. *Linguistische Berichte* 179, 350–60.

Reiffenstein, I. (1999) Sprachpflege und Sprachgeschichte. In J. Scharnhorst (ed.) *Sprachkultur und Sprachgeschichte: Herausbildung und Förderung von Sprachbewußtsein und wissenschaftlicher Sprachpflege in Europa.* Frankfurt/M.: Peter Lang.

Reiffenstein, I. (2000) Zur Orthographiegeschichte von daß. In S. Schmidt *et al.* (eds) *Specht und Gämse: Beiträge zur Rechtschreibung des Deutschen* (pp. 43–50). Göppingen: Kümmerle.

Richter, S. (2001) Schlechtere Rechtschreibleistungen nach Rechtschreibreform? Kritische Betrachtungen zu einer Untersuchung von Harald Marx. In M. Fölling-Albers, S. Richter, H. Brügelmann and A. Speck-Hamdan (eds) *Jahrbuch Grundschule III. Fragen der Praxis – Befunde der Forschung* (pp. 141–43). Velber.

Rigol, R. (1977). Schichtzugehörigkeit und Rechtschreibung. Versuch einer soziologischen Fehleranalyse. In G. Spitta (ed.) *Rechtschreibunterricht* (pp. 93–106). Braunschweig: Georg Westermann Verlag.

Rivers, J. and Young, C. (2001) Wer beherrscht die deutsche Sprache? Recht, Sprache und Autorität nach der Rechtschreibreform 1996. *Zeitschrift für Dialektologie und Linguistik* 68(2), 173–90.

Roellecke, G. (1997). Grundrecht auf richtiges Deutsch? Zur Unwesentlichkeit der Rechtschreibung. *Neue Juristische Wochenschrift* 38, 2500–501.

Roth, W. (1999) Zur Verwassungswidrigkeit der Rechtschreibreform: Zugleich Anmerkung zum Urteil des BVerfG vom 14. 07. 1998. *Bayrische Verwaltungsblätter* 130(9), 257–66.

Rothstein, R.A. (1977) Spelling and society: The Polish orthographic controversy of the 1930s. In B.A. Stolz (ed.) *Papers in Slavic Philology I. In Honor of James Ferrell* (pp. 225–36).

Russ, C.V.J. (1994) *The German Language Today.* London: Routledge.

Sauer, W.W. (1988) *Der 'Duden': Geschichte und Aktualität eines 'Volkswörterbuchs'.* Stuttgart: Metzler.

Sauer, W.W. and Glück, H. (1995) Norms and reforms: Fixing the form of the language. In P. Stevenson (ed.) *The German Language and the Real World* (pp. 69–93). Oxford: Clarendon Press.

Schaeder, B. (1989) Probleme der deutschen Rechtschreibung und ihre Neuregelung. *Deutsche Sprache* 1(89), 87–94.

Schaeder, B. (1997) Getrennt- und Zusammenschreibung – zwischen Wortgruppe und Wort, Grammatik und Lexikon. In G. Augst *et al.* (eds) *Zur Neuregelung der deutschen Orthographie. Begründung und Kritik* (pp. 157–208). Tübingen: Niemeyer.

Schaeder, B. (ed.) (1999a) *Neuregelung der deutschen Rechtschreibung: Beiträge zu ihrer Geschichte, Diskussion und Umsetzung.* Frankfurt/M.: Peter Lang.

Schaeder, B. (1999b) Neuregelung der deutschen Rechtschreibung – Chronik der laufenden Ereignisse. In B. Schaeder (ed.) *Neuregelung der deutschen Rechtschreibung: Beiträge zu ihrer Geschichte, Diskussion und Umsetzung* (pp. 11–34). Frankfurt/M.: Peter Lang.

Schaeder, B. (1999c) Neuregelung der deutschen Rechtschreibung – Begründung, Kritik und Erwiderung. In B. Schaeder (ed.) *Neuregelung der deutschen Rechtschreibung: Beiträge zu ihrer Geschichte, Diskussion und Umsetzung* (pp. 41–48). Frankfurt/M.: Peter Lang.

Scheuringer, H. (1996) *Geschichte der deutschen Rechtschreibung. Ein Überblick.* Vienna: Edition Praesens.

Scheuringer, H. (1997b) Letzte Zwistigkeiten ums Reförmchen. In H. Eichner, P. Ernst and S. Katsikas (eds) *Sprachnormung und Sprachplanung* (pp. 409–18). Vienna: Edition Praesens.

Schieffelin, B.B. and Doucet, R.C. (1994) The 'Real' Haitian creole: Ideology, metalinguistics, and orthographic choice. *American Ethnologist* 21(1), 176–200. (Reprinted in B.B. Schieffelin *et al.* (eds) *Language Ideologies: Practice and Theory* pp. 285–316. New York: Oxford University Press.)

Schieffelin, B.B., Woolard, K.A. and Kroskrity, P.V. (eds) (1998) *Language Ideologies: Practice and Theory.* New York: Oxford University Press.

Schiffman, H. (1998) Standardization or restandardization: The case for 'standard' spoken Tamil. *Language in Society* 27, 359–85.

Schlaefer, M. (1980) Grundzüge der deutschen Orthographiegeschichte vom Jahre 1800 bis zum Jahre 1870. *Sprachwissenschaft* 5, 276–319.

Schlaefer, M. (1981) Der Weg zur deutschen Einheitsorthographie vom Jahre 1870 bis zum Jahre 1901. *Sprachwissenschaft* 6, 391–438.

Schneider, H.-P. (1998) Vernunft wird Unsinn, Wohltat, Plage. *Neue Juristische Wochenschrift* 51, 2505–507.

Scholze-Stubenrecht, W. (1997) Warum der Duden die Rechschreibreform befürwortet. In H.-W. Eroms and H.H. Munske (eds) *Die Rechtschreibreform: Pro und Kontra* (pp. 205–208). Berlin: Erich Schmidt Verlag.

Scholze-Stubenrecht, W. (2001) Das morphematische Prinzip in der Umsetzung der Reform: Lexikographische Erfahrungen bei der Anwendung der neuen Rechtschreibregeln. *Sprachwissenschaft* 25(2), 141–51.

Schrodt, R. (ed.) (2000) *Dokumente zur neueren Geschichte der deutschen Orthographie in Österreich* (Documenta Orthographica, Band 8). Hildesheim: Georg Olms Verlag.

Scollon, R. (1998) *Mediated Discourse as Social Interaction: A Study of News Discourse.* London: Longman.

Sebba, M. (1998) Phonology meets ideology: The meaning or orthographic practices in British Creole. *Language Problems and Language Planning* 22(1), 19–47.

Sebba, M. (2000a) Orthography as literacy: How Manx was 'reduced to writing'. In N. Ostler and B. Rudes (eds) *Endangered Languages and Literacy* (pp. 63–70). Proceedings of the fourth FEL Conference, University of North Carolina, Charlotte, 21–24 September 2000.

Sebba, M. (2000b) Orthography and ideology: Issues in Sranan spelling. *Linguistics* 38(5), 925–48.

Shannon, S.M. (1999) The debate on bilingual education in the U.S.: Language ideology as reflected in the practice of bilingual teachers. In J. Blommaert (ed.) *Language Ideological Debates* (pp. 171–99). Berlin: Mouton de Gruyter.

Sidnell, J. (2001) Competence. In A. Duranti (ed.) *Key Terms in Language and Culture* (pp. 34–36). Oxford: Blackwell.

Silverstein, M. (1979) Language structure and linguistic ideology. In P. Clyne *et al.* (eds) *The Elements: A Parasession on Linguistic Units and Levels* (pp. 193–247). Chicago: Chicago Linguistic Society.

Silverstein, M. and Urban, G. (eds) (1996) *Natural Histories of Discourse.* Chicago: University of Chicago Press.

Simon, G. (1998) Zwei Rechschreibreformen im Dritten Reich. Zu Hiltraud Strunks Beitrag 'Gab es etwas einzustampfen?' *Der Deutschunterricht* 6, 86–92.

Sitta, H. (1997) Wie uneinheitlich dürfen unterschiedliche Rechtschreib-wörterbücher sein? In H.-W. Eroms and H.H. Munske (eds) *Die Rechtschreibreform: Pro und Kontra* (pp. 219–29). Berlin: Erich Schmidt Verlag.

Smalley, W.A. (1964) *Orthography Studies: Articles on New Writing Systems.* London: United Bible Societies.

Spitta, G. (ed.) (1977) *Rechtschreibunterricht.* Braunschweig: Georg Westermann Verlag.

Stanat, P., Artelt, C., Baumert, J., Klieme, E., Neubrand, M., Prenzel, M., Schiefele, U., Schneider, W., Schümer, G., Tillmann, K.-J. and Weiss, M. (2002) *PISA 2000: Overview of the Study: Design, Method and Results.* Berlin: Max Planck Institute for Human Development. On WWW at www.mpib-berlin.mpg.de/pisa/english.html. Retrieved 3.7.2003.

Staupe, J. (1986) *Parlamentsvorbehalt und Delegationsbefugnis.* Berlin: Duncker und Humblot.

Stebbins, T. (2001) Emergent spelling patterns in Sm'algyax (Tsimshian, British Columbia). *Written Language and Literacy* 4(2), 163–93.

Stenschke, O. (2001) Wissenstransfer und Emotion im Diskurs über die Rechtschreibreform. In S. Wichter and G. Antos (eds) *Wissens-*

transfer zwischen Experten und Laien: Umriss einer Transferwissenschaft (pp. 145–57). Frankfurt/M.: Peter Lang.

Stenschke, O. (2002) *Rechtschreiben, Recht sprechen, recht haben – Der Diskurs über die Rechtschreibreform. Eine linguistische Analyse des Streits in der Presse.* Unpublished PhD dissertation, University of Göttingen.

Stenschke, O. and Busch, A. (eds) (2004) *Wissenstransfer und gesellschaftliche Kommunikation. Festschrift für Sigurd Wichter zum 60. Geburtstag.* Frankfurt: Peter Lang.

Sternefeld W. (2000) Schreibgeminaten im Deutschen: Ein Fall für die Optimalitätstheorie. *Linguistische Berichte* 181, 35–54.

Stetter, C. (1990) Die Groß- und Kleinschreibung im Deutschen. Zur sprachanalytischen Begründung einer Theorie der Orthographie. In C. Stetter (ed.) *Zu einer Theorie der Orthographie: Interdisziplinäre Aspekte gegenwärtiger Schrift- und Orthographieforschung* (pp. 196–220). Tübingen: Niemeyer.

Stetter, C. (1997) *Schrift und Sprache.* Frankfurt/M.: Suhrkamp.

Stevenson, P. (2002) *Language and German Disunity: A Sociolinguistic History of East and West in Germany, 1945–2000.* Oxford: Oxford University Press.

Street, B. (1984) *Literacy in Theory and Practice.* Cambridge: CUP.

Street, B. (ed.) (1993) *Cross-Cultural Approaches to Literacy.* Cambridge: CUP.

Strunk, H. (1992) *Stuttgarter und Wiesbadener Empfehlungen. Entstehungsgeschichte und politisch–institutionelle Innenansichten gescheiterter Rechtschreibreformversuche von 1950 bis 1965.* Frankfurt/M.: Peter Lang.

Strunk, H. (ed.) (1998a) *Dokumente zur neueren Geschichte einer Reform der deutschen Orthographie. Die Stuttgarter und Wiesbadener Empfehlungen* (Documenta Orthographica, Band 10 1/2). Hildesheim: Georg Olms Verlag.

Strunk, H. (1998b) 'Gab es etwas einzustampfen?' Bemühungen des Reichserziehungsministers Rust um eine Rechtschreibreform während des Dritten Reiches. *Der Deutschunterricht* 51(2), 90–95.

Stubbs, M. (1980) *Language and Literacy: The Sociolinguistics of Reading and Writing.* London: Routledge and Kegan Paul.

Stubbs, M. (1992) Spelling in society: Forms and variants, users and uses. In R. Tracy (ed.) *Who Climbs the Grammar-Tree?* (pp. 221–34). Tübingen: Max Niemeyer Verlag.

Stuppnik-Bazzanella, E. (2000) Die Rechtschreibreform im Unterricht – 'Deutsch als Fremdsprache.' In S. Schmidt *et al.* (eds) *Specht und*

Gämse: Beiträge zur Rechtschreibung des Deutschen (pp. 155–64). Göppingen: Kümmerle.

Tauli, V. (1977) Speech and Spelling. In J. Fishman (ed.) *Advances in the Creation and Revision of Writing Systems* (pp. 17–35). The Hague: Mouton.

Tollefson, J.W. (1991) *Planning Language, Planning Inequality: Language Policy in the Community.* London: Longman.

Tönnies, F. (1887) *Gemeinschaft und Gesellschaft: Grundbegriffe der reinen Soziologie.* Darmstadt: Wissenschaftliche Buchgesellschaft.

Vachek, J. (1945–1949) Some remarks on writing and phonetic transcription. *Acta Linguistica* 5, 86–93.

Vachek, J. (1973) *Written Language: General Problems and Problems of English.* The Hague: Mouton.

Veith, W.H. (1997) Die deutsche Orthographie im Brennpunkt. *Sprachwissenschaft* 22(1), 19–44.

Veith, W.H. (2000) Bestrebungen der Orthographiereform im 18., 19., und 20. Jahrhundert. In W. Besch (ed.) *Sprachgeschichte: ein Handbuch zur Geschichte der deutschen Sprache und ihrer Erforschung* (Vol. 2, 2nd edition). Berlin: de Gruyter.

Verhandlungen (1876) *Verhandlungen der zur Herstellung größerer Einigung in der Deutschen Rechtschreibung berufenen Konferenz, Berlin, den 4. bis 15. Januar 1876.* Halle.

Vikør, L.S. (1988). *Perfecting Spelling: Spelling Discussions and Reforms in Indonesia and Malaysia, 1900–72.* Dordrecht: Foris.

Vikør, L.S. (1993) Principles of corpus planning – as applied to the spelling reforms of Indonesia and Malaysia. In E.H. Jahr (ed.) *Language Conflict and Language Planning* (pp. 279–96). Berlin/New York: de Gruyter.

Vološinov, V.N. (1973 [1986]) *Marxism and the Philosophy of Language.* Cambridge, MA: Harvard University Press.

von Polenz, P. (1978) *Geschichte der deutschen Sprache.* Berlin: de Gruyter.

von Polenz, P. (1991) *Deutsche Sprachgeschichte vom Spätmittelalter bis zur Gegenwart. Band 1: Einführung, Grundbegriffe, Deutsch in der frühbürgerlichen Zeit.* Berlin, New York: de Gruyter.

von Polenz, P. (1994) *Deutsche Sprachgeschichte vom Spätmittelalter bis zur Gegenwart. Band 2: 17. und 18. Jahrhundert.* Berlin, New York: de Gruyter.

von Polenz, P. (1999) *Deutsche Sprachgeschichte vom Spätmittelalter bis zur Gegenwart. Band 3: 19. und 20. Jahrhundert.* Berlin, New York: de Gruyter.

Wagner, V. (1998a) Mögliche Staatshaftungsansprüche der Schulbuchverlage im Falle eines Scheiterns der Rechtschreibreform – ein Gedankenspiel. *Neue Juristische Wochenschrift* 51(17), 1184–89.

Wagner, V. (1998b) Einzelfallentscheidung oder Paradigmenwechsel? Zum Verhältnis zwischen objektiver und subjektiver Funktion der Verfassungsbeschwerde nach dem Urteil des BVerfG zur Rechtschreibreform vom 14. 7. 1998. *Neue Juristische Wochenschrift* 51(36), 2368–40.

Weinberger, U. (2001) *The Spelling of Foreign Words in German after the 1996 Spelling Reform: Theoretical Overview and Empirical Study.* Assignment submitted for MA in Language Studies, Department of Linguistics, Lancaster University.

Weisgerber, L. (1964) *Die Verantwortung für die Schrift.* Mannheim: Bibliographisches Institut.

Wells, C. (1985) *German: A Linguistic History to 1945.* Oxford: OUP.

Wichter, S. (1999) Experten- und Laiensemantik. In J. Niederhauser and K. Adamzik (eds) *Wissenschaftssprache und Umgangssprache im Konflikt* (pp. 81–101). Frankfurt/M.: Peter Lang.

Wichter, S. and Stenschke, O. (eds) (2004) *Theorie, Steuerung und Medien des Wissenstransfers.* Frankfurt/M: Peter Lang.

Wiechers, S. (2001) 'Wir sind das Sprachvolk' – aktuelle Bestrebungen von Sprachvereinen und -initiativen. *Muttersprache* 2, 147–62.

Williams, G. (1992) *Sociolinguistics: A Sociological Critique.* London: Routledge.

Winer, L. (1990) Orthographic standardisation for Trinidad and Tobago: Linguistic and sociopolitical considerations in an English Creole community. *Language Problems and Language Planning* 14(3), 237–59.

Wittmann, R. (1999) *Geschichte des deutschen Buchhandels*, 2nd edition. Munich: Beck.

Woolard, K. (1992) Language ideology: Issues and approaches. *Pragmatics* 2(3), 235–50.

Woolard, K. (1998) Introduction: language ideology as a field of inquiry. In B. Schieffelin *et al.* (eds) *Language Ideologies: Practice and Theory* (pp. 3–47). Oxford: OUP.

Wynne, B. (1996a) Misunderstood misunderstandings: Social identities and the public uptake of science. In A. Irwin and B. Wynne (eds) *Misunderstanding Science* (pp. 19–46). Cambridge: CUP.

Wynne, B. (1996b) May the sheep safely graze? In S. Lash, B. Szerszynski and B. Wynne (eds) *Risk, Environment and Modernity* (pp. 44–83). Cambridge: Polity Press.

Zabel, H. (ed.) (1987) *Fremdwortorthographie. Beiträge zu historischen und aktuellen Fragestellungen.* Tübingen: Narr.

Zabel, H. (1989) *Der gekippte Keiser.* Bochum: Brockmeyer.

Zabel, H. (1996) *Keine Wüteriche am Werk. Berichte und Dokumente zur Neuregelung der deutschen Rechtschreibung.* Hagen: Rainer Padligur Verlage.

Zabel, H. (1997a) *Widerworte. 'Lieber Herr Grass, Ihre Aufregung ist unbegründet.' Antworten an Gegner und Kritiker der Rechtschreibreform.* Aachen: Shaker Verlag/AOL Verlag.

Zabel, H. (1997b) Der Internationale Arbeitskreis für Orthographie. In G. Augst *et al.* (eds) *Zur Neuregelung der deutschen Orthographie. Begründung und Kritik* (pp. 49–66). Tübingen: Niemeyer.

Zabel, H. (1997c) Die Geschichte der Reformbemühungen von 1970 bis 1995 in der BRD. In G. Augst *et al.* (eds) *Zur Neuregelung der deutschen Orthographie. Begründung und Kritik.* (pp. 7–14). Tübingen: Niemeyer.

Zabel, H. (1997d) Fremdwortschreibung. In G. Augst *et al.* (eds) *Zur Neuregelung der deutschen Orthographie. Begründung und Kritik* (pp. 141–56). Tübingen: Niemeyer.

Zemb, J.-M. (1997) *Für eine sinnige Rechtschreibung – eine Aufforderung zur Besinnung ohne Gesichtsverlust.* Tübingen: Narr.

Zemb, J.-M. (2001) Ein Wort? *Hypothese* beziehungsweise *Hyperthese*: nicht alles, was zusammengeschrieben wird, ist ein Wort. *Sprachwissenschaft* 26(1), 1–19.

Index

Page numbers in *italics* refer to tables, those in **bold** indicate main discussion; *n*/*ns* indicate chapter note(s); *passim* refers to numerous scattered mentions within page range.